PROGRAMED
SPELLING
AND
VOCABULARY

PROGRAMED SPELLING AND VOCABULARY
Words in Context

George W. Feinstein
Pasadena City College

Prentice-Hall, Inc., Englewood Cliffs, New Jersey 07632

Library of Congress Cataloging in Publication Data

Feinstein, George W.
    Programed spelling and vocabulary.

    1. Vocabulary--Programmed instruction. 2. Spellers--
Programmed instruction. I. Title.
PE1449.F39   1983   428.1'07'7   82-24112
ISBN 0-13-729855-2

            Editorial supervision: Chrys Chrzanowski
            Cover design: Ray Lundgren
            Manufacturing buyer: Harry P. Baisley

Printed in the United States of America

10 9 8 7 6 5 4 3 2 1

ISBN 0-13-729855-2

Prentice-Hall International, Inc., London
Prentice-Hall of Australia Pty. Limited, Sydney
Editora Prentice-Hall do Brasil, Ltda., Rio de Janeiro
Prentice-Hall Canada Inc., Toronto
Prentice-Hall of India Private Limited, New Delhi
Prentice-Hall of Japan, Inc., Tokyo
Prentice-Hall of Southeast Asia Pte. Ltd., Singapore
Whitehall Books Limited, Wellington, New Zealand

Contents

PREFACE TO THE STUDENT

An old man once said, "First I got appendicitis and mononucleosis. Later I got pneumonia and poliomyelitis. After that I was given inoculations, emetics, and hypodermics. What a spelling test!"

You'll be glad to learn that the programed spelling words in this book are not the long, hairy kind; rather, they are the common troublemakers. Likewise, the programed vocabulary terms are not the rare, outlandish variety; rather, they are useful derivatives of Latin and Greek roots and prefixes.

This book is designed to help a strong student become even stronger, yet give real help and hope to the student who can't spell DDT.

And why should spelling and vocabulary be studied together? (I'm glad you asked.) My answer is, Why not? Surely, spelling and vocabulary are joined like a pair of shears, and one blade is practically useless without the other. After all, a well-chosen word if misspelled is ridiculous, and a well-spelled word if misused is ridiculous. A word is yours, really all yours, only when you master both its meaning and its spelling.

The odd-numbered chapters in this book deal with the spelling of run-of-the-mill words like *angry, bargain, coming, lovely,* and *calendar.* We can assume that you already know the meaning of these ordinary words and so we will concentrate only on their spelling. Naturally, if you don't know what one of these words means you should look the word up in a dictionary.

The even-numbered chapters deal mainly with vocabulary that has come, like much of our language, from Greek and Latin--words like *benefactor, decathlon, eulogy,* and *panacea.* You will learn the meaning *and* the correct spelling of these words--yes, *and* the pronunciation, too. Some day soon--who knows?--you will slip some of these words into your conversation or your compositions and startle your friends or delight your history teacher. But just knowing the meaning of these words, and especially the Latin-Greek roots, will be like money in the bank when you study your college reading assignments.

The pronunciation of each Latin/Greek derivative is printed big because the pronunciation of a word has big importance and it must not be overlooked. As a fringe benefit you will also be picking up an easy familiarity with diacritical symbols (pronunciation markings) as used in dictionaries.

I once knew a man who was something less than a genius at spelling. His last name was Bolenkaczmarczyk. I asked him "Why is it that you've spelled *cow* with a *k* and yet you know how to spell *Bolenkaczmarczyk*?"--"Well," he answered, "I write my last name so many times that it's easy for me."

That was when I decided that practically anybody can learn to spell any word at all if he writes it often enough; also he can remember the meaning of any word if he deals with it often enough.

Thus the keynote of this program is drill, drill, drill. In this book you will handle the same vocabulary and spelling words again and again, until you can write each word automatically. You will be writing each word at least seven or eight times *mostly within phrases or sentences--that is, in context-- which is the preferred way.* If all that repetition doesn't nail the word down, you'll simply be expected to write the word a few dozen more times until you write it as naturally as you write your own name.

A word is troublesome to spellers because it has one or two trouble spots in it. For instance, the trouble spot in *receive* is the *ei*, and the *ei* causes 95% of the misspellings of that word. In *government* the trouble spot is the *n*; in *villain* the trouble spot is the *ai*. This textbook calls special attention to trouble spots, and it tests for them with combinations like *r-e-c-v-*, *g-o-v-m-n-t*, and *v-i-l-n-*, where you will have the pleasure of writing the complete word. So don't spend too much time studying the easy letters of a word--that's whipping a dead horse. Concentrate on the trouble spots because that's mainly what you'll be tested on.

Some textbooks print misspelled words for you to find and correct. But psychologists say that looking at a misspelling can burn that error into your mind. So this book does not print misspellings. What it does do is give you a word you have just studied but in skeletonized form and with hyphens in it-- like *d-v-i-n-* for *divine*--and the letters given will always be in the same order as they occur in the completed word.

A general assignment in this book consists of a pair of chapters, such as Chapters 1-2, 9-10, or 17-18. The odd-numbered chapter is usually a programing of spelling words 1-30; the even-numbered chapter is usually a programing of vocabulary words 31-50. At the end of each pair of chapters comes a Self-Test on 50 words. Your score in the Self-Test will tell you how well you are doing at home, but the grade will not count--yet. In class your instructor will give you the final test, most likely the official one from the Instructor's Manual, and then you'll be playing for real marbles.

The examples listed as "Other Derivatives" deserve close inspection and discussion. However, they are not included in quizzes or chapter tests.

This study program has two purposes: (1) to help you learn the spelling and the meaning of specific words that every college student should know, and (2) to spark your drive for vocabulary expansion and word accuracy in years to come. Your enthusiastic effort can make these aims a reality.

For their help and encouragement, I thank a galaxy of scholars, especially Professors Rae G. Ballard, Arthur J. Kelley, Margaret H. Marsh, Marion S. Murphy, Karen P. Norris, John D. Reib, Joseph Sierra, and Arthur H. Wright, Pasadena City College; Anne G. Phillips, Santa Monica College; Karen Houck, Bellevue Community College; Lisa Feinstein, California State University, Northridge; Cherie Lewis, University of Southern California; Margo Connolly, Chabot College; Richard O. Hale, University of North Dakota; J. Sheets, Lethbridge Community College, Alberta; Susan Gurman, Newbridge School; Margaret F. Sanders. Shelburne Falls, Mass.; also those conscientious editors J. Phil Miller, Chrys Chrzanowski, and Miranda Spencer of Prentice-Hall, Inc.

GEORGE W. FEINSTEIN
Pasadena, California

"Take heed, be wary how you place your words...."
(William Shakespeare, 1 King Henry VI, III, ii, 3)

A FEW SPELLING SUGGESTIONS

The trouble with most spelling rules is that the rules have exceptions, and even the exceptions have exceptions. Correct spelling should be automatic, like driving a car or playing concert piano, not a matter of clutching at imperfect rules with an imperfect memory. That is why this textbook stresses drill rather than rules.

However, a few generalizations about spelling are fairly reliable and are worth reviewing here. For instance--

1. FORMING PLURALS BY ADDING *S* OR *ES*

Most English words form their plurals by adding *s*.
EXAMPLES: *book < books; girl < girls; rock < rocks.*

Words that end in a hissing sound such as *s, x, z, ch,* or *sh* form the plural by adding *es*. EXAMPLES: *box < boxes; church < churches; dish < dishes; kiss < kisses.*

2. FORMING PLURALS OF WORDS ENDING IN *Y*

If a word ends in *y* with a vowel (*a, e, i, o,* or *u*) in front of it, you form the plural by simply adding *s*. EXAMPLES: *boy < boys; day < days; turkey < turkeys; valley < valleys.*

Otherwise, change the *y* to *i* and add *es*. EXAMPLES: *army < armies; baby < babies; city < cities; pony < ponies; library < libraries.*

3. ADDITIVE DOUBLING

When the last letter of a prefix such as *dis, mis,* and *un* is the same as the first letter of the root that follows, we have a doubling of letters. EXAMPLES: *dis + satisfy = dissatisfy; mis + spell = misspell; un + necessary = unnecessary.*

Otherwise, such doubling does not usually occur.
EXAMPLES: *dis + appear = disappear; mis + fortune = misfortune; un + dress = undress.*

4. WHEN TO DROP THE SILENT *E*

Words ending in silent *e* generally drop the *e* when adding a suffix beginning with a vowel (*ing, able, ion, ous,* etc.).
EXAMPLES: *take + ing = taking; prove + ing = proving; love + able = lovable; adore + ation = adoration; use + ing = using; desire + ous = desirous; conceive + able = conceivable.* EXCEPTIONS: *change + able = changeable; courage + ous = courageous; peace + able = peaceable.*

Words ending in silent *e* generally hang on to the *e* when adding a suffix beginning with a consonant (*ment, ful, ly,* etc.).
EXAMPLES: *care + less = careless; force + ful = forceful; sure + ly = surely; improve + ment = improvement.*

5. *I* BEFORE *E*, EXCEPT AFTER *C*

Write *i* before *e*, except after *c* or when sounded like *a* as in *neighbor* and *weigh*. EXAMPLES: *belief, brief, chief, piece, thief, deceive, receive, ceiling*. EXCEPTIONS: *either, neither, weird, seize, leisure, sheik, science*.

6. WHEN TO DOUBLE THE FINAL CONSONANT

If a word ends (1) in a single consonant, (2) preceded by a single vowel, and (3) is accented on that syllable, you should double the final consonant before adding a suffix (such as *ing* or *ed*) that begins with a vowel. EXAMPLES: *admit < admitted; shop < shopped; refer < referring; compel < compelling; omit < omitted; rap < rapping*.

But if a word does not follow all three conditions of the foregoing rule, then do not double the final consonant. EXAMPLES: *suggest < suggesting* (does not end in a single consonant); *appear < appeared* (not preceded by a single vowel); *benefit < benefited* (not accented on the last syllable).

HOW TO USE THIS MANUAL

1. READ INTRODUCTORY PAGES. Read the Preface, Spelling Suggestions, and Pronunciation Key. Now you are ready to begin.

2. STUDY WORD GROUP AND FILL BLANKS. Study each new word group (four to ten words) carefully, noting the trouble spots and/or the definitions, and write the words neatly in the blank spaces as directed.

3. TAKE QUIZ ON WORD GROUP. Cover the answers at the left side of each page with a strip of paper or with your hand. Complete a sentence with pen or pencil, then uncover just enough of the key at the left to check your answer. If your answer is correct, go on to the next sentence. If you make a mistake, correct your mistake and *study the word again* before going on.

4. LOOK OUT FOR TRAPS. You will be given a word with some holes in it, and you'll have to write the complete word correctly.

   EXAMPLE: The ___*sergeant*___ [s-r-g-n-t] tried to drown his

   sorrows but found they could ___*float*___ [f-1-o-t-].

   Each hyphen (short bar) can mean that one or more letters are missing there *or that no letters are missing there.* Notice that last hyphen in "[f-1-o-t-]." That extra hyphen was just thrown as bait to trap a sleepy student.

5. MEMORIZE LATIN/GREEK ROOTS AND PREFIXES. Memorize the Latin and Greek roots and prefixes as you go along, because you are going to start noticing them in an army of words, and they will benefit your vocabulary.

6. TAKE SELF-TESTS. Take the Self-Test after every even-numbered chapter and enter your score at the end of the test. You should be able to earn at least 90% in the Self-Test.

7. TAKE FINAL TESTS. Your teacher will give you a final test in class on each pair of chapters, based on the Instructor's Manual.

PRONUNCIATION KEY

a   as in   fat, grab, snack

ā   as in   āpe, hāte, jāil

ä   as in   cär, färce, lärd

e   as in   bend, leg, tent

ē   as in   bē, ēven, shē

i   as in   is, fling, hit

ī   as in   bīte, īce, wīne

o   as in   hop, odd, spot

ō   as in   gō, hōpe, telephōne

ô   as in   hôrse, ôrder, shôrt

oo   as in   book, shook, took

o͞o   as in   fo͞ol, no͞odle, sho͞ot

oi   as in   boil, oil, spoil

ou   as in   out, pout, shout

u   as in   bug, dust, up

û   as in   bûrn, chûrch, hûrt

NAMES OF DIACRITICAL MARKS: *macron* (‾), *circumflex* (^), *dieresis* (¨).

THE SCHWA (ə): The pronunciation symbol ə, which looks like an upside-down e, is called a *schwa*. It occurs in unaccented syllables and is pronounced "uh," though very lightly. Examples:

soda (sō′də), vanity (van′ə tē), listen (lis′ən), carbon (kär′bən)

ACCENT MARKS:

Primary accent (′), as in   bī′ped and spek′tā tər

Secondary accent (′), as in   ag′grə gā′shən and ben′ə fak′tər

SPELLING DEMONS: "ACCEPT" TO "CHOSE"

DIRECTIONS: Study the spelling of each word carefully, giving special attention to the trouble spots (underlined letters). Then write each word neatly three times.

1. a̲cc̲ept (verb): "to *accept* a gift" _*accept*_____

2. e̲xcept (prep.): "all *except* Max"_____

3. ac̲he _____ _____ _____

4. ac̲ross _____ _____ _____

5. advic̲e (noun): "take my *advice*"_____

6. advis̲e (verb): "*advise* him"_____

7. agg̲ain _____ _____ _____

8. all̲ right _____ _____ _____

9. a lo̲t _____ _____ _____

10. amon̲g̲ _____ _____ _____

Review words 1-10 until you are sure you can spell them. Then go on and take the quiz.

QUIZ

COVER THIS STRIP	FILL THE BLANKS
again	■ The tenor sang, "Kiss me _____ [a-g-n-]."
	■ A prizefighter must learn, _____ [a-m-n-g-]
among accept	other things, to _____ [-c-e-p-t-] a knock on the nose.
	■ Two silkworms raced _____ [a-c-r-s] a branch
across	and ended up in a tie.
ache	■ Grandpa's best tooth began to _____ [a-c-e-].
	■ The Salvation Army will _____ [-c-e-p-t-]
accept except	anything _____ [-c-e-p-t-] Confederate money.
	■ A person who works _____ [a-m-n-g-] sick
among a lot	people can pick up _____ [a-l-o-t-] of interesting diseases.
	■ "Take my _____ [a-d-v-i-]," said the man with
advice across	the gun, "and come _____ [a-c-r-s]."
	■ When their stomachs _____ [a-c-e-], we
ache advise	_____ [a-d-v-i-] them to eat fewer hot dogs.
	■ "You're _____ [a-l-r-g-t] in my book," said
all right	Kinsey.
advice	■ Stop smoking? That's good _____ [a-d-v-i-].
	■ Buster makes a _____ [a-l-o-t-] of noise for
a lot accept	only one baby, so _____ [-c-e-p-t-] our apologies.
	■ I enjoyed the rock music, _____ [-c-e-p-t-]
except ache	that it made my ears _____ [a-c-e-].
	■ A fish has only one life, but a frog croaks
again again	_____ [a-g-n-] and _____ [a-g-n-].

page 2

a lot	■ A cat that eats _____ [a-l-o-t-] of lemons is a sourpuss.
among	■ You'll find thorns _____ [a-m-n-g-] the roses.
advice	■ Wilmer wrote to "Dear Abby" for _____ [a-d-v-i-].
all right except	■ The quarterback now feels _____ [a-l-r-g-t] _____ [-c-e-p-t] for seeing double.
across	■ The stunt man jumped _____ [a-c-r-s] canyons.
all right advise	■ "You're out, _____ [a-l-r-g-t]," shouted the umpire, "and I _____ [a-d-v-i-] you to shut up!"
advise	■ Please _____ [a-d-v-i-] the boy to buy a drum and beat it.
again	■ *"When shall we three meet _____ [a-g-n-]* *In thunder, lightning, or in rain?"* (Macbeth, I, i, 2)

DIRECTIONS: Continue as before. Study the spelling carefully. Write each word three times.

11. an<u>g</u>ry   *angry*   _____   _____

12. ans<u>we</u>r   _____   _____   _____

13. an<u>x</u>ious   _____   _____   _____

14. arg<u>um</u>ent   _____   _____   _____

15. artic<u>le</u>   _____   _____   _____

16. at<u>hle</u>te   _____   _____   _____

17. attemp<u>t</u>   _____   _____   _____

18. barg<u>ai</u>n   _____   _____   _____

19. b<u>ea</u>utiful   _____   _____   _____

20. begi<u>nn</u>ing   _____   _____   _____

Review words 11-20. Then take the quiz.

COVER THIS STRIP	FILL THE BLANKS
argument	■ All night the dogs kept up an _____ [a-r-g-m-t].
	■ The salesman sold me a broken _____
article bargain	[a-r-t-c-l-] and convinced me I was getting a _____ [b-r-g-n-].
angry answer	■ When you get an _____ [a-g-r-y] question, try to give a mild _____ [a-n-s-r-].
attempt athlete	■ In his _____ [a-t-e-m-p-] to break the record, the _____ [a-t-h-l-t-] broke his leg.
beginning beautiful	■ "This might be the _____ [b-e-g-n-n-g]," said the stranger, "of a _____ [b-u-t-f-l-] friendship."
attempt article answer	■ I asked Father why he'd _____ [a-t-e-m-p-] to kill pests with an _____ [a-r-t-c-l-] such as a trap, and he said he didn't think a soft _____ [a-n-s-r-] turneth away rats.
athlete angry	■ The _____ [a-t-h-l-t-] swaggered into the cave, then ran out followed by _____ [a-g-r-y] wasps.
beginning anxious	■ The blizzard was _____ [b-e-g-n-n-g] to worsen, and the girl in the bikini was shivering and getting _____ [a-n-i-u-s].
beautiful angry	■ This bull is a _____ [b-u-t-f-l-] animal, but I'd rather not meet him when he is _____ [a-g-r-y].
beginning article bargain	■ In the _____ [b-e-g-n-n-g] God created the heavens; then man created an _____ [a-r-t-c-l-] known as smog as our part of the _____ [b-r-g-n-].

argument
answer

- Idiots love an _____ [a-r-g-m-t] over questions that have no _____ [a-n-s-r-].

- The _____ [a-t-h-l-t-] was so _____ [a-n-i-u-s] to hit a home run that he twisted himself into a pretzel in the _____ [a-t-e-m-p-].

athlete
anxious
attempt

- After a heated _____ [a-r-g-m-t] the tourist bought the rug, but it wasn't _____ [b-u-t-f-l] nor was it a _____ [b-r-g-n-].

argument
beautiful
bargain

- If you are _____ [a-n-i-u-s] to get rich, a career as poet is not the _____ [a-n-s-r-].

anxious
answer

- *"Thou art as wise as thou art _____ [b-u-t-f-l-]." (Midsummer Night's Dream, III, i, 151)*

beautiful

DIRECTIONS: Continue as before. Study the spelling carefully. Write each word three times.

21. believe *believe* _____ _____

22. brake *(noun)*: "Step on the *brake*." _____

23. break *(verb)*: "*Break* the glass." _____

24. business _____ _____ _____

25. busy _____ _____ _____

26. careless _____ _____ _____

27. carrying _____ _____ _____

28. children _____ _____ _____

29. choose *(verb, present tense)*: "Men who *choose* booze belong in zoos."

_____ _____ _____

30. chose *(verb, past tense)*: "Mose *chose* a rose and held it to his nose."

_____ _____ _____

Review words 21-30. Then take the quiz.

QUIZ

FILL THE BLANKS

---

carrying
children

- The bus was _____ [c-a-r-i-n-g] sixteen
_____ [c-h-i-l-d-n] and a goat.

believe
choose

- If you _____ [b-e-l-e-v-] in yourself, you
can succeed in anything you _____ [c-h-o-s-].

brake
break

- It's better to step on the _____ [b-r-k-] than
to _____ [b-r-k-] your neck.

busy
business

- Look at the _____ [b-s-y-] bee--now that's the
way to conduct your _____ [b-s-n-s-].

believe

- General Custer, I _____ [b-e-l-e-v-], was
wearing an arrow shirt.

children
break

- The hermit told the _____ [c-h-i-l-d-n-] to
vanish or he'd _____ [b-r-k-] their fingers.

business
choose

- Henry Ford, a _____ [b-s-n-s-] genius, said,
"You can have any car color you _____ [c-h-o-s-]
as long as it is black."

careless
break

- If you get _____ [c-r-l-e-s-] and
_____ [b-r-k-] this egg, the yolk will be on you.

busy
brake

- People who are too _____ [b-s-y-] to enjoy
life are like a car without a _____ [b-r-k-].

choose
business

- Why did Bill _____ [c-h-o-s-] to run a fish
_____ [b-s-n-s-]? Nobody gets close enough
to ask.

carrying
careless

- Anybody who is _____ [c-a-r-i-n-g] a load of
glass bulbs shouldn't get _____ [c-r-l-e-s-].

chose
believe

brake
careless

children
chose

busy
chose
carrying

believe

■ Last week Joe _____ [c-h-o-s-] to invent, I
_____ [b-e-l-e-v-], some low-calory pizza.

■ To drive from Mt. Wilson without a good _____
[b-r-k-] is extremely _____ [c-r-l-e-s-].

■ In the past the _____ [c-h-i-l-d-n] usually
_____ [c-h-o-s-] colas and other junk food.

■ Tom was _____ [b-s-y-] writing daily love
letters to Lulu, but she _____ [c-h-o-s-] to marry
the mailman who was _____ [c-a-r-i-n-g] Tom's
letters.

■ *"I am a great eater of beef and I* _____
[b-e-l-e-v-] that does harm to my wit."
                                        (Twelfth Night, I, iii, 90)

2

ALTER, ALTR: CHANGE; OTHER

31. **altercation** (ôl tər kā'shən) *n.* quarrel; a dispute (one with the other)

    The police stopped an *altercation* outside the tavern.
    The mother and daughter engaged in heated *altercations*.

    a noisy altercation   *a noisy altercation* _____
    (copy twice)

32. **alter ego** (ôl'tər ē'gō) another self; another aspect of one's self; a very close friend

    David's inseparable friend Jonathan is his *alter ego*.
    Kay's office partner acts as her *alter ego* when Kay isn't around.

    my alter ego   _____   _____

33. **alternative** (ôl tûr'nə tiv) *adj.* providing another choice
    n. a choice; another possibility

    Let me suggest some *alternatives*.
    We decided to take an *alternative* route.

    a second alternative   _____   _____

34. altruism (al'trōo iz'əm) *n.* unselfish concern for others

Sister Teresa, an *altruist*, devoted her life to the needy.
How rare today is an act of *altruism*.

<u>pure altruism</u>   _____   _____
(copy twice)

Review words 31-34. Then go on.

QUIZ

DIRECTIONS: Fill the blanks with words we studied that are derived from the Latin root ALTER, ALTR (change; other). Be sure you spell the words correctly.

COVER
THIS STRIP
_____

alter ego	■ We are inseparable friends. She is my _____ [a-l-g-o-].
alternative	■ The priest urged the couple to find a better _____ [a-l-t-v-] than divorce.
altercation alternative	■ The neighbors' wild _____ [a-l-c-t-n-] began at midnight, so I finally called the police. I had no _____ [a-l-t-v-].
altruism altercation	■ My warm-hearted aunt believes in _____ [a-l-t-m-], so she tried to stop the _____ [a-l-c-t-n-] between two dogs, and they both bit her.
alternative altruism	■ Albert Schweitzer suggested that in place of a give-me attitude we adopt a noble _____ [a-l-t-v-], a policy of _____ [a-l-t-m-].
alter ego	■ Damon was ready to die if necessary for his dear friend Pythias, his _____ [a-l-g-o-].
alter ego altercation	■ One twin boy is practically the _____ [a-l-g-o-] of the other, so I was amazed to find them in a bloody _____ [a-l-c-t-n-].

altruism	■ Shipley's contribution to the Brownies was not pure _____ [a-l-t-m-]. It was a tax deduction.
	■ *"Is't possible that so short a time can alter the condition of a man?" (Coriolanus, V, iv, 9)*

Non-test examples

OTHER DERIVATIVES OF ALTER, ALTR (CHANGE; OTHER):

alter (ôl'tər) *v.* to change; modify [*to alter plans*]

alteration (ôl'tə rā'shən) *n.* a change; result of altering ["*Love is not love / Which alters when it alteration finds." Sonnet 116*]

alternate (*adj.*, *n.* ôl'tər nit; *v.* ôl'tər nāt') *adj.* one and then the other; every other [*on alternate Sundays*] *v.* to take turns [*We alternated as drivers.*]

alternator (ôl'tər nāt'ər) *n.* a generator that produces alternating current

---

AM, AMAT: LOVE

35. **amatory** (am'ə tôr'ē) *adj.* having to do with love-making

> She threw him a warm, *amatory* look.
> Mr. Loudmouth bragged about his *amatory* conquests.

an amatory kiss _____ _____
  (copy twice)

36. **amiable** (ā'mē ə bəl) *adj.* friendly; good-natured

> His mother-in-law is an *amiable* woman.
> A cranky clerk makes fewer sales than an *amiable* one.

my amiable boss _____ _____

37. **amity** (am'i tē) *n.* friendship, as between nations or groups

> We pray for international *amity*.
> Ethnic groups shared the park in a spirit of *amity*.

spirit of amity _____ _____

38. amours (ə moors') *n.* love affairs

> Our TV soap operas depict endless *amours*.
> The story of Casanova's *amours* made steam come out of my ears.

secret amours   _____   _____
(copy twice)

Review words 35-38. Then go on.

QUIZ

DIRECTIONS: Fill the blanks with words we studied that are derived from the Latin root AM, AMAT (love). Be sure you spell the words correctly.

COVER
THIS STRIP

amity	■ The colonies tended to quarrel, but the new federal constitution restored _____ [a-m-y] among them.
amatory amours	■ The aging actors gave each other an _____ [a-m-r-y] embrace, then reminisced about youthful adventures and _____ [a-m-r-s].
amiable amity	■ An _____ [a-m-b-l-] tourist is like an ambassador who establishes _____ [a-m-y] between nations.
amiable amatory amours	■ I am of an easy-going and _____ [a-m-b-l-] disposition, and I wouldn't normally interfere with the _____ [a-m-r-y] relationships of the neighborhood cats; but I wish they'd do less yowling when they conduct their nightly _____ [a-m-r-s-].
amatory amity	■ When an _____ [a-m-r-y] affair has cooled, a civilized couple do not get spiteful; they maintain a spirit of _____ [a-m-y].

amiable
amours

amity

■ Early biographers were a respectful and _____
[a-m-b-1-] breed, whereas modern writers are happiest when
they expose the private _____ [a-m-r-s-] of
famous people.

■ *"...join your hearts in love and* _____ [a-m-y]*"*
    (1 Henry VI, III, i, 68)

Non-test examples

OTHER DERIVATIVES OF AM, AMAT (LOVE):

amateur (am'ə chər) *adj.* nonprofessional *n.* a person who performs for
pleasure, not pay; an unskillful person [*a blundering amateur*]

amative (am'ə tiv) *adj.* inclined to love, especially sexual love
[*amative moments*]

amoretto (am'ə ret'ō) *n.* a little cupid

amorist (am'ə rist) *n.* a lover, or one who writes about love

amorous (am'ər əs) *adj.* fond of making love [*an amorous couple*]

ANN, ENN: YEAR

39. annals (an'əlz) *n.* a historical record; a year-by-year account

    Beethoven's genius is unequaled in the *annals* of music.
    Few men in the *annals* of crime are as repulsive as Count de Sade.

    annals of war   _____   _____
    (copy twice)

40. annual (an'yōō əl) *adj.* yearly

    Thoreau refused to pay the *annual* poll tax.
    Welcome to our *annual* chili-making contest!

    annual vacation   _____   _____

41. annuity (ə nōō'ə tē) *n.* payments from an investment, at yearly or
    other intervals

    The trust fund provides an *annuity* for his children.
    On retirement the police officers get an *annuity*.

    a lifetime annuity   _____   _____

42. superannuated (so͞o'pər an'yo͞o ā'tid) *adj.* too old; outdated

>   Hobbling through the park was my *superannuated* friend.
>   We fought with *superannuated* biplanes.

superannuated cars _____ _____
    (copy twice)

Review words 39-42. Then go on.

QUIZ

DIRECTIONS: Fill the blanks with words we studied that are derived from the Latin root ANN, ENN (year). Be sure you spell the words correctly.

COVER
THIS STRIP

	■ Jesse Owens stands out in the _____ [a-n-s]
annals	of sports.
	■ Visitors gather at San Juan Capistrano for the
annual	_____ [a-n-1-] return of the swallows.
	■ When Jake got his _____ [a-n-t-y] he bought a
annuity superannuated	_____ [s-u-p-t-d] Oldsmobile.
	■ Businessmen love Christmas--it sends us on our
annual	_____ [a-n-1-] shopping spree.
	■ The white-haired, _____ [s-u-p-t-d] veteran
	had just received his _____ [a-n-t-y] from the
superannuated annuity	pension fund.
	■ This _____ [a-n-1-] rummage sale of our Ladies'
	Aid will go down in the _____ [a-n-s] of Coyote
annual annals	County.
	■ The _____ [a-n-s] of war are sprinkled with
	the innocent blood of infants and _____
annals superannuated	[s-u-p-t-d] citizens.
	■ *"Gives him three thousand crowns in* _____
annual	*[a-n-1-] fee!" (Hamlet, II, ii, 73)*

OTHER DERIVATIVES OF ANN, ENN (YEAR):

anniversary (an'ə vûr'sər ē) *n.* the yearly celebration of a past event [*The victim had forgotten his wedding anniversary.*]

anno Domini (an'ō dom'ə nī) lit., in the year of the Lord; A.D. [*invaded in A.D. 1066*]

annuitant (ə nōō'ə tənt) *n.* one who receives an annuity

biannual (bī an'yoo wəl) *adj.* coming twice a year

biennial (bī en'ē əl) *adj.* happening every two years *n.* a plant that lasts two years

centennial (sen ten'ē əl) *adj., n.* a hundredth anniversary or its celebration [*the 1876 Centennial fair*]

millenium (mi len'ē əm) *n.* a period of 1000 years--or of great happiness [*The millenium has arrived!*]

perennial (pə ren'ē əl) *adj.* year after year; everlasting; recurring [*perennial floods*] *n.* a plant that lives for years

---

AQUA: WATER

43. **aquarium** (ə kwer'ē əm) *n.* a tank for live water animals and plants

> The fish in that *aquarium* drink better water than I do.
> Your cat stole a goldfish from my *aquarium*.

aquarium plants   _____   _____
   (copy twice)

44. **aqueduct** (ak'wə dukt') *n.* a structure for bringing water

> Our farms need an *aqueduct* from swollen lakes.
> The Romans built *aqueducts* with cheap labor: slaves.

an ancient aqueduct   _____   _____

45. **aqueous** (ak'wē əs) *adj.* watery

> Dissolve honey in water to get an *aqueous* mixture.
> The priest recommends that the punch be *aqueous*, not alcoholic.

aqueous solution   _____   _____

46. **aquiculture** (ak'wə kul'chər) *n.* raising of water plants and animals
for food; hydroponics

> Excellent tomatoes can be grown by *aquiculture*.
> *Aquiculture* requires sunshine, chemicals, and a pool of water.

<u>art of aquiculture</u>   _____   _____.
   (copy twice)

Review words 43-46. Then go on.

QUIZ

DIRECTIONS: Fill the blanks with words we studied that are derived from the
Latin root AQUA (water). Be sure you spell the words correctly.

COVER
THIS STRIP

	■ Add water, because the formula calls for an
aqueous	_____ [a-q-s-] solution.
	■ The boy and the fish looked at each other through the
aquarium	glass walls of the _____ [a-q-m-].
	■ If we bring water to the desert with an _____
aqueduct aquiculture	[a-q-d-t], we could raise grapes by _____ [a-q-t-r-].
	■ Why are Fred's tropical fish floating upside down in his
aquarium	_____ [a-q-m-]?
	■ Pests don't bother tomatoes raised in an _____
aqueous aquiculture	[a-q-s-] solution--that is, by _____ [a-q-t-r-).
	■ Farmers can get mountain water with a pail, but it's
aqueduct	easier with an _____ [a-q-d-t-].
aqueous	■ Most of our earth's surface is _____ [a-q-s-].
	■ Colorado River water was brought to Los Angeles by means
aqueduct	of an _____ [a-q-d-t-].
	■ No, Johnny, I don't want you growing turnips by
aquiculture aquarium	_____ [a-q-t-r-] in my _____ [a-q-m-].
	■ *"give me some aqua vitae"* (*Romeo and Juliet, III, ii,* 88)

OTHER DERIVATIVES OF AQUA (WATER):

aquacade (ak'wə kād) *n.* a swimming and diving exhibition [*The coeds sponsored an aquacade*]

aqua fortis (fôr'təs) [<L.: lit., strong water] nitric acid

aqualung (ak'wə lung) *n.* apparatus for breathing underwater

aquamarine (ak'wə mə rēn') *adj.* bluish-green, like sea water [*She has aquamarine eyes.*]

aquanaut (ak'wə nôt') *n.* a skin diver

aquaplane (ak'wə plān) *n.* a surfboard towed by motorboat

aqua pura (pyoor'ə) pure water; distilled water

aqua regia (rē'jē ə) [<L.: lit., kingly water] a mixture of nitric and hydrochloric acids, which can dissolve gold and platinum [*The aqua regia melted our container.*]

aquarelle (ak'wə rel') *n.* a watercolor painting

aquarius (ə kwer'ē əs) [<L.: lit., water carrier] *n.* a sign of the Zodiac

aquatic (ə kwot'ik) *adj.* in or on water [*aquatic sports*]

aquatint (ak'wə tint') *n.* an etching that gives the effect of watercolor

aquavit (ak'wə vet') *n.* a Scandinavian liquor

aqua vitae (vīt'ē) [<L.: lit., water of life] alcohol; a liquor such as whiskey or brandy

aqueous humor (hyoo'mər) a watery fluid in the eye [*Infection of the aqueous humor isn't funny.*]

ARM: WEAPONS; ARMS

47. armada (är mä'də) *n.* a fleet of war vessels; a large force of military airplanes or vehicles

> The English navy defeated the Spanish *Armada* in 1588.
> An *armada* of tanks invaded Poland.

a mighty armada _____ _____
   (copy twice)

48. **armament** (är′mə mənt) *n.* military equipment; weapons for war

> Nuclear weapons became an essential of *armament*.
> The *armament* race has cost billions of dollars.

national armament   _____   _____
(copy twice)

49. **armistice** (är′mə stis) *n.* a temporary stopping of war by agreement; a truce

> World War I ended with an *armistice* on November 11, 1918.
> An *armistice* is usually followed by a peace treaty.

Armistice Day   _____   _____

50. **armory** (är′mər ē) *n.* a storage place for weapons; an arsenal

> The *armory* had sixty machine guns.
> The National Guard conducted drill in the *armory*.

armory supplies   _____   _____

Review words 47-50. Then go on.

QUIZ

DIRECTIONS: Fill the blanks with words we studied that are derived from the Latin root ARM (weapons). Be sure you spell the words correctly.

COVER
THIS STRIP

	■ After the _____ [a-m-s-t-] was signed, the
	great _____ [a-m-d-a-] of battleships returned
armistice	home peacefully, as though back from Sunday School.
armada	
	■ If we declare an _____ [a-m-s-t-], we'll
armistice	store our _____ [a-m-n-t-] in an _____
armament	
armory	[a-r-m-y] for use in the next war.
	■ The Kansas cornfields were invaded by an _____
armada	[a-m-d-a-] of grasshoppers.
	■ "Listen," said the senator, "how about getting some

armada
armament
armory

action out of that _____ [a-m-d-a-] of tanks and

all that other nice _____ [a-m-n-t-] that's

collecting dust in the big _____ [a-r-m-y]?

■ Small backward nations have no _____

[a-m-n-t-] in their _____ [a-m-r-y] except clubs;

so the big civilized nations kindly sell an _____

armament
armory
armada
armistice

[a-m-d-a-] of bombers to both sides--at a good profit,

naturally--and then the killing can proceed in a faster,

more civilized manner until both small countries bleed to

death or sign an _____ [a-m-s-t-].

■ *"...the goodliest weapons of his* _____

armory

[a-m-r-y]" (Titus Andronicus, IV, ii, 11)

Non-test examples

OTHER DERIVATIVES OF ARM (WEAPONS):

armadillo (är'mə dil'ō) *n.* a burrowing mammal protected by armorlike plates

armature (är'mə chər) *n.* the protective covering of an animal or plant; the part of a generator or motor in which an electromotive force is induced; any defensive covering such as the metal plating of warships and warplanes

armor (är'mər) *n.* a protective covering used as a defense against weapons [*a suit of armor*]

army (är'mē) *n.* a large body of soldiers organized to wage war; a multitude [*an army of grasshoppers*]

disarmament (dis är'mə mənt) *n.* reduction of military forces and equipment [*a disarmament agreement*]

disarming (dis är'ming) *adj.* tending to remove hostility [*a disarming smile*]

rearm (rē ärm') *v.* to arm again

Review words 1-50, spelling and vocabulary. Then take the Chapters 1-2 Self-Test.

DIRECTIONS: Write the words in full. Complete this entire test before you check and grade your answers.

1. I called Chloe, but she didn't [a-n-s-r-].
2. Somebody's horse walked [a-c-r-s-] my radishes.
3. Big Benny will now [a-t-e-m-p-] to run the ten-minute mile.
4. Never stop to argue with an [a-g-r-y-] bull.
5. The flood was [b-g-n-i-n-g] to reach the second floor.
6. Every baby looks [b-u-t-f-l-] to its mother.
7. Dropping the dodo bird's egg was [c-a-r-l-e-s] of me.
8. In 1928 Coolidge wisely [c-h-o-s-] to get out of politics.
9. Say a prayer for (c-h-i-d-r-n) who watch television.
10. Acupuncture cost me [a-l-o-t-] of pin money.
11. Everybody in our family has a vote [-c-e-p-t] Rover.
12. Baseball umpires win every [a-r-g-m-n-t]--but not at home.
13. You are retiring? Please [-c-e-p-t] this geranium pot.
14. The custodian says that [b-s-n-s] is picking up.
15. Our boss gives us a two-minute coffee [b-r-a-k-].
16. Grandma fell from the surfboard, but her baby is [a-l-r-i-t-].
17. Uncle doesn't give money; he gives [a-d-v-i-e].
18. My news [a-r-t-c-l-] was printed in the Daily Emetic.
19. Ten percent off on elephants? What a [b-a-r-g-n-]!
20. Our star [a-t-h-l-e-t-] gets a kick out of soccer.
21. Ferdinand sat [a-m-n-g-] the tulips.
22. We picked apples, and Dad was [c-a-r-i-n-g] a load.
23. For ten dollars, Madame Lazonga will [a-d-v-i-e] you.
24. Read, but don't [b-e-l-v-e] all you read.
25. Unusual exercise makes your muscles [a-c-e].
26. You don't have to [c-h-o-s-] a career. You can starve.
27. Two hours passed, and her telephone was still [b-s-y].
28. After my eye surgery I hope to see you [a-g-n].
29. The driver's last words were, "Gotta fix this [b-r-a-k-]."
30. The parachute didn't open, and I became quite [a-n-i-u-s].

Write correctly the words we studied that are derived from the Latin roots ALTER-ALTR, AM-AMAT, ANN-ENN, and AQU:

31. Water can be transported by means of an [a-q-t].
32. The general must surrender; he has no [a-l-t-v-].
33. The trip to Jupiter will live in the [a-n-l-] of science.
34. Tabloids love to gossip about the [a-m-r-s] of film stars.
35. Do we want military [a-r-m-n-t] or bread and butter?
36. Crops can be grown in this pond by [a-q-t-r-].
37. Stop the bombers! We've signed an [a-r-m-s-t-].
38. The crumbling, [s-u-p-r-n-t-d] building was condemned.
39. Mr. Two-Face is all smiles at the shop, but at home his [a-l-t-e-g-] asserts itself.
40. Sydney Carton lays down his life for Charles Darnay and Lucie Manette, an act of sheer [a-l-t-m].

Write the letter that indicates the best definition.

( ) 41. altercation   a. pertaining to lovemaking
( ) 42. amatory   b. friendship, as between nations
( ) 43. amiable   c. watery
( ) 44. amity   d. a fleet of warships
( ) 45. annual   e. yearly payment from an investment
( ) 46. annuity   f. a storehouse for military weapons
( ) 47. aquarium   g. a violent quarrel; dispute
( ) 48. aqueous   h. a tank for fish
( ) 49. armada   i. friendly; good-natured
( ) 50. armory   j. yearly

ANSWER KEY

Check your test answers by the following key. Deduct 2% per error from 100%.

1. answer	11. except	21. among	31. aqueduct	41. g
2. across	12. argument	22. carrying	32. alternative	42. a
3. attempt	13. accept	23. advise	33. annals	43. i
4. angry	14. business	24. believe	34. amours	44. b
5. beginning	15. break	25. ache	35. armament	45. j
6. beautiful	16. all right	26. choose	36. aquiculture	46. e
7. careless	17. advice	27. busy	37. armistice	47. h
8. chose	18. article	28. again	38. superannuated	48. c
9. children	19. bargain	29. brake	39. alter ego	49. d
10. a lot	20. athlete	30. anxious	40. altruism	50. f

Score: _____ %

Review carefully any words which you have missed in the foregoing Self-Test.

Your instructor will give you a final test on words 1-50 in Chapters 1 and 2.

SPELLING DEMONS: "CIGARETTE" TO "EXISTENCE"

3

DIRECTIONS: Study the spelling of each word carefully, giving special attention to the trouble spots (underlined letters). Then write each word neatly three times.

1. cig<u>a</u>rette *cigarette* _____ _____

2. cli<u>mb</u>ed _____ _____ _____

3. cloth<u>es</u> _____ _____ _____

4. coll<u>eg</u>e _____ _____ _____

5. col<u>o</u>r _____ _____ _____

6. co<u>mi</u>ng _____ _____ _____

7. coul<u>dn</u>'t _____ _____ _____

8. c<u>o</u>usin _____ _____ _____

9. cust<u>o</u>mer _____ _____ _____

10. da<u>ug</u>hter _____ _____ _____

Review words 1-10 until you are sure you can spell them. Then go on and take the quiz.

COVER THIS STRIP	FILL THE BLANKS
clothes color	■ When I find _____ [c-l-o-s-] that fit, they are the wrong _____ [c-l-r].
customer coming	■ Business is slow. Wake me up if you see a _____ [c-s-t-m-r] _____ [c-o-m-n-g].
cousin college	■ My _____ [c-u-s-n] nearly graduated from barber _____ [c-o-l-g-e], but he missed by a hair.
daughter couldn't clothes	■ McGinty told his _____ [d-a-t-r] that she _____ [c-d-n-t] go to the beach unless she put on more _____ [c-l-o-s-].
climbed cigarette	■ The hiker _____ [c-l-i-m-d] the mountain to reach sweet, clean air--then lit a _____ [c-i-g-r-t-].
couldn't customer coming	■ Sales _____ [c-u-d-n-t] be worse. Even the _____ [c-s-t-m-r] who doesn't pay his bills isn't _____ [c-o-m-n-g] in any more.
coming college cigarette	■ If you're _____ [c-o-m-n-g] into the _____ [c-o-l-g-e] library, you'd better put out your _____ [c-i-g-r-t-]--or they'll put you out.
daughter cousin couldn't	■ His _____ [d-a-t-r] Dixie has _____ [c-l-i-m-d] Mount Everest, but his _____ [c-u-s-n] Fudd _____ [c-d-n-t] stagger over the curb.
college couldn't color customer	■ The _____ [c-o-l-g-e] professors _____ [c-u-d-n-t] care less about a student's race, religion, or _____ [c-l-r]; they're only interested in the _____ [c-s-t-m-r] with brains.

climbed
color
clothes

- I _____ [c-l-i-m-d] the cliff to admire the _____ [c-l-r] of the eagle's eggs, and the eagle tore my _____ [c-l-o-s-].

daughter
cousin

- My _____ [d-a-t-r] married the grandfather of my _____ [c-u-s-n], which probably makes me my own stepmother.

cigarette
clothes

- Smoke a _____ [c-i-g-r-t-], and pretty soon your _____ [c-l-o-s-] smell like last week's socks.

daughter

- *"Have you married my* _____ *[d-a-t-r] without asking my good will?"* (Taming of the Shrew, V, i, 136)

DIRECTIONS: Continue as before. Study the spelling carefully. Write each word three times.

11. decent   *decent*   _____   _____

12. definite   _____   _____   _____

13. died   _____   _____   _____

14. doctor   _____   _____   _____

15. doesn't   _____   _____   _____

16. dollar   _____   _____   _____

17. dozen   _____   _____   _____

18. dropped   _____   _____   _____

19. drowned   _____   _____   _____

20. during   _____   _____   _____

Review words 11-20. Then take the quiz.

QUIZ

COVER
THIS STRIP

FILL THE BLANKS

---

doctor
dozen

- The _____ [d-o-c-t-r] recommended bananas, so I ate two _____ [d-z-n].

dropped
during
doesn't

- When bread is _____ [d-r-o-p-d] _____

[d-u-r-n-g] a meal, the peanut butter lands facing the rug.

Why _____ [d-s-n-t] some scientist explain that?

- One thing is _____ [d-e-f-n-t-]: A college

definite
decent

student must develop a _____ [d-c-n-t] command

of English.

- Mr. Murphy fell into the beer cask and _____

drowned
died

[d-r-o-n-d-], but he _____ [d-i-d-] with a smile.

- Junior said he'd be _____ [d-c-n-t] and good

if he was paid a _____ [d-o-l-r], but Mother told

decent
dollar

him to be good for nothing.

- Grandpa was a hundred years old today when he _____

[d-i-d-], but he _____ [d-s-n-t] look a day more

died
doesn't

than ninety-eight.

- Strike leaders report _____ [d-e-f-n-t-]

progress, and a settlement should be closer in a couple

definite
dozen

_____ [d-z-n] weeks.

- Angus _____ [d-r-o-p-d] a _____

dropped
dollar
drowned

[d-o-l-r] into the lake and almost _____

[d-r-o-n-d-] trying to get it out.

- The mayor _____ [d-s-n-t] ever say "yes" or

doesn't
definite

"no" but he gave us a _____ [d-e-f-n-t-] "maybe."

- In the Klondike, _____ [d-u-r-n-g] the Gold

during
dozen

Rush, a _____ [d-z-n] eggs were worth nuggets.

- The village _____ [d-o-c-t-r] _____

doctor
dropped
dollar

[d-r-o-p-d] over and told me I was as sound as a

_____ [d-o-l-r]. Then I knew I was in trouble.

drowned

- Nobody has actually _____ [d-r-o-n-d] in tears.

died
during
decent

- Hilda's faithful old dog _____ [d-i-d-]

_____ [d-u-r-n-g] the night, and she gave him a

_____ [d-c-n-t] burial near his favorite hydrant.

- *"By medicine life may be prolong'd, yet death*
  Will seize the _____ *[d-o-c-t-r] too."*
                          (Cymbeline, V, v, 29)

doctor

DIRECTIONS: Continue as before. Study the spelling carefully. Write each word three times.

21. e**a**ger   *eager*   _____   _____

22. **ea**rly   _____   _____   _____

23. eas**i**ly   _____   _____   _____

24. **E**nglish   _____   _____   _____

25. en**o**ugh   _____   _____   _____

26. equi**p**ment   _____   _____   _____

27. es**c**ape   _____   _____   _____

28. ever**y**thing   _____   _____   _____

29. e**xe**rcise   _____   _____   _____

30. ex**is**t**e**nce   _____   _____   _____

Review words 21-30. Then take the quiz.

QUIZ

FILL THE BLANKS

---

equipment
escape

- The prisoner received secret _____ [e-q-p-m-n-t]

in a pie, to help him _____ [e-c-a-p-].

eager
English

- Most immigrants to America were _____ [e-g-r]

to learn the _____ [-n-g-1-s-h] language.

everything
easily
existence

- If _____ [e-v-r-t-h-n-g] came to you too

_____ [e-s-1-y], what a dull _____ [e-x-s-t-n-c-]!

early
early
exercise

■ So _____ [e-r-l-y] to bed and _____ [e-r-l-y] to rise, and throw in some daily _____ [e-x-r-s-e].

escape

■ Travel to the moon and you still can't _____ [e-c-a-p-] from yourself.

enough
equipment

■ When my dentist puts _____ [e-n-g-h] _____ [e-q-p-m-n-t] into my mouth, he starts asking questions.

enough
easily

■ The bride invited _____ [e-n-g-h] guests to _____ [e-s-l-y] fill the Yankee Stadium.

eager
English

■ It's the _____ [e-g-r-] beaver who succeeds in this _____ [-n-g-l-s-h] class.

everything

■ My new diet lets me eat _____ [e-v-r-t-h-n-g] except the things I like.

existence
eager
early

■ Those who enjoy _____ [e-x-s-t-n-c-] are _____ [e-g-r] to get up _____ [e-r-l-y] in the morning, while others snore.

escape

■ A raving beauty! She made an _____ [e-c-a-p-] from an asylum.

equipment
exercise
everything

■ The gymnasium has _____ [e-q-p-m-n-t] to _____ [e-x-r-s-e] _____ [e-v-t-h-n-g] except your brains.

early

■ Light travels fast, and it gets here too _____ [e-r-l-y] in the morning.

enough
easily
existence

■ Lunatics have _____ [e-n-g-h] bombs so they can _____ [e-s-l-y] end human _____ [e-x-s-t-n-c-].

English
exercise

■ My _____ [-g-l-s-h] friend did all his _____ [e-x-r-s-e] with a knife and fork.

enough

■ *"Lay on, Macduff, and damned be him that first cries, 'Hold,* _____ *[e-n-g-h]!'" (Macbeth, V, viii, 34)*

LATIN ROOTS: "AUD" TO "CENT"

4

AUD, AUDIT: HEAR

31. **audible** (ô'də bəl) *adj.* able to be heard

    > The widow's sobs were *audible*.
    > His profanity was *audible* to mourners in the nearby church.

    <u>audible tones</u>   *audible tones*   _____
    (copy twice)

32. **audience** (ô'dē əns) *n.* those who hear or see a performance

    > The *audience* applauded without enthusiasm.
    > By act two we had lost our *audience*.

    <u>a live audience</u>   _____   _____

33. **audiophile** (ô'dē ə fīl') *n.* a person who is keenly interested in high-fidelity sound reproduction

    > The *audiophile* bought another tweeter and a woofer.
    > "A scratched record!" The *audiophile* sneered at me.

    <u>avid audiophiles</u>   _____   _____

34. **audition** (ô dish'ən) *n.* a trial hearing given to a musician, actor, etc. *v.* to take part in such a hearing

    > Van Cliburn amazed critics at his piano *audition*.
    > Judd *auditioned* for the role of Fagin.

vocal audition   _____   _____
   (copy twice)

35. **auditory** (ô′di tōr′ē)   *adj.* of the sense of hearing

> Luke's low grades are due to an *auditory* problem.
> Damage to *auditory* nerves can cause deafness.

<u>auditory nerves</u>   _____   _____

Review words 31-35. Then go on.

QUIZ

DIRECTIONS: Fill the blanks with words we studied that are derived from the Latin root AUD, AUDIT (hear). Be sure you spell the words correctly.

COVER
THIS STRIP

	■ The loud rock music was _____ [a-d-b-l-] in the next county, and it injured the _____ [a-d-t-y]
audible auditory	nerves of two farmers and a cow.
audition audience	■ I was the fifth amateur magician to _____ [a-d-t-n], and I made the _____ [a-d-n-c-] disappear.
	■ "That hiss should not be _____ [a-d-b-l-],"
audible audiophile auditory	complained the _____ [a-d-p-l-]. He had two ears like me but obviously greater _____ [a-d-t-y] talent.
	■ Jose smiled when the _____ [a-d-n-c-] sang,
audience	"Jose, can you see?"
audiophile	■ I listened with eyes shut, like an _____ [a-d-p-l-].
	■ A commencement speaker should quit when moans from the
audience audible	_____ [a-d-n-c-] become _____ [a-d-b-l-].
	■ Sheila was sobbing, her words hardly _____
audible audition	[a-d-b-l-]: "I--I won the _____ [a-d-t-n]."
	■ Surgery on the deaf boy's _____ [a-d-t-y]
auditory audiophile	nerve was successful. He became an _____ [a-d-p-l-].

audition	■ The competitive _____ [a-d-t-n] to play Santa Claus was won by an ex-convict.
audience	■ *"Their copious stories, oftentimes begun, End without _____ [a-d-n-c-], and are never done."* (Venus and Adonis, 845)

Non-test examples

OTHER DERIVATIVES OF AUD, AUDIT (HEAR):

audio-frequency (ô′dē ō frē′kwən sē) *n.* within the hearing range, about 20 to 20,000 cycles

audiogram (ô′dē ə gram′) *n.* a graph showing one's hearing loss

audiometer (ô′dē om′i tər) *n.* an instrument that tests hearing ability

audio-visual (ô′dē ō vizh′ōō əl) *adj.* involving both hearing and seeing [*audio-visual equipment*]

audiphone (ô′də fōn′) *n.* a hearing aid that transmits vibrations to the auditory nerves

audit (ô′dit) *n.* a formal checking of financial records [*a tax audit*]

auditor (ô′də tər) *n.* a listener; a person who audits accounts [*the county auditor*]

auditorium (ô′di tôr′ē əm) *n.* a hall or building for an audience

inaudible (in ô′də bəl) *adj.* not audible; not able to be heard

---

BEN, BENE: GOOD, WELL

36. **benediction** (ben′i dik′shən) *n.* a blessing

   The priest pronounced a *benediction.*
   The rain fell, like a *benediction,* upon the parched land.

   <u>holy benediction</u>   _____   _____
   (copy twice)

37. **benefactor** (ben′ə fak′tər) *n.* a kindly helper; one who gives a benefit

   Charles Edison was a *benefactor* of mankind.
   Do not bite the hand of your *benefactor.*

   <u>rich benefactor</u>   _____   _____

38. **beneficiary** (ben'ə fish'ər ē) *n.* one who receives benefits, as from a will or an insurance policy

> You are the sole *beneficiary*.
> When a man dies, his wife is usually his *beneficiary*.

legal beneficiary   _____   _____

39. **benevolence** (bə nev'ə ləns) *n.* good will to others; kindliness

> I was reassured by her *benevolent* smile.
> Krock's *benevolence* resulted in a Home for Wayward Cats.

act of benevolence   _____   _____

40. **benign** (bi nīn') *adj.* good-natured; gentle; *pathol.*, not malignant

> They loafed under the *benign* blue skies of Hawaii.
> Luckily, the growth was *benign*.

benign tumor   _____   _____

Review words 36-40. Then go on.

QUIZ

DIRECTIONS: Fill the blanks with words we studied that are derived from the Latin root BEN, BENE (good, well). Be sure you spell the words correctly.

COVER
THIS STRIP

	■ Please remain in your church pew until the final
benediction	_____ [b-n-d-n].
	■ In Dickens' *Great Expectations* Pip is the _____
beneficiary benefactor	[b-n-f-c-y] of money from an unknown _____ [b-n-f-c-t-].
	■ One Utah farmer assured me with a _____ [b-n-n]
benign beneficiary	smile that he was not the intended _____ [b-n-f-c-y] of Howard Hughes.
	■ The governor, in an act of _____ [b-n-v-l-],
benevolence	commuted Mugsy's sentence to life imprisonment.

page 30

benign benefactor	■ We have all seen the _____ [b-n-n] countenance of Benjamin Franklin, that public _____ [b-n-f-c-t-], on our postal stamps.
	■ John D. Rockefeller, in a burst of _____ [b-n-v-1-], made his caddy the _____ [b-n-f-c-y]
benevolence beneficiary	of a dime.
	■ The minister's _____ [b-n-d-n] may have helped;
benediction benign	at any rate, my tumor proved to be _____ [b-n-n].
	■ A parent is one's greatest _____ [b-n-f-c-t-], and the word "mother" falls on my ears like a _____
benefactor benediction	[b-n-d-n].
	■ Andrew Carnegie endowed 2800 free public libraries, an
benevolence	admirable act of _____ [b-n-v-1-].
	■ "O, look upon me, sir, And hold your hands in _____[b-n-d-n] o'er me."
benediction	*(King Lear, IV, vii, 58)*

Non-test examples

OTHER DERIVATIVES OF BEN, BENE (GOOD, WELL):

benedict (ben′i dikt) *n.* a newly married man, especially one who had
 long been a bachelor

benefaction (ben′ə fak′shən) *n.* a good deed

benefice (ben′ə fis) *n. Eccles.,* an endowed church office

beneficent (bə nef′i sənt) *adj.* doing good [*beneficent patrons*]

beneficial (ben′ə fish′əl) *adj.* advantageous; helpful [*beneficial rains*]

benefit (ben′ə fit) *n.* a help; an advantage *v.* to do good to

benignant (bi nig′nənt) *adj.* kind; gracious, especially to inferiors
 [*a benignant ruler*]

41. centennial (sen ten'ē əl) *adj., n.* a hundredth anniversary

> Colorado, admitted to the Union in 1876, is "The *Centennial* State."
> Invention of the airplane will be honored by a *centennial* in 2003.

centennial festival _____ _____
    (copy twice)

42. centigrade (sen'tə grād') *adj.* divided into one hundred degrees

> Physicists use a *centigrade* thermometer.
> Room temperature should be about 20° *centigrade*.

centigrade scale _____ _____

43. centimeter (sen'tə mē'tər) *n.* one hundredth of a meter

> One inch equals 2.54 *centimeters*.
> My new buzz saw neatly sliced off a *centimeter* of my thumb.

a centimeter wide _____ _____

44. centipede (sen'tə pēd) *n.* a many-legged crawler such as a caterpillar

> On the wall crawled a *centipede*.
> This *centipede* looks like an interurban train.

hairy centipede _____ _____

45. centurion (sen tyoor'ē ən) *n.* captain of a hundred Roman soldiers

> For bravery, Julius was promoted to *centurion*.
> Roman soldiers were quick to obey their *centurion*.

Roman centurion _____ _____

46. century (sen'chə rē) *n.* a hundred-year period

> Religious wars have been waged for *centuries*.
> A bloke named Doak planted this oak a *century* ago.

past centuries _____ _____

Review words 41–46. Then go on.

QUIZ

DIRECTIONS: Fill the blanks with words we studied that are derived from the Latin root CENT (hundred). Be sure you spell the words correctly.

COVER
THIS STRIP

century centimeter	■ Cyrano, who lived in the eighteenth _____ [c-t-r-y], had a nose that was a _____ [c-t-m-r-] or two too long.
centurion centipede	■ The Roman _____ [c-t-r-n-] didn't notice the _____ [c-t-p-d-] crawling up his leg.
centigrade centennial	■ If the temperature hits 40° _____ [c-t-g-d-], our _____ [c-t-n-1-] fair will be one hot failure.
centurion	■ Wambaugh's novel compares the police captain to an ancient _____ [c-t-r-n-].
century centipede	■ Alcoholic Al, at thirty-six, looks as though he's lived a _____ [c-t-r-y]. He's a shoe clerk and has nightmares about a _____ [c-t-p-d-] that wants a fitting.
centigrade	■ The temperature sank to 50° below on the _____ [c-t-g-d-] thermometer, a poor day for swimming.
century	■ My _____ [c-t-r-y] plant died at age two.
centipede centimeter	■ The _____ [c-t-p-d-] on my plate was a _____ [c-t-m-r-] long.
centennial centigrade	■ At the science _____ [c-t-n-1-], Abner learned that water freezes at 0° _____ [c-t-g-d-].
centimeter	■ One hundredth of a meter is a _____ [c-t-m-r-].
centennial centurion	■ At the _____ [c-t-n-1-] fair grounds stood a guard dressed as a Roman _____ [c-t-r-n-].
century	■ *"I ha' strew'd his grave* *And on it said a* _____ [c-t-r-y] *of prayers."* *(Cymbeline, IV, ii, 391)*

OTHER DERIVATIVES OF CENT (HUNDRED):

cent (sent) *n.* one hundredth of a dollar

centare (sen'târ) *n.* a square meter

centavo (sen tä'vō) *n.* one hundredth of a peso

centenarian (sen'tə ner'ē ən) *n.* a person at least one hundred years old

centesimal (sen tes'ə məl) *n.* a hundredth

centigram (sen'tə gram') *n.* one hundredth of a gram

centiliter (sen'tə lēt'ər) *n.* one hundredth of a liter

centillion (sen til'yən) *n.* a number represented in the United States by 1 followed by 303 zeros

centime (sän'tēm) *n.* one hundredth of a franc

centuple (sen'tə pəl) *adj.* a hundred times as many *v.* to increase a hundredfold

---

COGN: KNOW

47. cognizant (kog'nə zənt) *adj.* aware or conscious of something

> She is not *cognizant* of my existence.
> Is our president *cognizant* of the suffering in the slums?

cognizant of _____ _____
(copy twice)

48. cognomen (kog nō'mən) *n.* family name; a name by which one is known

> Johnson? That *cognomen* isn't unique in Minnesota.
> Somebody called him Alibi Ike, and the *cognomen* stuck.

familiar cognomen _____ _____

49. incognito (in kog'ni tō', in'kog nē'tō) *adj., adv.* under an assumed name; in disguise

> The prince visited the ghetto *incognito*.
> Garbo, in dark glasses, did her shopping *incognito*.

travel incognito _____ _____

50. **recognize** (rek′əg nīz′) *v.* to know by some detail; to acknowledge

> Mary *recognized* Marvin's little giggle.
> Management was asked to *recognize* the labor union.

<u>recognize talent</u>   _____   _____

Review words 47-50. Then go on.

QUIZ

DIRECTIONS: Fill the blanks with words we studied that are derived from the Latin root CENT (hundred). Be sure you spell the words correctly.

COVER
THIS STRIP

	▪ The prime minister attended a burlesque show
incognito	_____ [i-c-g-o-].
cognizant	▪ Skiers should be _____ [c-g-z-t] of dangers.
	▪ John Jones kept wishing he had a more distinctive
cognomen	_____ [c-g-n-m-], such as Antonio Vermicelli.
	▪ Einstein's teachers were not _____ [c-g-z-t]
cognizant	of his genius.
	▪ Mr. Kennedy, with a _____ [c-g-n-m-] like
	yours, you'll do well in politics. It's a name every
cognomen recognize	voter will _____ [r-c-g-z-].
	▪ Odysseus, in shabby clothes, returns _____
	[i-c-g-o-] to Ithaca, and the suitors of Penelope fail to
incognito recognize	_____ [r-c-g-z-] him.
cognomen	▪ Mortimer preferred the _____ [c-g-n-m-] Lefty.
	▪ The Beatles wanted to mingle _____ [i-c-g-o-]
incognito cognizant recognize	with the shoppers, but they were _____ [c-g-z-t] of
	difficulties. Someone would _____ [r-c-g-z-] them.
	▪ *"I will not be myself, nor have cognition*
	Of what I feel." (*Troilus and Cressida, V, ii, 63*)

cognition (kog nish'ən) *n.* the process of knowing or perceiving

cognizance (kog'nə zəns) *n.* knowledge; *Law*, the right of a court to hear a case

cognoscenti (kon'yə shen'tē) *n.* those who have superior knowledge; insiders; connoisseurs

recognizance (ri kog'ni zəns) *n.* *Law*, an obligation to do a particular act [*He was released on his own recognizance.*]

Review words 1-50, spelling and vocabulary. Then take the Chapters 3-4 Self-Test.

CHAPTERS 3-4: SELF-TEST

DIRECTIONS: Write the words in full. Complete this entire test before you check and grade your answers.

_____ 1. My [c-u-s-n-] was a big gun until he was fired.
_____ 2. A grown man used to work all day for a [d-o-l-r-].
_____ 3. It's twelve of one and a [d-z-n-] of the other.
_____ 4. One housewife [e-s-l-y] did the work of two mules.
_____ 5. You must create your own happy [[e-x-t-n-c-e].
_____ 6. Fido is old [e-n-g-h] to get social security.
_____ 7. My kindly aunt [d-r-o-n-d] the kittens in warm water.
_____ 8. One Siamese twin took poison and the other one [d-i-d-].
_____ 9. Fritz speaks [-n-g-l-s-h] with a German accent.
_____ 10. Jogging is an almost ideal [e-x-r-s-e].
_____ 11. My pet owl [d-o-s-n-t] give a hoot.
_____ 12. The near-sighted firefly made love to a [c-i-g-r-t-e-].
_____ 13. Joe swallowed a spoon and [c-u-d-n-t] stir for a week.
_____ 14. The seasick [d-o-c-t-r-] put on a tight collar.
_____ 15. Cynthia was expelled from a very fine [c-o-l-g-].
_____ 16. Get up [e-r-l-y] and you're sleepy all day.
_____ 17. Such a [c-u-s-t-m-r-] I send to my competitors.
_____ 18. Uncle's store teeth [d-r-o-p-d] into the lake.
_____ 19. The farmer drove his [d-a-t-r-] into the blizzard in act two.
_____ 20. It wasn't healthy to play the saxophone [d-u-r-n-g] Dad's nap.
_____ 21. The fish are so [e-g-r-] they jump into your boat.
_____ 22. Somebody stole our burglar alarm [e-q-i-p-n-t-].
_____ 23. The convict made his [e-c-a-p-e] through a sewer.
_____ 24. What will you do when you see the H-bomb [c-o-m-n-g]?
_____ 25. Tom [c-l-i-m-d-] barbed wire and had a ripping time.
_____ 26. Buy designer [c-l-o-s-] and pay through the nose.
_____ 27. The sun was the [c-l-r-] of an overripe tomato.
_____ 28. Kicking the pugilist was a [d-e-f-n-t-] mistake.
_____ 29. I may eat [e-v-r-t-h-n-g], unless it has calories.
_____ 30. "A very [d-e-c-n-t-] meal," burped the tramp.

Write correctly the words we studied that are derived from the Latin roots
AUD-AUDIT, BEN-BENE, CENT, and COGN:

_____ 31. Now a hundred years old, Bungville is celebrating its [c-t-1].
_____ 32. The governor put on a disguise and entered the inn [i-c-g-o-].
_____ 33. The pope held out his hands and gave us his [b-n-d-n-].
_____ 34. Is King Tut in the [a-d-n-c-]? Your mummy wants you.
_____ 35. I'll count the legs if you will hold the [c-t-p-d-].
_____ 36. The family name is Bzycrszh, a rather unusual [c-g-n-m-].
_____ 37. Thermometers are usually Fahrenheit or [c-t-g-d-].
_____ 38. The telltale heart was [a-d-b-1-] to the mad killer.
_____ 39. The billionaire passed away, and you're his sole [b-n-f-c-y].
_____ 40. On tryout day, Fanny brought her tuba for the [a-d-t-n-].

Write the letter that indicates the best definition.

( ) 41. audiophile   a. one hundredth of a meter
( ) 42. auditory   b. not malignant (of a tumor)
( ) 43. benefactor   c. aware of; conscious
( ) 44. benevolence   d. captain of 100 Roman warriors
( ) 45. benign   e. kindness; good will to others
( ) 46. centimeter   f. a hundred-year period
( ) 47. centurion   g. a lover of high-fidelity sound
( ) 48. century   h. to know by some detail
( ) 49. cognizant   i. a generous helper
( ) 50. recognize   j. pertaining to hearing

ANSWER KEY

Check your test answers by the following key. Deduct 2% per error from 100%.

1. cousin	11. doesn't	21. eager	31. centennial	41. g
2. dollar	12. cigarette	22. equipment	32. incognito	42. j
3. dozen	13. couldn't	23. escape	33. benediction	43. i
4. easily	14. doctor	24. coming	34. audience	44. e
5. existence	15. college	25. climbed	35. centipede	45. b
6. enough	16. early	26. clothes	36. cognomen	46. a
7. drowned	17. customer	27. color	37. centigrade	47. d
8. died	18. dropped	28. definite	38. audible	48. f
9. English	19. daughter	29. everything	39. beneficiary	49. c
10. exercise	20. during	30. decent	40. audition	50. h

Score _____ %

Review carefully any words which you have missed in the foregoing Self-Test.

Your instructor will give you a final test on words 1-50 in Chapters 3 and 4.

5

DIRECTIONS: Study the spelling of each word carefully, giving special attention to the trouble spots (underlined letters). Then write each word neatly three times.

1. exper<u>ie</u>nce *experience* _____ _____

2. fin<u>a</u>lly _____ _____ _____

3. fr<u>ie</u>nd _____ _____ _____

4. g<u>h</u>ost _____ _____ _____

5. gro<u>c</u>ery _____ _____ _____

6. g<u>ue</u>ss _____ _____ _____

7. ha<u>v</u>ing _____ _____ _____

8. h<u>ei</u>ght _____ _____ _____

9. hop<u>i</u>ng _____ _____ _____

10. hun<u>dr</u>ed _____ _____ _____

Review words 1-10 until you are sure you can spell them. Then go on and take the quiz.

COVER THIS STRIP	FILL THE BLANKS

■ Hamlet asks the _____ [g-o-s-t-] whether he comes as a _____ [f-r-n-d-] or a foe.

ghost
friend

■ Farmer Dingle is _____ [h-a-v-n-g] us dig a well, and he's _____ [h-o-p-n-g] you'll drop in.

having
hoping

■ Their basketball center was eight feet in _____ [h-i-t-], and I _____ [f-i-n-l-y] bit his kneecap.

height
finally

■ My _____ [f-r-n-d-] was hit by lightning--it was a shocking _____ [e-x-p-r-n-c-].

friend
experience

■ Gaston pointed to the _____ [g-o-s-t-] and said, "That's the spirit."

ghost

■ Hank has the same _____ [h-i-t-] as Abe Lincoln, but not the same character.

height

■ The little pigs _____ [f-i-n-l-y] went hogwild.

finally

■ Jim sent Linda a note with "a _____ [h-n-d-r-d] kisses," which his _____ [f-r-n-d-] Sam delivered.

hundred
friend

■ We spent a _____ [h-n-d-r-d] dollars at the _____ [g-r-o-r-y] store, and _____ [g-e-s-] what we're _____ [h-a-v-n-g] for supper--spinach.

hundred
grocery
guess
having

■ To get the job at the _____ [g-r-o-r-y] store, I had to be twenty years old and have a _____ [h-n-d-r-d] years of _____ [e-x-p-r-n-c-].

grocery
hundred
experience

■ Here's _____ [h-o-p-n-g] that we can _____ [f-i-n-l-y] cure our malaria. I'll shake to that.

hoping
finally

■ At his _____ [g-r-o-r-y] market, the political candidate _____ [f-i-n-l-y] handed us some baloney.

grocery
finally

ghost
height
guess

■ I met a _____ [g-o-s-t-] that was ten feet in _____ [h-i-t-], I _____ [g-e-s-], but I didn't hang around to measure.

hoping
having

■ Mr. Philander wrote his wife: "Here's _____ [h-o-p-n-g] you are well. Am _____ [h-a-v-n-g] a wonderful time. Wish you were her."

friend

■ *"He was my _____ [f-r-n-d-], faithful and just to me: / But Brutus says he was ambitious."*
(Julius Caesar, III, ii, 89)

DIRECTIONS: Continue as before. Study the spelling carefully. Write each word three times.

11. hun**gr**y   *hungry*   _____   _____

12. inst**ea**d   _____   _____   _____

13. int**e**rest   _____   _____   _____

14. i**ts** *(possessive)*: "wags *its* tail"   _____

15. i**t's** *(means "it is")*: "*it's* hot"   _____

16. **k**new   _____   _____   _____

17. **k**nock   _____   _____   _____

18. l**ai**d   _____   _____   _____

19. l**ea**d *(verb, present tense)*: "to *lead* the way"; *(noun)*: "a hunk of *lead*"

_____   _____   _____

20. l**ed** *(verb, past tense)*: "Last week she *led* me"   _____

Review words 11-20. Then take the quiz.

QUIZ

COVER
THIS STRIP

FILL THE BLANKS

laid
knock
it's

■ The little hen _____ [l-a-d-] an egg as big as an apple and said, "Well, don't _____ [-n-o-k-] it, because _____ [i-t-s-] the best I can do."

it's
knew

hungry

led
lead

instead
knock

laid
instead
interest

lead
it's

hungry
knew

lead
led
lead

its
interest

knew
hungry
interest

led
its

hungry
instead

■ The baby is two, and _____ [i-t-s-] high time he _____ [-n-e-w] the alphabet.

■ Schubert's horse named Sarah was _____ [h-n-g-r-y], so Schubert's Sarah neighed.

■ Marvin _____ [l-e-d] the parade slowly, as though he had _____ [l-e-d] in his pants.

■ A Puritan child who was dozing _____ [i-n-s-t-d] of listening to the sermon got a _____ [-n-o-k-] on the head.

■ Silas Marner _____ [l-a-d-] his gold coins away in a secret spot where they collected dust and flies _____ [i-n-s-t-d] of _____ [i-n-t-r-s-t].

■ Don't _____ [l-e-d] me into temptation, because _____ [i-t-s-] the only thing I can't resist.

■ The _____ [h-n-g-r-y] vultures _____ [-n-e-w] that I would be a tasty snack.

■ "Just _____ [l-e-d] us on!" shouted Ned; and the old miner Fred _____ [l-e-d] Ned into a shed that was full of _____ [l-e-d].

■ The alligator showed _____ [i-t-s-] teeth, and I lost _____ [i-n-t-r-s-t] in catching it.

■ I _____ [-n-e-w] the lost boy scouts were _____ [h-n-g-r-y] when they began to take an _____ [i-n-t-r-s-t] in the cactus plants.

■ The little dog _____ [l-e-d] the blind man to _____ [i-t-s-] favorite garbage can.

■ The Cyclops was so _____ [h-n-g-r-y] that he ate two sailors for lunch _____ [i-n-s-t-d] of one.

laid
its
knock

■ The little chimp _____ [l-a-d-] the coconut on

_____ [i-t-s] mother's toes and then gave it a good

_____ [-n-o-k-] with a rock.

knew

■ *"Alas, poor Yorick! I _____ [-n-e-w] him,*
Horatio: a fellow of infinite jest." (Hamlet, V, i, 179)

DIRECTIONS: Continue as before. Study the spelling carefully. Write each word three times.

21. less_o_n   *lesson*   _____   _____

22. li_st_en   _____   _____   _____

23. lon_e_ly   _____   _____   _____

24. lo_si_ng   _____   _____   _____

25. m_a_ny   _____   _____   _____

26. marr_ia_ge   _____   _____   _____

27. ma_y_be   _____   _____   _____

28. mi_dd_le   _____   _____   _____

29. min_u_te   _____   _____   _____

30. na_tu_ral   _____   _____   _____

Review words 21-30. Then take the quiz.

QUIZ

COVER
THIS STRIP   FILL THE BLANKS

marriage
lonely

■ The old bachelor avoided _____ [m-r-a-g-e],

and now he's a _____ [l-o-n-l-y] man.

middle
lesson

■ Luckily the fire drill came in the _____

[m-i-d-l-] of a hard _____ [l-e-s-n-].

listen
many
lesson
maybe

■ If we _____ [l-i-s-n-] to the busy bee, we can

learn _____ [m-n-y] a valuable _____ [l-e-s-n-]

about work, and _____ [m-a-b-e-] we'll get stung, too.

■ If religion doesn't change you, _____ [m-a-b-e-]

maybe

you should change your religion.

■ A Hollywood _____ [m-r-a-g-e] was supposed to

marriage
many

last forever—and it often did last _____[m-n-y] weeks.

losing

■ On my diet I was _____ [l-o-s-n-g] only my temper.

■ Excellent photos can be taken in the _____

middle
natural

[m-i-d-l-] of a _____ [n-a-t-r-l-] setting.

■ They hanged the cattle rustler and said that _____

maybe
lesson

[m-a-b-e-] that would teach him a _____ [l-e-s-n-].

■ I thought I was a _____ [n-a-t-r-l-] cheer-

leader; then I led a yell in the _____ [m-i-d-l-]

natural
middle
minute
losing

of a game and in less than a _____ [m-i-n-t-] our

team was _____ [l-o-s-n-g].

■ Wilbur speaks German with a _____ [n-a-t-r-l-]

natural

accent—an English accent, that is.

■ The world is full of _____ [l-o-n-l-y] people;

lonely
listen
minute

one should _____ [l-i-s-n-] to them, if only for a

_____ [m-i-n-t-].

■ Abe Lincoln, too, was a _____ [l-o-n-l-y] man,

lonely
marriage

and his _____ [m-r-a-g-e] didn't cheer him up.

■ Rest your mouth once in a while and _____

listen

[l-i-s-n-].

■ A moron speeds through traffic, and _____ [m-n-y]

a time his gamble saves a whole _____ [m-i-n-t-],

many
minute
maybe
losing

but _____ [m-a-b-e-] he ends up _____

[l-o-s-n-g] fifty years of his life.

marriage

■ *"Hasty* _____ *[m-r-a-g-e] seldom proveth well."*
                              (3 King Henry VI, IV, i, 18)

6

DIC, DICT: SAY

31. contradict (kon'trə dikt') *v.* to say the opposite; deny

> Galileo's strange theory *contradicted* the popular belief.
> I never dared to *contradict* my father.

contradict rumors   *contradict rumors*
   (copy twice)

32. diction (dik'shən) *n.* style of speaking or writing; choice of words

> A newscaster must use clear, correct *diction*.
> Sloppy *diction* is considered a mark of ignorance.

poetic diction

33. edict (ē'dikt) *n.* an official public command; decree

> The peasants obeyed the *edict* of the king.
> The Vatican issued a papal *edict*.

military edict

34. indict (in dīt') *v.* to accuse of a crime; make a formal legal accusation

> The grand jury has *indicted* the murder suspect.
> You can *indict* my client, but you won't prove him guilty.

indict for burglary

35. **jurisdiction** (joor'is dik'shən) *n.* the legal power to decide cases; the authority to administer justice

> Our town was in Judge Schnapp's *jurisdiction*.
> The Senate has *jurisdiction* in matters of impeachment.

<u>local jurisdiction</u> _____ _____

36. **malediction** (mal'ə dik'shən) *n.* a curse; slander; evil talk about someone

> The coach heaped *maledictions* on the umpire.
> The rival gangs exchanged *maledictions*.

<u>flung maledictions</u> _____ _____

Review words 31-36. Then go on.

QUIZ

DIRECTIONS: Fill the blanks with words we studied that are derived from the Latin root DIC, DICT (say). Be sure you spell the words correctly.

COVER
THIS STRIP

	■ The hog was stolen in Utah, and this Chicago court has
jurisdiction	no _____ [j-r-d-n] in this case.
	■ Demosthenes practiced oratory with pebbles in his mouth,
diction	to improve his _____ [d-c-n].
	■ "I don't aim to _____ [c-t-d-t] you," said the
contradict indict	little lawyer, "but you can't _____ [i-n-d-t-] my client just because he has shifty eyes."
	■ Upon hearing the Czar's latest _____ [e-d-t-],
edict	the peasants groaned a mighty groan.
malediction	■ The opposite of a benediction is a _____ [m-1-d-n].
	■ We would _____ [i-n-d-t-] the Boston Strangler,
indict jurisdiction	but our Texas courts have no _____ [j-r-d-n] in the case.

contradict malediction	■ The only man who dared to _____ [c-t-d-t] the Godfather and even to hurl a _____ [m-l-d-n] at him was my brave brother Gino—-may he rest in peace. ■ The church of Rome, which is international in its _____ [j-r-d-n], has issued an _____ [e-d-t-] against abortion.
jurisdiction edict	
malediction diction	■ The angry prisoner cast a _____ [m-l-d-n] or three at the guards, nor did he use the cleanest _____ [d-c-n].
edict contradict	■ When the emperor issued an _____ [e-d-t-] in Latin, the uneducated villagers could not _____ [c-t-d-t] him.
indict	■ In a democracy we can even _____ [i-n-d-t-] our president. The process is called impeachment.
diction	■ Englishmen take pride in precise _____ [d-c-n].
contradict	■ *"A greater power than we can _____ [c-t-d-t] Hath thwarted our intents"* *(Romeo and Juliet, V, iii, 153)*

Non-test examples

OTHER DERIVATIVES OF DIC, DICT (SAY):

addict (ad′ikt) *n.* a habitual user, as of narcotics [*a confirmed addict*]

dictate (dik′tāt) *v.* to say something for another to write down [*dictate a letter*]

dictator (dik′tā tər) *n.* a ruler with absolute power [*a Roman dictator*]

dictum (dik′təm) *n.* a formal opinion; a pronouncement [*dictum of science*]

interdict (in tər dikt′) *v.* to forbid with authority; prohibit [*interdict the divorce*]

predicate (pred′ə kit) *n. Gram.*, the part of a sentence that says something about the subject [*a compound predicate*]

prediction (pri dik′shən) *n.* a forecast; a foretelling of what may happen [*a weather prediction*]

valedictorian (val'i dik tōr'ē ən)   *n.* a student, usually ranking
highest in scholarship, who delivers the farewell speech at the
commencement exercises   [*a valedictory talk*]

verdict (vur'dikt)   *n.* a court decision; a judgment [*verdict of guilty*]

FID: FAITH; TRUST

37. affidavit (af'i dā'vit)   *n.* a sworn written statement

> A notary public witnessed the *affidavit*.
> Here's an *affidavit* from an absent witness.

a notarized affidavit _____ _____
    (copy twice)

38. confidence (kon'fi dəns)   *n.* full trust; faith; self-assurance

> The coach has great *confidence* in his 329-pound wrestler.
> Clara told me this in *confidence*.

vote of confidence _____ _____

39. fidelity (fi del'i tē)   *n.* loyalty; faithfulness

> His wife's *fidelity* is beyond question.
> The violin solo was reproduced with *fidelity*.

high fidelity _____ _____

40. infidel (in'fə dəl)   *n.* somebody without religious faith; an unbeliever

> Christians and Moslems regard each other as *infidels*.
> The missionary converted the *infidels*.

damned infidels _____ _____

41. perfidious (pər fid'ē əs)   *adj.* treacherous; deceitful

> Benedict Arnold did a *perfidious* thing.
> The *perfidious* plot of Guy Fawkes was discovered.

perfidious advice _____ _____

Review words 37-41.   Then go on.

QUIZ

DIRECTIONS: Fill the blanks with words we studied that are derived from the Latin root FID (faith; trust). Be sure you spell the words correctly.

COVER
THIS STRIP

affidavit confidence	■ This court _____ [a-f-v-t-] regarding your excellent character gives me some _____ [c-n-f-d-] that you will not be hanged.
fidelity	■ Early radios had such poor _____ [f-d-t-y] that Enrico Caruso sounded like a cat fight.
infidel perfidious	■ The Puritans looked upon the Indian as an _____ [i-f-d-l-], whereas the Indian looked upon the tricky white man as _____ [p-f-d-s-].
confidence fidelity	■ Julius Caesar expressed complete _____ [c-n-f-d-] as to his wife Calpurnia's _____ [f-d-t-y].
affidavit perfidious	■ The lawyer read one signed _____ [a-f-v-t-] after another testifying to the _____ [p-f-d-s-] activities of Sam the Snitch.
confidence infidel	■ Jonathan Edwards predicted with _____ [c-n-f-d-] that every _____ [i-f-d-l-] would sizzle in hell.
fidelity	■ The artist drew my big ears with _____ [f-d-t-y].
affidavit	■ I lost my birth certificate, but I have my uncle's _____ [a-f-v-t-] to prove that I was born.
infidel perfidious	■ Thomas Paine, a critic of the Bible, was regarded as an _____ [i-f-d-l-] of the most _____ [p-f-d-s-] sort.
infidel	■ *"What a pagan rascal is this! an* _____ *[i-f-d-l-]!"* (1 Henry IV, II, iii, 32)

confide (kən fīd') *v.* to trust by sharing secrets [*confide troubles to a friend*]

confidential (kon'fə den'shəl) *adj.* telling of private or secret matters [*a confidential report*]

diffident (dif'i dent) *adj.* shy; timid; lacking self-confidence [*a diffident applicant for a job*]

fiduciary (fi dōō'shē er'ē) *adj.* held in trust [*fiduciary property*]

perfidy (pur'fi dē) *n.* betrayal of trust; treachery [*an act of perfidy*]

GREG: FLOCK

42. aggregation (ag'grə gā'shən) *n.* a group; a mass of individuals

> The football *aggregation* came by bus.
> The dead fish attracted an *aggregation* of flies.

vast aggregation _____   _____
  (copy twice)

43. congregate (kong'grə gāt') *v.* to assemble; flock together

> The strikers *congregated* at the factory entrance.
> The priest addressed his *congregation*.

congregate for prayer _____   _____

44. egregious (i grē'jəs) *adj.* remarkably bad; flagrant

> What an *egregious* liar!
> Buying the swampland was an *egregious* blunder.

egregious errors _____   _____

45. gregarious (grə ger'ē əs) *adj.* sociable; fond of the company of others; living in flocks

> Sheep are *gregarious*.
> Dance halls attract *gregarious* people.

gregarious partygoers _____   _____

46. segregate (seg′rə gāt′) *v.* to separate from the group; isolate

> Some schools *segregate* their more gifted students.
> Jails *segregate* criminals from society.

<u>to segregate the aged</u> _____ _____

Review words 42-46. Then go on.

QUIZ

DIRECTIONS: Fill the blanks with words we studied that are derived from the Latin root GREG (flock). Be sure you spell the words correctly.

COVER
THIS STRIP

gregarious	■ My _____ [g-r-g-s-] aunt should never have married the hermit.
segregate aggregation	■ The parking attendant decided to _____ [s-e-g-t-] my jalopy from the _____ [a-g-t-n] of Cadillacs.
egregious	■ Washing his feet in the punch bowl was one of Harpo's more _____ [e-g-r-s-] social errors.
segregate	■ A Supreme Court decision struck at those who would _____ [s-e-g-t-] students because of color.
egregious gregarious congregate	■ The saloon was an _____ [e-g-r-s-] den of sin, and the more _____ [g-r-g-s-] cowboys and miners tended to _____ [c-n-g-t-] there.
egregious segregate	■ Two of the parrots used such _____ [e-g-r-s-] profanity that we had to _____ [s-e-g-t-] them from the more innocent birds.
congregate aggregation	■ College teachers began to _____ [c-n-g-t-] at the convention center, and from a tiny taxicab poured a dense _____ [a-g-t-n] of professors.

page 50

■ Our dog Mildred was extremely amiable and _____

[g-r-g-s-]; and she generally played tag with an

_____ [a-g-t-n] of her friends who used to

gregarious
aggregation
congregate

_____ [c-n-g-t-] near the butcher shop.

■ *"You give me most* _____ [e-g-r-s-] *indignity."*

egregious

(All's Well that Ends Well, II, iii, 228)

ANOTHER DERIVATIVE OF GREG (FLOCK):

aggregate (ag'rə git) *adj.* formed by a collection of particulars into a sum; total [*the aggregate profits*] *n.* the gross amount [*the aggregate for the year*]

LITERA: LETTER

47. **alliteration** (ə lit ə rā'shən) *n.* repetition of an initial sound in a word group, as in *Billy Bungle's Bigtime Band*

Poets make constant use of *alliteration.*
Alliteration occurs in "summer skies" and "dark despair."

poetic alliteration _____ _____
(copy twice)

48. **illiterate** (i lit'ər it) *adj.* not knowing how to read and write; unlettered; ignorant

Many are *illiterate* because of television.
Illiterate citizens usually get low-paying jobs.

illiterate laborers _____ _____

49. **literally** (lit'ər ə lē) *adv.* actually; word for word

Jessica translated the Greek passage *literally.*
Dunkle was *literally* suffocated by the volcanic ash.

literally amazed _____ _____

50. **literature** (lit'ər ə chər) *n.* outstanding imaginative poetry and prose

Poe and Hawthorne contributed to American *literature.*
Dramatic *literature* is incomplete without Ibsen's plays.

modern literature _____ _____

Review words 47-50. Then go on.

QUIZ

DIRECTIONS: Fill the blanks with words we studied that are derived from the Latin root LITERA (letter). Be sure you spell the words correctly.

COVER
THIS STRIP

literature illiterate	■ A student who hasn't read the _____ [l-t-r-e] of Mark Twain might as well be _____ [i-l-r-t-].
literature alliteration	■ Poe's poetic _____ [l-t-r-e], with its "weak and weary" and "surcease from sorrow," is crammed with _____ [a-l-t-n].
alliteration	■ "Fee, fie, foe, fum!" said the giant in an outburst of _____ [a-l-t-n].
illiterate literature	■ Many immigrants were _____ [i-l-r-t-] when they arrived, yet some later wrote great _____ [l-t-r-e].
literally	■ Don't translate poetry too _____ [l-t-l-y].
literally	■ If a child was sinful, the Puritans _____ [l-t-l-y] "beat the hell" out of him.
illiterate alliteration	■ "Peter Piper picked a peck..."--even an _____ [i-l-r-t-] child can enjoy such _____ [a-l-t-n].
literally	■ A court reporter must record even the stupidest remarks _____ [l-t-l-y] and without change.
illiterate	■ *"O _____ [i-l-r-t-] loiterer!...this proves that thou canst not read."* (The Two Gentlemen of Verona, IV, i, 296)

Non-test examples

OTHER DERIVATIVES OF LITERA (LETTER):

literacy (lit′ər ə sē) *n.* ability to read and write [*literacy in Italy*]

literalism (lit′ər ə liz′əm) *n.* sticking to the exact letter in interpretation; realism in art or literature [*literalism in Bible commentary*]

literary (lit′ə rer′ē) *adj.* having to do with polished writing
[*literary works*]

literate (lit′ər it) *adj.* able to read and write; well-educated
[*highly literate young women*]

literati (lit ə rot′ē) *n.* scholarly people; intellectuals [*the literati
of Paris*]

transliteration (trans lit ər ā′shən) *n.* writing words in corresponding
letters of another language [*transliteration of Arabic into English*]

Review words 1-50, spelling and vocabulary. Then take the Chapters 5-6
Self-Test.

CHAPTERS 5-6: SELF-TEST

DIRECTIONS: Write the words in full. Complete this entire test before you
check and grade your answers.

_____ 1. Joe forgot his lines in the [m-i-d-l-] of act one.
_____ 2. The stranger [l-a-d-] four aces on the table.
_____ 3. Never stop to debate with a [h-n-g-y] tiger.
_____ 4. The chief cause of divorce is [m-r-a-g-e].
_____ 5. My beagle hound stepped on [i-t-s-] own ears.
_____ 6. One [f-r-n-d] is better than two enemies.
_____ 7. Eat yoghurt [i-n-s-t-d] of ice cream.
_____ 8. Basketball requires speed and [h-i-g-t-].
_____ 9. Fernando had [n-a-t-r-l-] talent.
_____ 10. My old history professor [-n-e-w-] Abe Lincoln.
_____ 11. Money stinks, but [m-n-y] people like the smell.
_____ 12. "Do you believe in people?" asked the little [g-o-s-t-].
_____ 13. The bloodhound [l-e-d] the officers to a dead catfish.
_____ 14. If one team is winning, another must be [l-o-s-n-g].
_____ 15. She returned my photo, saying she wasn't that [l-o-n-l-y].
_____ 16. Speedy Sam can type sixty mistakes per [m-i-n-t-].
_____ 17. These guides will [l-e-d] you to the crocodiles.
_____ 18. The desert temperature dipped to one [h-u-n-r-d-].
_____ 19. The executioner says that [i-t-s-] about time.
_____ 20. Butch has gone to take his ballet [l-e-s-n-].
_____ 21. Shut up and [l-i-s-n-] to the mockingbird.
_____ 22. You remember details only if you take an [i-n-t-r-s-t].
_____ 23. Our pilot [f-i-n-l-y] sobered up.
_____ 24. Some people talk to avoid [h-a-v-n-g] to think.
_____ 25. Touching the bare wire was a hair-raising [e-x-p-r-n-c-].
_____ 26. Prices hit the ceiling at the [g-r-o-r-y] store.
_____ 27. I'm [h-o-p-n-g] you feel better than you look.
_____ 28. Food is so expensive that [m-a-b-e-] we should eat money.
_____ 29. Grandpa lost his marbles—[g-e-s-] how many.
_____ 30. A skateboard spill can [-n-o-k-] out one's teeth.

Write correctly the words we studied that are derived from the Latin roots
DIC-DICT, FID, GREG, and LITERA:

_____	31. The gates of paradise won't open for an [i-f-d-l-].
_____	32. A news commentator must use flawless [d-c-n].
_____	33. Petting the rattlesnake was an [e-g-s] mistake.
_____	34. The plot of O'Neill's play comes from Greek [l-i-t-r-].
_____	35. The title Pride and Prejudice is an example of [a-l-t-n].
_____	36. The notary public signed and recorded the [a-f-v-t].
_____	37. The farm was [l-t-r-y] eaten up by grasshoppers.
_____	38. "Curses!" was the strongest [m-l-d-n] in the melodrama.
_____	39. Politicians are handshakers, [g-r-g-s] by nature.
_____	40. They were losers--drunk, jobless, and [i-l-t-r-].

Write the letter that indicates the best definition.

( ) 41. aggregation   a. deceitful; treacherous
( ) 42. confidence   b. to separate from the flock
( ) 43. congregate   c. faithfulness in marriage; loyalty
( ) 44. contradict   d. to gather together; assemble
( ) 45. edict   e. the authority to judge cases
( ) 46. fidelity   f. self-assurance; optimism; trust
( ) 47. indict   g. a group of individuals
( ) 48. jurisdiction   h. to say the opposite
( ) 49. perfidious   i. an official command
( ) 50. segregate   j. to accuse of a crime

ANSWER KEY

Check your test answers by the following key. Deduct 2% per error from 100%.

1. middle	11. many	21. listen	31. infidel	41. g
2. laid	12. ghost	22. interest	32. diction	42. f
3. hungry	13. led	23. finally	33. egregious	43. d
4. marriage	14. losing	24. having	34. literature	44. h
5. its	15. lonely	25. experience	35. alliteration	45. i
6. friend	16. minute	26. grocery	36. affidavit	46. c
7. instead	17. lead	27. hoping	37. literally	47. j
8. height	18. hundred	28. maybe	38. malediction	48. e
9. natural	19. it's	29. guess	39. gregarious	49. a
10. knew	20. lesson	30. knock	40. illiterate	50. b

Score: _____ %

Review carefully any words which you have missed in the foregoing Self-Test.

Your instructor will give you a final test on words 1-50 in Chapters 5 and 6.

7

DIRECTIONS: Study the spelling of each word carefully, giving special attention to the trouble spots (underlined letters). Then write each word neatly three times.

1. ne<u>c</u>essary *necessary* _____ _____

2. nin<u>e</u>ty _____ _____ _____

3. occa<u>s</u>ion _____ _____ _____

4. opi<u>ni</u>on _____ _____ _____

5. p<u>ai</u>d _____ _____ _____

6. pa<u>ss</u>ed *(verb, past tense of "pass")*: "The bus *passed* me"

_____ _____ _____

7. pas<u>t</u> *(prep.)*: "The bus sailed *past* me" _____

8. pen<u>c</u>il _____ _____ _____

9. pe<u>o</u>ple _____ _____ _____

10. p<u>e</u>rform _____ _____ _____

Review words 1-10 until you are sure you can spell them. Then go on and take the quiz.

QUIZ

COVER THIS STRIP	FILL THE BLANKS

COVER THIS STRIP — FILL THE BLANKS

people
opinion
paid

■ Some _____ [p-e-p-1-] give you a free _____ [o-p-i-n-], and it's worth what you _____ [p-a-d-].

ninety
occasion

■ Grandma was _____ [n-i-n-y] today, and she celebrated the _____ [o-c-s-o-n] by jumping the hedge.

pencil

■ Ida scribbled sharp words with a dull _____ [p-n-1-].

opinion
necessary
perform

■ "In my _____ [o-p-i-n-]," chuckled my dentist, "it's _____ [n-e-s-r-y] to _____ [p-r-f-o-m] a root canal."

past
passed
ninety

■ As Dad jogged _____ [p-a-s-] the school, a little girl _____ [p-a-s-] him. She was sprinting about _____ [n-i-n-y] miles an hour.

pencil
perform

■ Give a talented freshman a hunk of paper and a _____ [p-n-1-], and he'll _____ [p-r-f-o-m] brilliantly.

paid

■ Nick _____ [p-a-d-] for the lingerie and gave his wife the slip.

necessary
paid
ninety
past

■ "This visit wouldn't be _____ [n-e-s-r-y]," grunted the piano mover, "except that your bill was to be _____ [p-a-d-] in _____ [n-i-n-y] days and now it is ten hours _____ [p-a-s-] due."

occasion
passed
occasion
passed

■ I heard the bullet twice: The first _____ [o-c-a-s-n] was when the bullet _____ [p-a-s-] me, and the second _____ [o-c-a-s-n] was when I _____ [p-a-s-] it.

necessary

■ Baby swallowed ten aspirins, so it was _____ [n-e-s-r-y] to give him a headache.

page 56

pencil people past	■ The blind man sold a _____ [p-n-l-] to several unwilling _____ [p-e-p-l-] who were walking _____ [p-a-s-].
opinion necessary people paid perform	■ In Mother's _____ [o-p-i-n-] it's hardly _____ [n-e-s-r-y] that grown _____ [p-e-p-l-] be _____ [p-a-d-] a million dollars to _____ [p-r-f-o-m] in a game with a ball and a stick.
people	■ *"How beauteous mankind is! O brave new world,* *That has such* _____ *[p-e-p-l-] in't."* *(The Tempest, V, i, 184)*

DIRECTIONS: Continue as before. Study the spelling carefully. Write each word three times.

11. poss**ib**le   *possible*   _____   _____

12. privi**l**ege   _____   _____   _____

13. prob**ab**ly   _____   _____   _____

14. promi**se**   _____   _____   _____

15. qu**ie**t *(adj.):* "a *quiet* scene"   _____   _____

16. re**a**dy   _____   _____   _____

17. rec**ei**ve   _____   _____   _____

18. rem**em**ber   _____   _____   _____

19. saf**e**ty   _____   _____   _____

20. sep**a**rate   _____   _____   _____

Review words 11-20. Then take the quiz.

QUIZ

COVER THIS STRIP	FILL THE BLANKS
quiet probably	■ A child who is always _____ [q-i-t-] as a mouse is _____ [p-r-o-b-l-y] not normal.
probably	■ Tweezers will _____ [p-r-o-b-l-y] do in a pinch.

privilege
receive
safety

- Driving a car is a _____ [p-r-i-v-l-g-], and nobody should _____ [r-e-c-v-e] a driver's license who sneers at _____ [s-a-f-t-y].

remember
possible
separate

- When we _____ [r-e-m-b-r-] how Clym loved Eustacia, it doesn't seem _____ [p-o-s-b-l-] that they would _____ [s-e-p-r-t-].

safety

- Is that a red necktie or did Jim's _____ [s-a-f-t-y] razor slip?

ready
receive
remember

- The bride was now _____ [r-e-d-y] to _____ [r-e-c-v-e] the wedding ring, but the groom couldn't _____ [r-e-m-b-r] where he'd put it.

promise
quiet
promise

- The parents made a _____ [p-r-o-m-s-] that their baby would be _____ [q-u-i-t-] at the concert, but the baby didn't make any _____ [p-r-o-m-s-].

receive
possible

- To _____ [r-e-c-v-e] such photos of Saturn hardly seemed _____ [p-o-s-b-l-].

ready
safety
receive

- When the plane is _____ [r-e-d-y] to take off, please fasten your _____ [s-a-f-t-y] belt or you may _____ [r-e-c-v-e] a bump on the noggin.

promise

- The janitors _____ [p-r-o-m-s-] to make sweeping reforms.

separate
safety
privilege

- The thug threatened to _____ [s-e-p-r-t-] me from my teeth; so, fearing for my _____ [s-a-f-t-y], I assured him that it was a _____ [p-r-i-v-l-g-] to contribute my wallet toward his personal needs.

ready
separate
probably

- The tightrope walker is _____ [r-e-d-y] to juggle nine _____ [s-e-p-r-t-] eggs while he whistles "Dixie," but he _____ [p-r-o-b-l-y] won't be in tune.

quiet
possible

■ The kids were now so _____ [q-u-i-t-] that it was

almost _____ [p-o-s-b-l-] to hear a firecracker.

■ The Siamese twins in Prague were cut apart, and now

separate

they're _____ [s-e-p-r-t-] Czechs.

■ "Oh, darling," wrote Mike, "_____ [p-r-o-m-s-]

to _____ [r-e-m-b-r-] me after I become a war hero

promise
remember
probably
privilege

and have _____ [p-r-o-b-1-y] lost my legs for the

_____ [p-r-i-v-l-g-] of walking in freedom."

■ Death Valley was so dry that Dinah attached the postage

safety

stamp to the envelope with a _____ [s-a-f-t-y] pin.

■ *"Out of this nettle, danger, we pluck this flower,*
_____ [s-a-f-t-y]"

safety

(1 King Henry IV, II, iii, 11)

DIRECTIONS: Continue as before. Study the spelling carefully. Write each
word three times.

21. simil**a**r   *similar*   _____   _____

22. s**i**nce   _____   _____   _____

23. str**ai**ght   _____   _____   _____

24. stud**y**ing   _____   _____   _____

25. su**r**prise   _____   _____   _____

26. th**a**n *(conj.):* "bigger *than* Joe"   _____

27. th**e**n *(adv.):* "and *then* we met"   _____

28. the**i**r *(possessive):* "*their* dog"   _____

29. the**r**e *(adv., interj., noun):* "go *there*"   _____

30. the**y**'re *(contraction):* "*they're* gone"   _____

Review words 21-30. Then take the quiz.

COVER THIS STRIP	FILL THE BLANKS
	■ Those hillbillies over _____ [t-h-r-] are so far from civilization that _____ [t-h-r-] using kerosene to run _____ [t-h-r-] TV sets.

there
they're
their

straight
then
than

studying
straight
surprise
their

then
their

they're
similar
since
than

there
since
similar

surprise
their
they're
studying
their

■ Those hillbillies over _____ [t-h-r-] are so

far from civilization that _____ [t-h-r-] using

kerosene to run _____[t-h-r-] TV sets.

■ Washington threw a dollar _____ [s-t-r-a-t-]

across the Delaware, but money went further _____

[t-h-n] _____ [t-h-n] it does now.

■ Two athletes started _____ [s-t-u-d-n-g] and

earned a _____ [s-t-r-a-t-] A, and the

_____ [s-u-p-r-i-s-] caused _____ [t-h-r-]

coach to go into shock.

■ Old people travel; _____ [t-h-n] they lose

_____ [t-h-r-] grip.

■ Although _____ [t-h-r-] twins, the pair aren't

exactly _____ [s-i-m-l-r-], especially

_____ [s-n-c-e] Don is taller _____ [t-h-n]

Donna.

■ Mary won't eat _____ [t-h-r-] any more at the

Boots Cafe _____ [s-n-c-e] being served a

hamburger _____ [s-i-m-l-r-] to boot leather.

■ What a pleasant _____ [s-u-p-r-i-s-] to find

that Hans and Fritz have broken _____ [t-h-r-]

television set and that _____ [t-h-r-] both

_____ [s-t-u-d-n-g] _____ [t-h-r-]

vocabulary lesson.

their
than
there
since

■ I don't know why they think _____ [t-h-r-]

baseball team is better _____ [t-h-n] ours, but

we haven't been invited over _____ [t-h-r-] to

play them _____ [s-n-c-e] they beat us 31 to 0.

■ All week Joe and Flo were _____ [s-t-u-d-n-g]

theorems about _____ [s-t-r-a-t-] angles and

studying
straight
similar
then
surprise

_____ [s-i-m-l-r-] triangles; and _____

[t-h-n-], to their _____ [s-u-p-r-i-s-] the

final test was on circles.

their
their

■ *"They have* _____ *[t-h-r-] exits and*
_____ *[t-h-r-] entrances"*
                    (As You Like It, II, vii, 141)

8

MAL: BAD

31. **maladroit** (mal'ə droit') *adj.* awkward; clumsy

> The ballet master said I was a *maladroit* clown.
> The violin is not an ideal instrument for the *maladroit*.

maladroit skaters *maladroit skaters* _____
     (copy twice)

32. **malefactor** (mal'ə fak'tər) *n.* an evildoer or criminal

> The *malefactor* was placed behind bars.
> A license number led to the arrest of the *malefactor*.

catch the malefactor _____ _____

33. **malice** (mal'is) *n.* evil intent; desire to harm another

> "With *malice* toward none; with charity for all," said Lincoln.
> Did he trip you accidentally or in *malice*?

malice toward none _____ _____

34. **malignant** (mə lig'nənt) *adj.* very harmful; evil

> One must remove a *malignant* tumor.
> The devil cast a *malignant* glance at Faustus.

malignant fate _____ _____

35. malnutrition (mal noo trish'ən) *n.* faulty nourishment caused by poor food or insufficient food

> Candy and cola diets can lead to *malnutrition*.
> Children in India died of *malnutrition*.

fight malnutrition _____ _____

36. malpractice (mal prak'tis) *n.* injurious or neglectful treatment, as of a patient by a professional

> The drunken surgeon was guilty of *malpractice*.
> Removing the kidney from the wrong patient was *malpractice*.

legal malpractice _____ _____

Review words 31-36. Then go on.

QUIZ

DIRECTIONS: Fill the blanks with words we studied that are derived from the Latin root MAL (bad). Be sure you spell the words correctly.

COVER
THIS STRIP

	■ The lawyer bribed a witness? That's _____ [m-p-c-e]!
malpractice	
	■ Flo's toes were flattened by her _____ [m-l-d-t] dancing partner.
maladroit	
	■ Although Alice lives in a Dallas palace, I bear Alice no _____ [m-l-c-].
malice	
	■ Cyrano was so skillful that he made other swordsmen look _____ [m-l-d-t].
maladroit	
	■ Is it possible that a _____ [m-g-n-t] growth might be caused by faulty nourishment, that is, by
malignant malnutrition	_____ [m-l-t-n]?
	■ The security guard caught a skinny burglar inside the bakery; the _____ [m-f-t-r] was apparently
malefactor malnutrition	suffering from _____ [m-l-t-n].

malpractice	■ A psychiatrist who blabbed about his patient's secrets has been sued for _____ [m-p-c-e].
malignant	■ Dirty Dumbo flung me a _____ [m-g-n-t] scowl.
malefactor	■ Should a young offender be imprisoned with a hardened old _____ [m-f-t-r]?
malice	■ Love your neighbor, even though he displays _____ [m-1-c-] toward you.
malnutrition malignant	■ Siberian food had given Igor a bad case of _____ [m-1-t-n] and, possibly, a _____ [m-g-n-t] disease or two.
maladroit malpractice malice malefactor	■ The surgeon left a sponge and two tickets to "Star Wars" in Billy's belly. How _____ [m-1-d-t] can a physician be? Certainly he was guilty of _____ [m-p-c-e]. Luckily, Billy liked the movie and bore no _____ [m-1-c-] toward the _____ [m-f-t-r].
malefactor	■ *"Fie upon 'But yet'!* *'But yet' is as a gaoler to bring forth* *Some monstrous _____ [m-f-t-r]."* (Antony and Cleopatra, II, v, 53)

Non-test examples

OTHER DERIVATIVES OF MAL (BAD):

maladjusted (mal'ə jus'tid) *adj.* badly adjusted, especially to one's environment [*a maladjusted child*]

maladminister (mal əd min'ə stər) *v.* to manage badly [*maladminister the estate*]

malaise (ma lāz') *n.* vague physical discomfort, as early in an illness [*overcome by malaise*]

malapropism (mal'ə prop iz'əm) *n.* a ridiculous misuse of words that sound similar [named after Mrs. Malaprop, a comic word-blunderer in Sheridan's *The Rivals* (1775)]; examples: "take it for granite," "Socrates died of an overdose of wedlock," "The secret lovers in *The Scarlet Letter* broke the seventh amendment."

malaria (mə ler'ē ə) *n.* an infectious disease, spread by mosquitoes, formerly blamed on the bad air of swamps

malcontent (mal′kən tent′) *n.* a dissatisfied or rebellious person [*the malcontents threatened mutiny*]

malediction (mal ə dik′shən) *n.* a curse; a calling down of evil on someone [*she flung maledictions at us*]

malevolent (mə lev′ə lənt) *adj.* wishing evil to others [*malevolent aims*]

malfeasance (mal fē′zəns) *n.* wrongdoing by a public official [*accused of malfeasance in office*]

malformed (mal fôrmd′) *adj.* badly formed [*a malformed child*]

malign (mə līn′) *v.* to speak evil of; slander [*I was maligned by critics.*]

malinger (mə ling′ger) *v.* to pretend to be ill in order to avoid working [*Yossarian malingered in the hospital.*]

malocclusion (mal′ə klōō′zhən) *n.* faulty meeting of the lower and upper teeth [*a case of malocclusion*]

malodorous (mal ō′dər əs) *adj.* stinking [*an aging, malodorous fish*]

MOR, MORT: DEATH

37. immortal (i môr′təl) *adj.* deathless; everlasting *n.* a person who has undying fame

> Remember the *immortal* words of Patrick Henry.
> Michelangelo is one of Italy's *immortals*.

immortal heroes   _____   _____
 (copy twice)

38. mortgage (môr′gij) *n.* the pledging of property as security

> If I stop payments, the bank will foreclose the *mortgage*.
> Our soldiers *mortgage* their lives for our country.

mortgage payments   _____   _____

39. mortician (môr tish′ən) *n.* an undertaker; funeral director

> Funeral arrangements are handled by the *mortician*.
> A *mortician* has to pass a stiff examination.

soft-voiced morticians   _____   _____

40. **post-mortem** (pōst môr′təm) *n.* done after death; an evaluation after the end of something

> The *post-mortem* revealed an overdose of cocaine.
> Critics conducted a *post-mortem* on the play.

<u>post-mortem analysis</u> _____ _____

Review words 37-40. Then go on.

QUIZ

DIRECTIONS: Fill the blanks with words we studied that are derived from the Latin root MOR, MORT (death). Be sure you spell the words correctly.

COVER
THIS STRIP

mortgage immortal	■ We've made house payments for thirty years, but the _____ [m-r-g-] seems _____ [i-m-t-l-].
	■ After the coroner conducted a _____
post-mortem mortician	[p-s-m-t-m-] on the body, it was turned over to the _____ [m-t-c-n-].
	■ If you buy on credit, you _____ [m-r-g-] your
mortgage	future.
	■ "When I kick the bucket," I told the _____
mortician immortal	[m-t-c-n-], "I'd enjoy having the organist play the _____ [i-m-l-] melodies of Bach."
	■ The coroner charged so much for doing _____
post-mortem mortgage	[p-s-m-t-m-] examinations that he soon lifted the _____ [m-r-g-] from his second mansion.
	■ The blacksmith was so powerful we thought he was _____ [i-m-l-], but the friendly _____
immortal mortician post-mortem	[m-t-c-n-] told us that the blacksmith, according to the _____ [p-s-m-t-m-], had died of a bee sting.

immortal

■ *"Oh, I have lost my reputation. I have lost the _____ [i-m-l-] part of myself, and what remains is bestial." (Othello, II, iii, 263)*

OTHER DERIVATIVES OF MOR, MORT (DEATH):

moribund (mor'ə bund') *adj.* dying; reaching extinction [*moribund custom*]

mortal (môr'təl) *adj.* deadly [*a mortal wound*] *n.* a being that will eventually die [*a mere mortal*]

mortality (môr tal'ə tē) *n.* the condition of having eventually to die; death rate [*a high mortality rate*]

mortify (mor'tə fī') *v.* to cause body tissue to decay; to humiliate [*a mortifying defeat*]

mortuary (môr'choo er'ē) *n.* a funeral home or morgue [*a mortuary for domestic pets*]

rigor mortis (rig'ər môr'tis) the stiffening of the body after death [*Rigor mortis had set in.*]

OMNI: ALL

41. omnibus (om'ni bus') *n.* a bus that carries many passengers; a book of collected stories and articles

    We saw London from the top of an *omnibus*.
    Please read the *omnibus* volume of Conan Doyle.

    omnibus edition
      (copy twice)   _____   _____

42. omnipotent (om nip'ə tənt) *adj.* all-powerful

    Every religion looks to an *omnipotent* Being.
    Hitler thought he was *omnipotent*.

    omnipotent ruler   _____   _____

43. omnipresent (om'nə prez'ənt) *adj.* being everywhere at the same time; all-enveloping

    In India one meets the *omnipresent* beggar.
    The laws of nature are *omnipresent*.

    omnipresent smog   _____   _____

44. omniscient (om nish'ənt) *adj.* knowing all things

> Nobody is *omniscient*.
> Some computers seem almost *omniscient*.

an omniscient God _____ _____

45. omnivorous (om niv'ər əs) *adj.* eating all foods; taking in everything, as with the mind

> Human beings eat meat and vegetables. We're *omnivorous*.
> An *omnivorous* reader gets an excellent education.

omnivorous locusts _____ _____

Review words 41-45. Then go on.

QUIZ

DIRECTIONS: Fill the blanks with words we studied that are derived from the Latin root OMNI (all). Be sure you spell the words correctly.

COVER
THIS STRIP

---

omnibus	■ The legislature passed an _____ [o-m-b-s-] bill.
	■ As he was attacking his second ham sandwich in the study hall, my _____ [o-m-v-s-] friend Blimpy was
omnivorous omnipresent	nabbed by the _____ [o-m-p-s-] principal.
	■ Like every child, I thought my daddy was _____
omnipotent omniscient omnibus	[o-m-p-t-] and _____ [o-m-s-n-]--until the day the conductor kicked him off the _____ [o-m-b-s-].
	■ The evangelist proclaimed that the Almighty is all-powerful, all-knowing, and all-pervasive; in other words,
omnipotent omniscient omnipresent	God is _____ [o-m-p-t-], _____ [o-m-s-n-], and _____ [o-m-p-s-].
	■ Sheep are herbivorous (plant-eating); tigers are carnivorous (meat-eating); but man--_____
omnipotent omnivorous	[o-m-p-t-] man--is _____ [o-m-v-s-].

page 68

omniscient	■ My friend tore his **hair** whenever he misspelled a word; I guess Baldy wasn't _____ [o-m-s-n-].
omnibus omnipresent omnivorous	■ Tourists kept pouring out of each _____ [o-m-b-s-]. They were _____ [o-m-p-s-] and, judging by the swill they ate, _____ [o-m-v-s-].
omnipotent	■ "O _____ [o-m-p-t-] *Love!"* *(The Merry Wives of Windsor, V, v, 8)*

Non-test examples

OTHER DERIVATIVES OF OMNI (ALL):

omnicompetent (om'nə kom'pə tənt) *adj.* all-capable [*my omnicompetent Aunt Sophie*]

omnicredulous (om'nə krej'ə ləs) *adj.* tending to believe anything; completely gullible [*omnicredulous yokels*]

omnidirectional (om'nē de rek'shə nəl) *adj.* sending or receiving signals in all directions [*an omnidirectional antenna*]

omniferous (om nif'ərəs) *adj.* producing all kinds [*omniferous fruit trees*]

omni-ignorant (om'nə ig'nər ənt) *adj.* completely uneducated; totally ignorant [*an omni-ignorant newcomer*]

omnilingual (om'nə ling'gwəl) *adj.* speaking all languages [*an omnilingual European*]

omnium-gatherum (om'nē əm gath'ər əm) *n.* a miscellaneous collection [*an omnium-gatherum of old clothes*]

omnivore (om'nə vōr') *n.* an animal that eats all varieties of food

---

PED: FOOT

46. **biped** (bī'ped) *n.* a two-footed creature

> I talk to my mynah bird, as one *biped* to another.
> Aristotle said that man is "a featherless *biped.*"

<u>featherless biped</u>   _____   _____
     (copy twice)

47. **expedite** (ek'spi dīt') *v.* to speed up the action of; facilitate

> Please *expedite* our order.
> Roman army captains would remove fetters from (*ex-*) each prisoner's foot (*ped*) to *expedite* the march.

expedite delivery _____ _____

48. **impediment** (im ped'ə mənt) *n.* an obstruction; obstacle; hindrance

> Land mines were an *impediment* to the army's progress.
> The child had a speech *impediment*.

speech impediment _____ _____

49. **pedestrian** (pə des'tri ən) *n.* a walker; one who goes by foot; dull and unimaginative

> In Chicago a *pedestrian* must be agile to survive.
> Theodore Dreiser has a *pedestrian* literary style.

pedestrian crosswalk _____ _____

50. **quadruped** (kwod'roo ped') *n.* a four-footed animal

> A *quadruped* in a fur coat stole chocolates from our tent last night.
> The zebra, a strange *quadruped*, looks like a horse in pajamas.

a rare quadruped _____ _____

Review words 46-50. Then go on.

QUIZ

DIRECTIONS: Fill the blanks with words we studied that are derived from the Latin root PED (foot). Be sure you spell the words correctly.

COVER
THIS STRIP

	■ My canary Sheila is a _____ [b-p-d] like me,
biped	but she sings better.
	■ The blacksmith said he'd _____ [e-p-d-t-] the
expedite	job, but he pointed out that a _____ [q-p-d] needs
quadruped	
biped	twice as many shoes as a _____ [b-p-d].

expedite quadruped	■ To _____ [e-p-d-t-] communication on the war front, our signal corps sometimes used a messenger dog named Choo-Choo, a most faithful _____ [q-p-d].
impediment pedestrian	■ Mountains of fresh snow served as an extra _____ [i-p-d-t] to the _____ [p-d-t-n].
impediment	■ Demosthenes overcame a speech _____ [i-p-d-t].
expedite quadruped pedestrian	■ Although Henry put an airmail stamp on his love letter in order to _____ [e-p-d-t-] delivery, he found that a swift _____ [q-p-d] or perhaps even an elderly _____ [p-d-t-n] could have delivered his note faster.
pedestrian biped quadruped impediment	■ The average _____ [p-d-t-n] has two legs and is, therefore, a _____ [b-p-d]; his dog has four legs and is a _____ [q-p-d]. Unfortunately, the leash between them acts as an _____ [i-p-d-t] to cross-traffic.
impediment	■ *"Let his lack of years be no* _____ *[i-p-d-t]."* (*Merchant of Venice, IV, i, 162*)

Non-test examples

OTHER DERIVATIVES OF PED (FOOT):

centipede (sen'tə pēd') *n.* a many-legged crawling thing; a myriapod

expedient (ik spē'dē ənt) *adj.* advisable [*Gassing the roaches seemed expedient.*] *n.* a prudent course of action [*a useful expedient*]

expedition (ek'spə dish'ən) *n.* a journey, as for exploration; those taking part in such a journey; promptness [*She acted with expedition.*]

pedal (ped'l) *n.* a foot-operated lever, as on a bicycle

pedestal (ped'is təl) *n.* a support, as for a statue or vase

pedicure (ped'i kyoor') *n.* care of the feet; trimming and polishing toenails

pedometer (pə dom'ə tər) *n.* an instrument that measures distance walked

Review words 1-50. Then take the Chapters 7-8 Self-Test.

CHAPTERS 7-8: SELF-TEST

DIRECTIONS: Write the words in full. Complete this entire test before you check and grade your answers.

_____ 1. Believe in yourself, and everything is [p-o-s-b-l-].
_____ 2. I took a memory course, but I can't [r-m-b-r] if I passed.
_____ 3. It will [p-r-o-l-y] be sunny, if it doesn't rain.
_____ 4. My stony-faced friend was [s-t-d-n-g] geology.
_____ 5. Yesterday Gale [p-a-s-] me with her nose in the air.
_____ 6. Dogs pollute, but not as much as [p-e-p-l-].
_____ 7. The landlord wants coin, not just a [p-r-o-m-s-].
_____ 8. Butch spends his salary before it's [p-a-d-] to him.
_____ 9. The taxi driver told me to go [s-t-r-a-t-] to a hot place.
_____ 10. Opportunity knocks once, so be [r-e-d-y].
_____ 11. The dogs bark at night to test [t-h-r-] lungs.
_____ 12. Are firebombs [n-s-r-y] on the Fourth of July?
_____ 13. Our fingerprints are [s-i-m-l-r-] but not identical.
_____ 14. A good name is better [t-h-n] riches.
_____ 15. "For, lo! the winter is [p-a-s-], the rain is over and gone."
_____ 16. Tom asks for my honest [o-p-i-n-], so he can ignore it.
_____ 17. Finding half a worm in my apple was a [s-r-p-r-s-].
_____ 18. See the lovely tombstone over [t-h-r-].
_____ 19. Why pity lunatics if [t-h-r-] happy?
_____ 20. When Holmes was [n-i-n-y] he said, "Oh, to be eighty again!"
_____ 21. Max shook his bad habits [s-n-c-e] he got malaria.
_____ 22. Gunder cut himself with a [s-f-t-y] razor.
_____ 23. Everybody was [q-u-i-t-] except the librarians.
_____ 24. The dinner guest belched politely now and [t-h-n].
_____ 25. In death they went [s-e-p-r-t-] ways. She went to heaven.
_____ 26. The landlady told me not to [p-r-f-m] on my tuba at dawn.
_____ 27. To attend college is a marvelous [p-r-v-l-g-].
_____ 28. Write with a sharp mind as well as a sharp [p-e-n-l-].
_____ 29. You'll [r-c-v-e] a special award: a parking ticket.
_____ 30. I held a job, on one [o-c-a-s-n], as lifeguard in a carwash.

Write correctly the words we studied that are derived from the Latin roots MAL, MOR-MORT, OMNI, and PED.

_____ 31. Our small house is covered by a big [m-o-r-g-].
_____ 32. Snurd's subcompact car hit a [p-d-t-n] in the ankle.
_____ 33. The ice cream will melt unless we [e-p-d-t-] delivery.
_____ 34. My [m-l-d-t] friend tripped on his tennis racket.
_____ 35. The [m-r-t-n-] is a grave man.
_____ 36. Eating devitalized food leads to [m-l-n-t-n].
_____ 37. Hebrews believe in an [o-m-p-t-] Jehovah.
_____ 38. Thank heavens, the lump is not [m-l-g-t].
_____ 39. Steaks, lobster, onions! The starving man was [o-m-v-s-].
_____ 40. "Giddap, Homer," said the farmer to his faithful [q-d-r-p-].

Write the letter that indicates the best definition.

( )	41.	biped	a. an obstacle; hindrance
( )	42.	immortal	b. neglectful treatment by a professional
( )	43.	impediment	c. an after-death analysis
( )	44.	malefactor	d. found in all places
( )	45.	malice	e. everlasting; undying
( )	46.	malpractice	f. a large public transport
( )	47.	omnibus	g. a criminal
( )	48.	omnipresent	h. knowing everything
( )	49.	omniscient	i. desire to do harm; vindictiveness
( )	50.	post-mortem	j. a creature with two legs

ANSWER KEY

Check your test answers by the following key. Deduct 2% per error from 100%.

1. possible	11. their	21. since	31. mortgage	41. j
2. remember	12. necessary	22. safety	32. pedestrian	42. e
3. probably	13. similar	23. quiet	33. expedite	43. a
4. studying	14. than	24. then	34. maladroit	44. g
5. passed	15. past	25. separate	35. mortician	45. i
6. people	16. opinion	26. perform	36. malnutrition	46. b
7. promise	17. surprise	27. privilege	37. omnipotent	47. f
8. paid	18. there	28. pencil	38. malignant	48. d
9. straight	19. they're	29. receive	39. omnivorous	49. h
10. ready	20. ninety	30. occasion	40. quadruped	50. c

Score: _____ %

Review carefully any words which you have missed in the foregoing Self-Test.

Your instructor will give you a final test on words 1-50 in Chapters 7 and 8.

9

DIRECTIONS: Study the spelling of each word carefully, giving special attention to the trouble spots (underlined letters). Then write each word neatly three times.

1. thr<u>ew</u> *(verb)*: "*threw* snowballs" *threw* _____

2. thr<u>ough</u> *(prep.)*: "*through* Omaha" _____

3. to<u>ge</u>ther _____ _____ _____

4. to<u>m</u>orrow _____ _____ _____

5. t<u>o</u>n<u>gue</u> _____ _____ _____

6. t<u>o</u> *(prep.)*: "*to* college" _____

7. t<u>oo</u> *(adv.)*: "*too* big" _____

8. t<u>wo</u> *(adj., noun)*: "*two* men" _____

9. tr<u>ou</u>ble _____ _____ _____

10. tr<u>ul</u>y _____ _____ _____

Review words 1-10 until you are sure you can spell them. Then go on and take the quiz.

COVER THIS STRIP	FILL THE BLANKS

FILL THE BLANKS

■ "I won't be _____ [t-r-1-y] happy until we are

_____ [t-o-g-t-r-]," said the hungry cat

_____ [t-o-] the mouse.

truly
together
to

■ The pitcher stuck out his _____ [t-n-g-],

then _____ [t-h-r-] his fast ball _____ [t-o-]

Guerrero, and _____ [t-o-] runs scored.

tongue
threw
to
two

■ Oscar is _____ [t-r-1-y] unfit for aviation; he

goes _____ [t-h-r-] dizzy spells when the barber

pumps his chair _____ [t-o-] high.

truly
through
too

■ During wartime a _____ [t-n-g-] that wags

_____ [t-o-] easily can cause _____

[t-r-b-1-] and sink ships.

tongue
too
trouble

■ The vandal who _____ [t-h-r-] a rock

_____ [t-h-r-] the bank window will get _____

[t-o-] months in a jail without any windows, starting

_____ [t-o-m-r-o-].

threw
through
two
tomorrow

■ My jalopy and I have _____ [t-r-1-y] been

_____ [t-h-r-] much joy and _____

[t-r-b-1-] _____ [t-o-g-t-r-], but I'd part with

my dimpled companion _____ [t-o-m-o-r-o-] for

about _____ [t-o-] dollars.

truly
through
trouble
together
tomorrow
two

■ "We've faced _____ [t-r-b-1-] _____

[t-o-g-t-r-] before," said the condemned prisoner _____

[t-o-] his wife, "but what I face _____ [t-o-m-r-o-]

morning is just _____ [t-o-] shocking."

trouble
together
to
tomorrow
too

trouble threw tongue	■ Blabber's _____ [t-r-b-1-] was that he _____ [t-h-r-] his _____ [t-n-g-] into gear before his brain warmed up.
tongue	■ _"I would my horse had the speed of your _____ [t-n-g-]."_ _(Much Ado About Nothing, I, i, 142)_

DIRECTIONS: Continue as before. Study the spelling carefully. Write each word three times.

11. un<u>c</u>le _____<u>uncle</u>_____ _____ _____

12. use<u>d</u> _____ _____ _____

13. us<u>e</u>less _____ _____ _____

14. us<u>u</u>al _____ _____ _____

15. v<u>e</u>ry _____ _____ _____

16. vill<u>ai</u>n _____ _____ _____

17. w<u>a</u>g<u>o</u>n _____ _____ _____

18. we<u>a</u>ther _(noun, verb)_: "rainy _weather_" _____

19. wh<u>e</u>ther _(conj.)_: "_whether_ or not" _____

20. wh<u>e</u>re _____ _____ _____

Review words 11-20. Then take the quiz.

QUIZ

COVER THIS STRIP	FILL THE BLANKS
uncle villain used wagon	■ My _____ [u-n-c-] looks like the movie _____ [v-i-1-n-] who _____ [u-s-] to shoot at the covered _____ [w-a-g-n-].
	■ "It's only ten below," said the Eskimo. "This warm
weather very	_____ [w-t-h-r] is _____ [v-r-y] uncomfortable."

- A home _____ [w-e-r-] the buffalo roam isn't easy to keep clean.

- Linda _____ [u-s-] to wonder _____ [w-t-h-r] to hitch her _____ [w-a-g-n] to a star or to a mud fence. She wanted _____ [v-r-y] much to escape the _____ [u-s-a-l] fate of farm women.

- A refrigerator might seem _____ [u-s-l-e-s] in the Arctic, _____ [w-e-r-] the _____ [w-t-h-r] is below zero; but the refrigerator can be _____ [u-s-] to keep food from freezing.

- The hermit said he would take his _____ [u-s-a-l] annual bath, _____ [w-t-h-r] he needed it or not.

- Clara can predict the _____ [w-t-h-r] _____ [v-r-y] accurately in Death Valley, _____ [w-e-r-] she lives. The _____ [u-s-a-l] summer day will melt your fillings.

- We buried the _____ [v-i-l-n] face downward so he could see _____ [w-e-r-] he was going.

- Because Hamlet's _____ [u-n-c-] is a _____ [v-i-l-n], Hamlet becomes _____ [v-r-y] depressed. He feels that life is _____ [u-s-l-e-s] and debates _____ [w-t-h-r] "to be or not to be."

- My own _____ [u-n-c-] _____ [u-s-] to drive a horse and _____ [w-a-g-n]. He claimed a car was as _____ [u-s-l-e-s] as a second navel.

- "...one may smile, and smile, and be a
  _____ [v-i-l-n]."
                    (Hamlet, I, v, 106)

DIRECTIONS: Continue as before. Study the spelling carefully. Write each word three times.

21. wh_ich   *which*   _____   _____

22. _whole   _____   _____   _____

23. who_'s *(who is)*: "Who's there" _____

24. who_se *(possessive)*: "whose car" _____

25. wom_en   _____   _____

26. wri_ti_ng   _____   _____

27. _wrong   _____   _____

28. y_oung   _____   _____

29. yo_ur *(possessive)*: "your hat" _____

30. you_'re *(you are)*: "You're cute." _____

Review words 21-30. Then take the quiz.

QUIZ

COVER THIS STRIP	FILL THE BLANKS
wrong	■ Ringo rang the _____ [-r-o-n-g-] number.
you're writing	■ I hear that _____ [y-u-r-] _____ [-r-i-t-n-g] an essay on clocks, and it's about time.
who's whose	■ Let's get this straight--_____ [w-h-o-s-] riding in _____ [w-h-o-s-] car?
whole writing which	■ Lovesick Looey spent a _____ [-h-o-l-] day _____ [-r-i-t-n-g] a love poem _____ [w-c-h] is four lines long.
young women your	■ If you _____ [y-n-g] _____ [w-m-n] want to drive trucks, I won't stand in _____ [y-u-r-] way.

you're
young
whole

who's
whose

your
which
which
wrong

young
your
wrong

young
whole
who's

women
whose
writing
your

young

- When _____ [y-u-r-] very _____ [y-n-g], a month seems like a _____ [-h-o-1-] year.

- Say, _____ [w-h-o-s-] the clown _____ [w-h-o-s-] wet overshoes are on my term paper?

- When you take _____ [y-u-r-] false-true test, please don't flip coins to decide _____ [w-c-h] statements are right and _____ [w-c-h] are _____ [-r-o-n-g-].

- You _____ [y-n-g] men and women must make _____ [y-u-r-] own career choices, because to follow the _____ [-r-o-n-g-] advice is disastrous.

- The _____ [y-n-g] boy ate the _____ [-h-o-1] bottle of chocolate pills. He's the one _____ [w-h-o-s-] having his stomach pumped.

- Emily Dickinson is one of those _____ [w-m-n] _____ [w-h-o-s-] high voltage _____ [-r-i-t-n-g] curls _____ [y-u-r-] hair.

- *"I never knew so _____ [y-n-g] a body with so old a head."*
  (Merchant of Venice, IV, i, 164)

10

SCRIB, SCRIPT: WRITE

31. **conscription** (kən skrip'shən) *n.* a draft; enrollment for compulsory service in the armed forces

> The president ordered the *conscription* of two million men.
> Flynn fled to Canada to avoid *conscription*.

military conscription *military conscription* _____
       (copy twice)

32. **inscribe** (in skrīb') *v.* to write, engrave, or sign, as on a photograph or book

> Mark Twain *inscribed* his name on the flyleaf.
> Please *inscribe* "Rest in Peace" on Ivan's tombstone.

inscribe your name _____ _____

33. **manuscript** (man'yə skript') *n.* a handwritten or typed document, especially as submitted to a publisher

> The stupid editor rejected Mike's great *manuscript*.
> Shepherds found an ancient *manuscript* in a cave.

a typed manuscript _____ _____

34. nondescript (non'di skript) *adj.* so ordinary as to be hard to
describe

> A *nondescript* dog was ravaging a garbage can.
> The houses have no character—they're simply *nondescript*.

nondescript soup _____   _____

35. postscript (pōst'skript') *n.* a note added below the signature line
of a letter

> Melvin had an afterthought and added a *postscript*.
> The *postscript* was brief: "I love you."

short postscript _____   _____

36. scribe (skrīb) *n.* a penman; copyist; writer

> Testimony was recorded by a courtroom *scribe*.
> The *scribe* wrote until his hand was weary.

faithful scribe _____   _____

Review words 31-36. Then go on.

QUIZ

DIRECTIONS: Fill the blanks with words we studied that are derived from the
Latin root SCRIB, SCRIPT (write). Be sure you spell the words correctly.

COVER
THIS STRIP

nondescript	■ Main Street shops were plain and _____ [n-d-p-t].
	■ Geometry students can _____ [i-n-c-b-] a
inscribe	circle in a triangle.
	■ Mother's "note" of advice stretched into a ten-page
manuscript postscript	_____ [m-s-p-t], to which she added a quarter-mile _____ [p-s-c-t].
	■ Unknown actors _____ [i-n-c-b-] the most words
inscribe	on their photograph.
postscript	■ P.S. stands for _____ [p-s-c-t].

■ Wealthy Howard Hughes wore _____ [n-d-p-t]

nondescript   clothing.

■ The copyist, known as a _____ [s-c-b-], toiled

scribe
manuscript   over an illuminated _____ [m-s-p-t].

■ Young Russians sometimes hacked off a finger to avoid

conscription   military _____ [c-n-s-p-] by the Czar.

■ The news reporter, a gifted _____ [s-c-b-],

scribe
manuscript
conscription   wrote a book-length _____ [m-s-p-t] about the

war, beginning with his _____ [c-n-s-p-].

■ The office Romeo would _____ [i-n-c-b-] a

sugary message in each valentine and add a red-hot

inscribe
postscript   _____ [p-s-c-t] that burned a hole in the envelope.

■ From hills and farms came a _____ [n-d-p-t]

nondescript
conscription   flock of young men, summoned by _____ [c-n-s-p-].

■ The Torah is a religious _____ [m-s-p-t] that

manuscript
scribe   has been penned by a dedicated _____ [s-c-b-].

■ *"Jove and my stars be praised! Here is yet a*
_____ [p-s-c-t]."

postscript   *(Twelfth Night, II, v, 188)*

Non-test examples

OTHER DERIVATIVES OF SCRIB, SCRIPT (WRITE):

ascribe (ə skrīb′) *v.* to assign, as to a source; attribute; impute
[*plays ascribed to Shakespeare*]

circumscribe (sur′kəm skrīb′) *v.* to draw a line around; encircle [*to circumscribe a triangle*]

describe (di skrīb′) *n.* to tell or write about; to picture in words
[*describe the incident*]

prescribe (pri skrīb′) *v.* to order or advise, as of a medicine; to lay
down rules [*prescribe a change of diet*]

scribble (skrib′əl) *v.* to write hastily or carelessly; to make
meaningless marks [*scribble a note*]

scrip (skrip) *n.* a brief writing, usually of a right to receive something; paper money

script (skript) *n.* handwriting; the text of a film or show [*revise the play script*]

scripture (skrip'chər) *n.* the books of the Old and New Testament; a passage from the Bible [*quote Scripture*]

subscribe (səb skrīb') *v.* to sign one's name as indication of consent, approval, or support [*subscribe to the women's liberation movement*]

subscript (sub'skript) *n.* a symbol written below and to the side of another

transcribe (tran skrīb') *v.* to make a written copy of spoken material or of a text; to translate [*to transcribe the shorthand notes*]

transcription (tran skrip'shən) *n.* an arrangement of a piece of music for instruments other than that for which it was originally written [*transcription of the piano sonata for oboe and flügelhorn*]

typescript (tīp'skript') *n.* typewritten copy

SPEC, SPECT: LOOK

37. circumspect (sur'kəm spekt') *adj.* careful; cautious

    Nancy tiptoed in *circumspect* fashion through the puddles.
    A rash investor! He should be more *circumspect*.

    circumspect manner _____ _____
      (copy twice)

38. introspection (in trə spek'shən) *n.* a looking into one's mind and feelings; self-analysis

    The moody student was given to *introspection*.
    Hamlet was more inclined to *introspection* than to action.

    habit of introspection _____ _____

39. perspective (pər spek'tiv) *n.* a view of things from a particular standpoint; a visible scene

    From the peak we had a splendid *perspective* of Pumpkin Valley.
    Huck Finn describes Mississippi life from a fresh *perspective*.

    unique perspective _____ _____

40. retrospect (ret′rə spekt′) *n.* a looking back at past events

> The old woman now saw her life in *retrospect*.
> In *retrospect* I feel my Edsel agency was a mistake.

<u>in retrospect</u> _____ _____

41. spectator (spek′tā tər) *n.* one who watches; an onlooker

> One *spectator* shouted "Home run!" and pounded my head.
> The wrong people get exercise in *spectator* sports.

<u>role of spectator</u> _____ _____

Review words 37-41. Then go on.

QUIZ

DIRECTIONS: Fill the blanks with words we studied that are derived from the Latin root SPEC, SPECT (look). Be sure you spell the words correctly.

COVER
THIS STRIP

spectator perspective	■ As the parade began, one _____ [s-p-t-r-] climbed a tree to get a better _____ [p-r-s-v-].
	■ Betty is impulsive and outgoing, but her sister is quite _____ [c-r-s-p-c-] and has an inner life of
circumspect introspection	_____ [i-n-t-p-n].
spectator	■ An irate _____ [s-p-t-r-] bit the umpire.
	■ The cosmonauts saw Earth from a new _____
perspective	[p-r-s-v-].
	■ During a war we lose our _____ [p-r-s-v-], and our judgment doesn't return until we see things in
perspective retrospect	_____ [r-t-r-s-t].
	■ After a period of _____ [i-n-t-p-n], the convict said he felt, in _____ [r-t-r-s-t],
introspection retrospect circumspect	that he should have been more _____ [c-r-s-p-c-].

introspection	■ Examine your feelings; take time for _____ [i–n–t–p–n].
spectator circumspect retrospect	■ At the game a foul ball hit an overeager _____ [s–p–t–r–] on the nostrils. "I should have been more _____ [c–r–s–p–c–]," he said in _____ [r–t–r–s–t].
circumspect	■ *"let not his smoothing words Bewitch your hearts; be wise and* [c–r–s–p–c–]." (2 King Henry *VI, I, i, 157*)

Non-test examples

OTHER DERIVATIVES OF SPEC, SPECT (LOOK):

aspect (as'pekt) *n.* the way something looks; facial expression
[*a gloomy aspect*]

inspect (in spekt') *v.* to look at carefully, especially for defects
[*inspect the brakes*]

prospect (pros'pekt) *n.* the outlook; the chance for future success
[*a cheerful prospect*]

prospector (pros'pek tər) *n.* one who looks for valuable minerals, etc.

prospectus (prə spek'təs) *n.* a summary or outlook of a proposed literary or business undertaking [*to issue a prospectus*]

respectable (ri spek'tə bəl) *adj.* socially acceptable; of moderate excellence; good enough to be seen [*a respectable showing*]

respectively (ri spek'tiv lē) *adv.* in the order named [*First and second prizes went to Helen and Leo respectively.*]

spectacle (spek'tə kəl) *n.* something to look at; an impressive sight [*an inspiring spectacle*]

spectacular (spek tak'yə lər) *adj.* thrilling to see; impressive and dramatic [*spectacular display of fireworks*]

specter (spek'tər) *n.* a ghost or phantom [*haunted by a midnight specter*]

spectroscope (spek'trə skōp') *n.* an optical device for observing and analyzing the nature of light waves

spectrum (spek'trəm) *n.* the band of colors observed when white light is broken into its parts; an entire range of characteristics [*the political spectrum*]

42. **contemporary** (kən tem'pə rer'ē) *adj.* living or happening in the same period of time; modern *n.* a person living in the same period as another

> Ben Franklin was a *contemporary* of Washington and Jefferson.
> Read the best of *contemporary* fiction.

contemporary authors _____ _____
    (copy twice)

43. **extemporaneous** (ĭk stem pə rā'nē əs) *adj.* spoken or done without preparation; offhand; impromptu

> The professor gave *extemporaneous* lectures.
> The prizefighter's *extemporaneous* remarks were unprintable.

extemporaneous speech _____ _____

44. **temporary** (tem'pə rer'ē) *adj.* lasting for a time only; not permanent

> We used a pup tent as a *temporary* shelter.
> Joe's job as plum picker is quite *temporary*.

temporary jobs _____ _____

45. **temporize** (tem'pə rīz') *v.* to be indecisive in order to gain time; to delay

> Patrick Henry wanted us to revolt, not to *temporize*.
> Strikers demanded a raise, but the employers *temporized*.

Let's not temporize. _____ _____

Review words 42-45. Then go on.

QUIZ

DIRECTIONS: Fill the blanks with words we studied that are derived from the Latin root TEMP, TEMPOR (time). Be sure you spell the words correctly.

COVER
THIS STRIP
_____

	■ We're making _____ [t-m-p-y] use of boxes;
	some day we'll buy real _____ [c-n-p-r-y]
temporary contemporary	furniture.

extemporaneous temporize	■ In an _____ [-x-p-r-n-s] outburst, O'Brian demanded that our governor act, not _____ [t-m-p-z-].
contemporary	■ Walt Whitman admired his great _____ [c-n-p-r-y], Abe Lincoln.
contemporary extemporaneous	■ Groucho Marx pelted _____ [c-n-p-r-y] audiences with _____ [-x-p-r-n-s] puns.
temporize	■ The filibuster is used in Congress to _____ [t-m-p-z-], so that action on a bill becomes impossible.
temporary temporize	■ Aspirins give _____ [t-m-p-y] relief from pain; but if pains persist, don't _____ [t-m-p-z-]— see a doctor.
extemporaneous temporary	■ A creative pianist, Brenda played _____ [-x-p-r-n-s] melodies as a _____ [t-m-p-y] escape.
temporize	■ *"If I could _____ [t-m-p-z-] with my affection...."* *(Troilus and Cressida, IV, iv, 6)*

Non-test examples

OTHER DERIVATIVES OF TEMP, TEMPOR (TIME):

contretemps (kon trə täng′) *n.* an awkward, embarrassing mischance; an untimely mishap [*tripping on the altar step, a minor contretemps*]

extemporize (ik stem′pəriz′) *v.* to speak, compose, or perform without preparation; to improvise [*to extemporize at the drums*]

pro tem (prō tem′) for the time being; temporarily [*chairman pro tem*]

tempo (tem′pō) *n.* the rate of speed of a musical passage; pace [*the tempo of city life*]

temporal (tem′pərəl) *adj.* lasting for only a limited time; earthly, not spiritual or everlasting [*temporal power*]

tempus fugit (tem′pəs fyoo′jit) time flies [*My twenty-first birthday! Tempus fugit.*]

46. **avocation** (av'ə kā'shən) *n.* a hobby; something done for pleasure in addition to one's regular work

>   Mountain climbing was her *avocation*.
>   Without *avocations* retirement is a bore.

favorite avocation _____ _____
     (copy twice)

47. **convocation** (kon'və kā'shən) *n.* an assembly; a group that has been called together

>   The church ministers met in *convocation*.
>   The college president spoke to a *convocation* of professors.

annual convocation _____ _____

48. **equivocal** (i kwiv'ə kəl) *adj.* having two or more meanings; vague; ambiguous; misleading

>   The oracle gave an *equivocal* answer.
>   Our landlord mumbled some *equivocal* promises.

equivocal reply _____ _____

49. **vocation** (vō kā'shən) *n.* an occupation; profession; calling

>   Choose a *vocation* you will enjoy.
>   Aunt Edna's *vocation*? She drives a truck.

lifelong vocation _____ _____

50. **vociferous** (vō sif'ər əs) *adj.* loud; crying out noisily; boisterous

>   The mess sergeant ignored the *vociferous* complaints.
>   *Vociferous* children chased the ice cream truck.

vociferous crowd _____ _____

Review words 46-50. Then go on.

DIRECTIONS: Fill the blanks with words we studied that are derived from the Latin root VOC, VOCAT (call). Be sure you spell the words correctly.

COVER
THIS STRIP

convocation	■ I felt like a mouse at a _____ [c-v-c-n] of cats.
avocation vocation	■ Debra's _____ [a-v-c-n] was tennis, and she played so well that it became her _____ [v-c-n].
vociferous equivocal	■ "Mary, Mary, come back to me!" begged the _____ [v-c-f-s] young man, but the girl merely gave him an _____ [e-q-v-l] glance. Her name was Susan.
vocation avocation	■ If your _____ [v-c-n] confines you to an office chair, better choose an _____ [a-v-c-n] like golf.
convocation equivocal vociferous	■ Pinchum was quizzed by a _____ [c-v-c-n] of union workers; and his _____ [e-q-v-l] replies resulted in _____ [v-c-f-s] booing.
equivocal convocation vocation avocation	■ "I wish to be clear, not _____ [e-q-v-l]," said the dean to the _____ [c-v-c-n] of students. "You should love your _____ [v-c-n] as much as your _____ [a-v-c-n]."
vocation *vocation*	■ *"Why, Hal, 'tis my _____ [v-c-n], Hal; 'tis no sin for a man to labor in his _____ [v-c-n]."* *(1 Henry IV, I, ii, 116)*

Non-test examples

OTHER DERIVATIVES OF VOC, VOCAT (CALL):

advocate (ad'və kāt) *n.* a lawyer or person who pleads in support of something *v.* to speak or write in favor of; to support [*advocate a truce*]

evoke (i vōk') *v.* to call forth; extract; elicit [*to evoke laughter*]

invocation (in və kā'shən) *n.* a calling on a deity, spirit, etc., for blessing or aid [*Milton's "Paradise Lost" begins with an invocation.*]

irrevocable (i rev′ə kə bəl) *adj.* unalterable; unable to be repealed or called back [*a victim of irrevocable fate*]

provocative (prə vok′ə tiv) *adj.* stimulating; tending to call forth anger, lust, or other feelings [*a provocative glance*]

revoke (ri vōk′) *v.* to repeal; cancel; annul; abolish [*revoke a license*]

vocable (vō′kə bəl) *n.* a word or term; a combination of sounds or letters [*The baby emitted vocables.*]

vocabulary (vō kab′yə ler′ē) *n.* the stock of words used by a particular person or by a class of people; the words of a language [*Spanish vocabulary*]

vocal (vō′kəl) *adj.* pertaining to the voice; spoken; sung [*a vocal quartet*]; inclined to express one's self insistently [*a vocal member of the opposition*]

Review words 1–50, spelling and vocabulary. Then take the Chapters 9–10 Self-Test.

CHAPTERS 9-10: SELF-TEST

DIRECTIONS: Write the words in full. Complete this entire test before you check and grade your answers.

_____ 1. Some men are almost as intelligent as [w-m-n].
_____ 2. We aren't musical, but we play [v-r-y] loud.
_____ 3. The doctor told me to stick out my [t-o-n-g-], so I did.
_____ 4. He sold me a car [w-c-h] has no transmission.
_____ 5. Thomas Paine was up to his ears in [t-r-u-b-1-].
_____ 6. I wonder [w-h-o-s-] socks are in the hash.
_____ 7. Hang [t-g-t-r-], advised Franklin, or we'll hang separately.
_____ 8. Bran and wheat germ are Slim's [u-s-a-1] diet.
_____ 9. An offer that sounds [t-o-] good to be true probably is.
_____ 10. Hungry Harry ate the [-h-o-1-] watermelon.
_____ 11. A sane person knows right from [-r-n-g-].
_____ 12. The boss [t-h-r-] out my coat, and I was in it.
_____ 13. Count the kids. Who fell out of our station [w-g-n]?
_____ 14. Letters generally end with "Yours [t-r-1-y]."
_____ 15. "Some [v-i-1-n]," she said, "stole my false teef."
_____ 16. I answered Einstein's question--[w-e-r-] is the bathroom?
_____ 17. Dr. Cuttum will operate [w-t-h-r-] you need it or not.
_____ 18. If [y-u-r-] leaving, say goodby and leave.
_____ 19. I've been [t-h-r-] poverty and wealth, and wealth is better.
_____ 20. "Well, I must be off," said the [y-u-n-g-] lunatic.
_____ 21. My old [u-n-c-] had a sparring partner, my aunt.
_____ 22. Stanley [u-s-] to bend bars with his hands: Hershey bars.
_____ 23. Keep a journal. Start [-r-i-t-n-g] a page a day.
_____ 24. As pilot I was [u-s-1-e-s-] because heights gave me nosebleed.
_____ 25. The average baseball fan eats [t-o-] hot dogs.
_____ 26. North Dakota [w-t-h-r-] is fine except for the temperature.

_____ 27. A cello seems [t-o-] be a violin with mumps.
_____ 28. This sweater won't shrink, unless it rains [t-o-m-r-o-].
_____ 29. Do you stand on [y-r-] head to make an upside-down cake?
_____ 30. A man [w-h-o-s-] bald can comb his head with a rag.

Write correctly the words we studied that are derived from the Latin roots
SCRIB-SCRIPT, SPEC-SPECT, TEMP-TEMPOR, and VOC-VOCAT:

_____ 31. In a helicopter you see Shmaltzville from a new [p-r-s-v-].
_____ 32. The museum has a [m-n-c-p-] copy of Mozart's concerto.
_____ 33. Idiots often [-n-c-r-b-] their initials on toilet walls.
_____ 34. The diplomat's answer was vague and [-q-v-c-1-].
_____ 35. Maria has a talent for making [-x-t-m-p-s-] speeches.
_____ 36. Kit Marlowe was a [c-n-t-p-r-y] of Shakespeare.
_____ 37. Engineering was Jenny's chosen [v-c-t-n].
_____ 38. She signed the letter, then added a [p-s-c-t].
_____ 39. Historians judge events better in [r-t-o-p-t].
_____ 40. My dentist put in a [t-m-p-r-y] filling.

Write the letter that indicates the best definition.

( ) 41. avocation   a. an assembly
( ) 42. circumspect   b. an onlooker
( ) 43. conscription   c. a hobby
( ) 44. convocation   d. a penman or copyist
( ) 45. introspection   e. military draft
( ) 46. nondescript   f. to delay purposely
( ) 47. scribe   g. self-analysis
( ) 48. spectator   h. cautious; careful
( ) 49. temporize   i. noisy; boisterous
( ) 50. vociferous   j. very ordinary in appearance

ANSWER KEY

Check your test answers by the following key. Deduct 2% per error from 100%.

1. women	11. wrong	21. uncle	31. perspective	41. c
2. very	12. threw	22. used	32. manuscript	42. h
3. tongue	13. wagon	23. writing	33. inscribe	43. e
4. which	14. truly	24. useless	34. equivocal	44. a
5. trouble	15. villain	25. two	35. extemporaneous	45. g
6. whose	16. where	26. weather	36. contemporary	46. j
7. together	17. whether	27. to	37. vocation	47. d
8. usual	18. you're	28. tomorrow	38. postscript	48. b
9. too	19. through	29. your	39. retrospect	49. f
10. whole	20. young	30. who's	40. temporary	50. i

Score: _____ %

Review carefully any words which you have missed in the foregoing Self-Test.

Your instructor will give you a final test on words 1-50 in Chapters 9 and 10.

SUPPLEMENTARY SPELLING LIST (BASIC)

These 250 basic words are a supplement to the spelling demons programed
in previous chapters. Study of this extra-credit list is recommended
if you had trouble handling the demons. In any case, make sure you can
spell these much-used words.

An old-fashioned classroom spelldown based on this list can be entertaining
and instructive.

address	debt	goes	marrying	president	special
airplane	December	group	match	pretty	square
almost	degree	guest	material	priest	steady
although	dentist	guilty	measure	private	strength
always	describe	handkerchief	million	problem	student
American		happiness	mistake	prompt	style
animal	didn't	haven't	money	pupil	sugar
ankle	difference	healthy	month	purpose	swimming
anybody	dinner	heaven	motor	quality	talent
August	direction	heavy	mountain	quarrel	teacher
aunt	distance	heroes	much	question	therefore
avenue	doesn't		native	quick	thirst
backward	done	history	neither	radio	thousand
because	don't	honest	niece	realize	tiger
beggar	double	honor	nineteen	really	tonight
beneath	driving	hour	noise	reckon	total
bigger	dropping	huge	obey	region	trial
bottle	earth	humor		regular	Tuesday
bottom	easy	husband	oblige	relative	ugly
breast	edge	idea	ocean	replies	until
bridge	educate	important	odor	rescue	valley
brief	empty	increase	often	revenge	victory
brother	engine	inquiry	once	ribbon	village
build	error	insane	orange		water
bundle	etc.	iron	ordinary	rival	Wednesday
button	everybody	January	ourselves	river	welcome
can't	example	journey	parcel	roar	wisdom
captain	faith	juice	pardon	robber	yours
careful	family	kingdom	parent	rotten	yourselves
chair	famous	kitchen	pattern	rough	
cheese	fasten	kitten	peach	sailor	
chicken	fault	knives	peanut	salary	
choice	favorite	labor	penny	sandwich	
cities	fellow	ladies	piano	Saturday	
coffee	female	lawyer	pistol	says	
collect	field	learn	planning	search	
common	figure	leaves	pleasant	sentence	
copies	flight	length	pledge	service	
correct	forty	liberty	plumber	shoulder	
cottage	freedom	likely	pocket	shouldn't	
cotton	frighten	little	poetry	silence	
cough	funny	lively	police	smoking	
country	further	loving	popular	soap	
danger	gallon	maiden	powerful	soldier	
death	garden	making	prayer	soup	

11

DIRECTIONS: Study the following sets of words carefully. Note the differences in spelling and meaning. Then fill each blank with the word that fits the meaning.

COVER
THIS STRIP

---

1. **adapt** *v.* to adjust to new circumstances
   adopt *v.* to take into one's family; take up and use

■ The childless jungle family decided to (1) _adopt_ a chimpanzee and learn whether it could (2) _____ to their household and also (3) _____ to their social life. They wrote a book about the outcome. Perhaps our psychology class could (4)_____ the book as a textbook and even (5) _____ the story to television. Now, all we need is a chimp.

1. adopt
2. adapt
3. adapt
4. adopt
5. adapt

2. **addition** *n.* a joining of one thing to another; an increase
   edition *n.* a printing of a book, magazine, or newspaper; a copy

■ Little Luke, the latest (1) _____ to the banker's family, looks like a tiny (2)_____ of his father, and already does little problems in subtraction and (3) _____ on the computer. The little whiz kid is mentioned in the morning (4) _____ of the Daily Bugle and also, I believe, in the evening (5) _____.

1. addition
2. edition
3. addition
4. edition
5. edition

3. **affect** *v.* to influence; act upon
   effect *n.* the result *v.* to bring about; achieve

1. effect
2. affect
3. affect
4. effect
5. effect

■ Intense desert heat has a bad (1) _____ on your
body and can even (2) _____ your judgment....
Would sudden wealth (3) _____ me? Well, it might
(4) _____ an improvement in my mode of transportation. After all, my skateboard has had a depressing
(5) _____ on my self-image.

4. **aisle** *n.* a passageway between rows of seats
   isle *n.* a small island

1. isle
2. aisle
3. aisle
4. aisle
5. isle

■ The movie dealt with Melville's life on a cannibal
(1) _____; and, arriving late, I stumbled blindly
down the dark theater (2) _____, up the next
(3) _____, then sat down in a stranger's lap.
Meanwhile my friends Al and Sal were walking down a church
(4) _____ and rushing off to honeymoon on a
Pacific (5) _____.

5. **alley** *n.* a narrow lane behind rows of buildings
   ally *n.* a friendly nation or associate *v.* to unite or
      connect by some bond

1. alley
2. ally
3. alley
4. alley
5. ally

■ I was attacked in the (1) _____ by a Doberman
and his four-footed (2) _____, so I sped out of
that (3) _____ like a guided missile. I noticed,
though, that the food we Americans throw away as garbage in
the (4) _____ could feed an American (5) _____.

6. **allowed** *v.* permitted
   aloud *adv.* audibly; loudly

1. aloud
2. allowed
3. aloud
4. aloud
5. allowed

■ During the math test a student prayed (1) _____
and his teacher told him that school prayers were not
(2) _____ if spoken (3) _____. Then
another student sobbed (4) _____ when he learned
that smoking in the classroom would not be (5) _____.

7. **allusion** *n.* a casual reference or mention
   illusion *n.* a misconception; delusion; a misleading
      image

1. illusion
2. allusion
3. illusion
4. illusion
5. allusion

■ Macbeth thinks he sees the ghost of Banquo; it's a kind
of psychological (1) _____. In his fright
Macbeth makes a dramatic public (2) _____ to the
(3) _____. I myself once crawled a mile toward
a lake that turned out to be an optical (4) _____
and am usually embarrassed by any (5) _____
to that incident.

8. **altar** *n.* a raised place used for religious rituals
   alter *v.* to change; modify

1. altar
2. alter
3. alter
4. altar
4. alter

■ The simple words "I do," spoken at the (1) _____ will truly (2) _____ your life--yes, and (3) _____ it for the better, I trust. The minister told us how Pacific natives would sometimes sacrifice a pig on an (4) _____, a custom that missionaries have tried to (5) _____.

9. **anecdote** *n.* a short, entertaining story
   antidote *n.* a remedy for a poison or other evil

1. anecdote
2. antidote
3. antidote
4. anecdote
5. antidote

■ The warden told an (1) _____ about an alcoholic that let a snake bite him because he expected to get whiskey as an (2) _____. Unfortunately, whiskey was no longer prescribed as an (3) _____ for snakebite. You'll hear many a merry (4) _____ such as that at the Greasy Plate Cafe, but if you eat the food there you'll need an (5) _____.

10. **angel** *n.* a heavenly spirit
    angle *n.* The shape made by two straight lines
        meeting at a point

1. angle
2. angel
3. angel
4. angle
5. angel

■ From any camera (1) _____ Anita looked like an (2) _____, yes, like a lovely, smiling (3) _____. In fact, Diamond Jim stared at her and finally asked, "What's your (4) _____, (5) _____?"

11. **ascent** *n.* the act of rising or climbing
    assent *n.* agreement; consent *v.* to agree; consent

1. assent
2. ascent
3. assent
4. ascent
5. assent

■ Will the mountain climbers (1) _____ to my taking part in their (2) _____ of the glacier? My boss will (3) _____ to my taking a week off and has offered me a pair of slippery boots. Actually, I'd rather make the (4) _____ in a balloon if my congressman will (5) _____ to supply the hot air.

12. **assistance** *n.* aid; help
    assistants *n.* helpers

1. assistance
2. assistants
3. assistants
4. assistants
5. assistance

■ I broke both legs and, at long last, was given minor (1) _____ by two carpenter (2) _____. Then the star actress stubbed her toe and five medical (3) _____ and three stage (4) _____ rushed madly to her (5) _____.

13. **bare** *adj.* naked *v.* to expose; reveal
    bear *n.* a large furry mammal *v.* to carry; endure

1. bear
2. bare
3. bear
4. bare
5. bare
6. bear

■ The grizzly (1) _____ swam toward me, and I was as (2) _____ as a doorknob. Suddenly the (3) _____ began to (4) _____ his teeth—I'm giving you the (5) _____ facts—and my fear was almost more than I could (6) _____.

14. **base** *adj.* vile *n.* a foundation; a baseball bag
    bass *adj.* low in pitch *n.* low-pitched musical tones

1. base
2. bass
3. base
4. bass
5. bass
6. base

■ Dusty slid into second (1) _____, and a (2) _____ voice shouted, "You're out!"—"You're a (3) _____ villain!" Dusty told the umpire.—"Scram!" said the (4) _____ voice. "Go to your locker room and fool with your (5) _____ guitar. I'm ump, and I (6) _____ my decisions on facts."

15. **beach** *n.* a sandy shore
    beech *n.* a tree

1. beach
2. beech
3. beech
4. beach
5. beach

■ The only shade on the hot sands of the (1) _____ came from a (2) _____ tree and a telephone post. I lay under the branches of the (3) _____, but Leatherneck Louie lay on the flat, burning (4) _____ because he was a regular son of the (5) _____.

16. **beat** *v.* to pound; defeat; punish
    beet *n.* a vegetable

1. beet
2. beat
3. beet
4. beat
5. beet

■ Farmer John held up a big (1) _____ in the courtroom and said, "You can't (2) _____ a (3) _____ like this." — "That's irrelevant," shouted the lawyer. "Just answer yes or no—do you still (4) _____ your wife?" Farmer John was silent now and turned red as a (5) _____.

17. **berth** *n.* a bunk in a ship or sleeping car; a job on a ship
    birth *n.* the act of being born

1. berth
2. birth
3. berth
4. birth
5. berth

■ The sailor slept soundly in the lower (1) _____ while his poor wife gave (2) _____ to twins in the upper (3) _____. Annoyed by the (4) _____ of the wailing infants, the heartless man accepted a (5) _____ on a whaling ship.

18. **board** *n.* a slab of wood; a managing group; meals
    bored *adj.* uninterested; tired of the dullness

1. board
2. bored
3. board
4. bored
5. board

■ Leaning back against a (1) _____, Benny was soon (2) _____ by the endless discussions of the school (3) _____. "If a student looks (4) _____," said one irate parent, "the teacher should hit him on the head with a (5) _____."

19. **boarder** *n.* somebody who gets regular meals for pay
    border *n.* boundary *v.* to lie next to

1. boarder
2. boarder
3. border
4. boarder
5. border

■ Next to me at the table, when I was a regular (1) _____, sat Mr. Lopez, a (2) _____ from south of the (3) _____. He and another (4) _____ at our rooming house bought the two vacant lots that (5)_____ the fertilizer factory.

20. **born** *adj.* brought into life
    borne *pp. of bear* carried; endured

1. born
2. borne
3. borne
4. borne
5. born

■ As soon as he was (1) _____, the little prince was (2) _____ on a pillow to the throne of the king. Meanwhile, the queen thought of the insults she had (3) _____ and the pain she had (4) _____ and wished that she had never been (5) _____.

21. **breath** *n.* the air to and from the lungs
    breathe *v.* to take air into the lungs and let it out; inhale and exhale

1. breathe
2. breath
3. breath
4. breath
5. breathe

■ The joggers began to (1) _____ noisily, and my plump companion was gasping for (2) _____. Ah, the sweet (3) _____ of life! But sometimes a jogger takes a big (4) _____ of California smog and he doesn't want to (5) _____ any more.

22. **bridal** *adj.* having to do with a bride or a wedding
    bridle *n.* the headgear by which a horse is controlled
    v. to show quick resentment out of offended pride

1. bridal
2. bridle
3. bridal
4. bridle
5. bridal

■ When the bride's father saw the bill for the (1) _____ veil, he began to (2) _____ at the milliner. But the (3) _____ pair did look handsome. Afterwards, the happy couple adjusted the horse's saddle and (4) _____ and set forth on their (5) _____ tour.

23. canvas   *n.* a firm, closely-woven cloth
    canvass   *v.* to cover a district to determine
    opinions or solicit votes

1. canvas
2. canvass
3. canvas
4. canvas
5. canvass

■ From the (1) _____ tent went the candidate's
backers to (2) _____ the town. Among them were
two elderly women in (3) _____ tennis shoes,
carrying (4) _____ bags, who proceeded to
(5) _____ the supermarket customers for votes.

24. capital   *adj.* excellent [*a capital idea*]; written
    large [*capital letters*]; involving execution [*capital
    punishment*] *n.* a city serving as a seat of government;
    accumulated assets
    capitol   *n.* the building in which the legislators
    meet; statehouse

1. capital
2. capitol
3. capital
4. capitol
5. capital

■ Arriving in Austin, the (1)_____ of Texas,
the old senator immediately ascended the steps of the
(2) _____. "I have a (3) _____
suggestion," he told reporters. "Let's gild the dome of
our (4) _____ building. The project may cost a
nice bit of (5) _____ ,but I know a contractor ...."

25. carton   *n.* a cardboard box
    cartoon   *n.* a humorous drawing

1. cartoon
2. cartoon
3. carton
4. cartoon
5. carton

■ I prefer a political (1) _____ , but I recently
did enjoy an old Mickey Mouse (2) _____ comedy.
Mickey ate a whole (3) _____ of cheese, then
drew a (4) _____ of an ugly cat on the side of a
(5) _____ of dog chow.

Review those exercises in this chapter where you made errors. Then go on.

12

DIRECTIONS: Study the following sets of words carefully. Note the differences in spelling and meaning. Then fill each blank with the word that fits the meaning.

COVER
THIS STRIP

---

26. **ceiling** *n.* the inside top part of a room
     sealing *adj.* closing tightly

1. ceiling
2. sealing
3. sealing
4. sealing
5. ceiling

■ Plaster fell from the (1) _*ceiling*_ and dirtied the gift package which I was (2) _____. When I told Mother that I'd thrown out the (3) _____ wax after (4) _____ the gift package, she hit the (5) _____.

27. **censor** *n.* an official who checks writing or entertainment for offensive material *v.* to delete or ban objectionable material
    censure *n.* condemnation; the act of blaming *v.* to blame; find fault with

1. censure
2. censure
3. censor
4. censor
5. censure

■ "You may (1) _____ me if you feel that I deserve (2) _____," said Ingersoll, "but do not (3) _____ my writing." Nowadays the town librarian often acts as a (4) _____ of books, an arrangement which has drawn public (5) _____.

28. **cheap** *adj.* at low cost; having little value; stingy
    cheep *n.* a weak chirp, as of a young bird *v.* to chirp or squeek

■ When the baby canary let out a (1) _____, Chuck dickered and bought the bird (2) _____ and also bought a (3) _____ cage for it. But when his wife heard the canary go (4) "_____," she said, "I wanted a parrot. You're just a (5) _____ guy, Chuck."

1. cheep
2. cheap
3. cheap
4. cheep
5. cheap

29. **chord** *n.* a harmonious blend of tones
    cord *n.* a heavy string

■ Elvis struck a romantic (1) _____ on his guitar, then another (2) _____, and we had to put up a heavy (3) _____ to hold back the screaming girls. Later, the pianist hit a faulty (4) _____ and Elvis began looking for a (5) _____ with which to strangle him.

1. chord
2. chord
3. cord
4. chord
5. cord

30. **cite** *v.* to summon to law court; quote; refer to
    sight *n.* a view; the act of seeing
    site *n.* a location; a piece of land

■ We visited the burned-out (1) _____, a sad (2) _____ indeed. Nearby stood an aging woman who had lost her (3) _____ but who could (4) _____ Biblical passages by memory. Catching (5) _____ of us, the security man told us to leave the construction (6) _____ or he would (7) _____ us.

1. site
2. sight
3. sight
4. cite
5. sight
6. site
7. cite

31. **coarse** *n.* rough in texture; crude
    course *n.* a path; a way of behaving

■ The gambler told a few (1) _____ jokes in his usual (2) _____ language, then left for the race (3) _____. He left me a bread made of (4) _____ flour, and of (5) _____ I ate it.

1. coarse
2. coarse
3. course
4. coarse
5. course

32. **complement** *n.* something that fills up or completes *v.* to fill in or to complete
    compliment *n.* words of praise *v.* to praise

■ Gail's shoes (1) _____ her purse, and Melvin paid her a (2) _____. Then he told old Mrs. Flynn that her cheeks seemed to (3) _____ her red roses, and she said, "What a sweet (4) _____, Melvin! One (5) _____ like that makes me feel like a girl of forty again."

1. complement
2. compliment
3. complement
4. compliment
5. compliment

33. **council** *n.* a group that meets to discuss and advise; a deliberative meeting
   counsel *n.* advice *v.* advise

1. council
2. counsel
3. counsel
4. counsel
5. council

■ A (1) _____ of tribal chiefs gave me some excellent (2) _____ : "Get out of the jungle!" I accepted their (3) _____ . Now I'm writing to Dear Abby for further (4) _____ : Should I run for city (5) _____ ?

34. **costume** *n.* a set of clothes worn for the stage or a special occasion
   custom *n.* a habit

1. costume
2. custom
3. custom
4. costume
5. costume

■ The country boys swam in the (1) _____ of Adam and Eve, as was the (2) _____ . But on Halloween they had a (3) _____ of putting on a scary (4) _____ --except Ugly Rufus who didn't need a (5) _____ .

35. **dairy** *n.* a producer of milk products
   diary *n.* a record of daily activities

1. dairy
2. diary
3. diary
4. dairy
5. dairy

■ Sally, the manager of the (1) _____ , keeps a (2) _____ . In her (3) _____ she writes about a new employee of the (4) _____ who seems much more attractive to her than the (5) _____ cows.

36. **dammed** *adj., v.* held back by a barrier or dam
   damned *adj., v.* cursed; condemned to eternal punishment

1. dammed
2. damned
3. dammed
4. dammed
5. damned

■ "Those beavers have (1) _____ the river," said the forest ranger. "Well, I'll be (2) _____ !" The fact is that rivers are often (3) _____ , lakes are (4) _____ , but sinners are (5) _____ .

37. **dear** *adj.* beloved; costly *n.* a beloved person
   deer *n.* an animal such as the moose or elk

1. dear
2. deer
3. deer
4. dear
5. deer
6. dear

■ "Under my stocking, (1) _____ Santa Claus," wrote Susan, "I left some hay for your (2) _____ ." But our butcher told Susan: "No longer do the (3) _____ and the antelope play, and that, my (4) _____ , is why (5) _____ meat is so (6) _____ ."

38. **deceased** *adj.* dead *n.* a dead person
    diseased *adj.* sick; infected

■ The veterinarian opened a hospital for (1) _____
animals and a pet cemetery for the (2) _____
(a lovely cemetery--dogs dying to get in). He warns that
if skinny, (3) _____ cattle and (4) _____
chickens aren't given enough water and food they will also
soon be (5) _____ .

1. diseased
2. deceased
3. diseased
4. diseased
5. deceased

39. **desert** *n.* a dry wasteland *v.* to abandon one's duty
    dessert *n.* a pastry or other delicacy served at the
              end of a meal

■ We will eat dates for (1) _____ when we camp
here in the sandy (2) _____ . But you soldiers
who (3) _____ the rest of us in this
(4) _____ oasis will not ever again share our
(5) _____ --and may you get (6) _____ sand
in your navel.

1. dessert
2. desert
3. desert
4. desert
5. dessert
6. desert

40. **device** *n.* something designed for a purpose; a
              contrivance; a plan or trick
    devise *v.* to plan; invent; contrive

■ This mousetrap--what a clever (1) _____ ! Only
a genius like me could (2) _____ such a flawless
mechanical (3) _____ . But curses! Leave it to
those mice to (4) _____ a way to steal my cheese
without getting trapped in my "foolproof" (5)_____ .

1. device
2. devise
3. device
4. devise
5. device

41. **dew** *n.* condensed moisture
    do *v.* to accomplish; perform
    due *adj.* owed; scheduled to arrive

■ I get up early while the (1) _____ is on the grass,
and I (2) _____ everything I can (3) _____ to pay
bills that are (4) _____ . As I (5) _____ my work,
the sweat stands like (6) _____ upon my brow. The
landlord has to be paid, and my motto is, Give the devil
his (7) _____ .

1. dew
2. do
3. do
4. due
5. do
6. dew
7. due

42. **dual** *adj.* double; twofold
    duel *n.* combat between two persons

■ Fritz has a (1) _____ personality. He can sing
in the choir and he can (2) _____ to the death.
His car has (3) _____ carburetion and (4) _____
exhaust pipes, and Fritz has driven his Shebang-V8 in many
a racing (5) _____ . Personally, I'd rather
(6) _____ with water pistols at fifty paces.

1. dual
2. duel
3. dual
4. dual
5. duel
6. duel

43. **dyeing** *pres.participle* coloring fabrics, hair, etc.
    dying *pres.participle* about to die

1. dying
2. dyeing
3. dying
4. dyeing
5. dyeing
6. dying

■ "I am (1) _____, Julia," said Mrs. Jones, "while you, my ungrateful daughter, stand there (2) _____ your hair." -- "I'm truly sorry, Mother, if you're (3) _____, but your doctor says that you're really as healthy as a buzzsaw. Well, I've been (4) _____ my shoes and (5) _____ my dress, and I'm just (6) _____ to try them on."

44. **eminent** *adj.* famous; outstanding
    imminent *adj.* about to happen; threatening

1. eminent
2. imminent
3. imminent
4. eminent
5. eminent

■ An (1) _____ scientist predicts that an earthquake is (2) _____. Even more gloomy is the notion that a nuclear holocaust may be (3) _____, a conviction held by certain (4) _____ military generals and some (5) _____ statesmen. Good news for cockroaches: they will survive.

45. **envelop** *v.* to wrap; enclose
    envelope *n.* a paper container for letters

1. envelope
2. envelope
3. envelop
4. envelop
5. envelope

■ The mailman handed me a large (1) _____ and a small (2) _____; then I saw the fog (3) _____ him like a blanket. Later that day came the fire. As flames began to (4) _____ the postoffice, a little man drove up and pushed a stamped (5) _____ under the smoking door.

46. **fair** *adj.* just and honest; blond *n.* a festival
    fare *n.* money paid for transportation; food

1. fair
2. fair
3. fare
4. fair
5. fare

■ It didn't seem (1) _____ to me to be sent to the county (2) _____ with little more than my bus (3) _____. I met two girls, one dark and one (4) _____, and I took them to lunch. Believe me, we had pretty scant (5) _____.

47. **flea** *n.* a small, bloodsucking insect
    flee *v.* to run away

1. flea
2. flee
3. flee
4. flea
5. flea
6. flee
7. flea

■ When a (1) _____ attacks a dog, that dog must scratch or (2) _____. But the dog can't really (3) _____ from a (4) _____ because that (5) _____ has taken up light housekeeping in the dog's fur....Seeing a spray can coming toward the fireplace, a fly said, "Let us (6) _____," and the (7) _____ said, "Let us fly." So they flew through a flaw in the flue.

48. **flour** *n.* a fine powder produced by grinding grain
    flower *n.* a blossoming plant; a bloom

1. flour
2. flour
3. flower
4. flower
5. flour

■ This fine bread baked from corn (1) _____ and whole wheat (2) _____ goes to the gringo with the (3) _____ in his lapel. Little Rosita, who looks like a (4) _____ in a garden, ground the (5) _____ herself.

49. **formally** *adv.* in a proper, conventional fashion; ceremoniously
    formerly *adv.* at an earlier time

1. formerly
2. formally
3. formally
4. formally
5. formerly
6. formerly

■ A young woman (1) _____ did not talk to a man until they had been (2) _____ introduced. Weddings are still conducted (3) _____ and graduation exercises are conducted (4) _____, just as was done (5) _____, but sweat shirts and jeans now blossom where they were (6) _____ unthinkable.

50. **forth** *adv.* forward; out into view
    fourth *adj.* following three others in a series

1. forth
2. fourth
3. fourth
4. fourth
5. forth

■ Belinda burst (1) _____ into glorious song and won (2) _____ prize. She would have won third except that the (3) _____ note of the (4) _____ stanza was too high and it wouldn't come (5) _____.

Review word sets 1-50, spelling and vocabulary, particularly where you may have made errors. Then take the Chapters 11-12 Self-Test.

CHAPTERS 11-12: SELF-TEST

DIRECTIONS: Write the words in full. Complete this entire test before you check and grade your answers.

_____ 1. I never promised you a [f-l-o-r-] garden.
_____ 2. Kissing each cheek was an Italian [c-s-t-m-].
_____ 3. Mail your check in the enclosed [e-n-v-l-o-p-].
_____ 4. Rudy scribbled her name in his [d-i-r-y].
_____ 5. The sculptors ate their [d-e-s-r-t-]: marble cake.
_____ 6. I told the drunkard not to [b-r-e-t-h-] on me.
_____ 7. England was our [a-l-y] in two world wars.
_____ 8. Harry Truman had [f-o-r-m-l-y] been a shirt salesman.
_____ 9. The wetback slipped past the [b-o-r-d-r] patrol.
_____ 10. This is where the [d-e-r] and the antelope play.
_____ 11. Would your grandmother [a-s-e-n-t] to pose for *Playboy*?
_____ 12. Approach of Hurricane Buster was [-m-i-n-e-n-t].

_____ 13. Those little vandals need [c-o-n-s-1].
_____ 14. Should we [a-d-p-t] a child or buy a dog?
_____ 15. Our generals will [d-e-v-i-] a plan of attack.
_____ 16. I admired the [b-a-s-] drum and Rocky told me to beat it.
_____ 17. When you pick roses, wear [c-a-n-v-s-] gloves.
_____ 18. In the theater [-i-l-e] I stumbled over a wooden leg.
_____ 19. The [c-h-e-p] meal gave me an expensive illness.
_____ 20. The old man laughed at his own [a-n-d-o-t-e].
_____ 21. The grass was wet with morning [d-e-].
_____ 22. We built an [-d-i-t-i-o-n] at the farm: an inside toilet.
_____ 23. I painted the walls and the [-e-l-i-n-g], ruining the rug.
_____ 24. Read editorials, not just the [c-a-r-t-n] page.
_____ 25. Abner's profanity didn't [a-l-t-r] the mule's attitude.
_____ 26. Gloria hit a home run in the [f-o-t-h] inning.
_____ 27. Afraid of heights, I chose the lower [b-r-t-h].
_____ 28. Location can [-f-e-c-t] property values. So can termites.
_____ 29. Jim loves cigarettes, despite his [d-e-a-s-e-d] lungs.
_____ 30. Tourists posed on the steps of the state [c-a-p-t-1].
_____ 31. I hope to be a heavenly [a-n-g-1-], so I practice the harp.
_____ 32. The widow sobbed [a-1-o-d] when her cat died.
_____ 33. Victorians were shocked to see [b-a-r-] legs.
_____ 34. The pianist banged out an opening [c-o-r-d].
_____ 35. A nuclear plant was erected on the [s-i-t-] of the church.
_____ 36. To encourage the donkey, Pancho [b-e-t] it with a stick.
_____ 37. The president loved the golf [c-o-r-s-] and was happy.
_____ 38. The Red Baron fought many a [d-u-1] in the sky.
_____ 39. Ben Jonson made a glowing [-1-u-s-o-n] to Shakespeare.
_____ 40. Pay the bus [f-a-r-] or get off the bus.
_____ 41. Lincoln was [b-o-r-n-] on a national holiday.
_____ 42. Under the [b-e-c-h] tree we arranged a shady deal.
_____ 43. The military [c-e-n-s-r-] enjoyed reading intimate lines.
_____ 44. Our sinking ship needs immediate [a-s-i-s-t-n-].
_____ 45. Rover's blood was siphoned off by a thirsty [f-1-e-].
_____ 46. His green face and red eyes [c-o-m-p-1-m-t] each other.
_____ 47. Children are [b-o-r-d] by films without gore.
_____ 48. The horse disliked me, and I hung tight to the [b-r-d-1-].
_____ 49. Fish were [d-y-n-g] in Lake Erie.
_____ 50. "Out, [d-a-m-d] spot! out, I say!" (Macbeth, V, 1, 39)

ANSWER KEY

Check your test answers by the following key. Deduct 2% per error from 100%.

1. flower	11. assent	21. dew	31. angel	41. born
2. custom	12. imminent	22. addition	32. aloud	42. beech
3. envelope	13. counsel	23. ceiling	33. bare	43. censor
4. diary	14. adopt	24. cartoon	34. chord	44. assistance
5. dessert	15. devise	25. alter	35. site	45. flea
6. breathe	16. bass	26. fourth	36. beat	46. complement
7. ally	17. canvas	27. berth	37. course	47. bored
8. formerly	18. aisle	28. affect	38. duel	48. bridle
9. border	19. cheap	29. diseased	39. allusion	49. dying
10. deer	20. anecdote	30. capitol	40. fare	50. *damned*

Score: _____%

13

DIRECTIONS: Study the following sets of words carefully. Note the differences in spelling and meaning. Then fill each blank with the word that fits the meaning.

COVER
THIS STRIP

51. **foreword** *n.* a preface; an introductory statement
    forward *adv.* toward what is ahead

1. foreword
2. forward
3. foreword
4. forward
5. foreword
6. forward

■ Read the (1) _____ before plunging
(2) _____ into the body of the textbook. In
other words, the table of contents and the (3) _____
suggest what you can look (4) _____ to; so first
check a book's (5)_____, then (6) _____
march!

52. **foul** *adj.* dirty; not fair; not according to the
    rules
    fowl *n.* a domestic bird such as a chicken or goose

1. foul
2. fowl
3. fowl
4. fowl
5. foul

■ The farm boy batted a (1) _____ ball which
missed one frightened (2) _____ but struck another
(3) _____ in the head. The dead (4) _____
rotted where it lay, and before long it gave off a
(5) _____ odor.

53. **have** *v.* to possess--*also used as auxiliary in phrases like "should have won," "might have worked," "could have died"*
of *prep.* from; relating to--*as in "Jones of Nevada," "plays of Ibsen," "tub of lard"*

1. of
2. have
3. have
4. of
5. have
6. of

■ One (1)_____ our fielders should (2)_____ caught the ball, and he would (3)_____ caught it, too, except that he slid into a puddle (4)_____ water. I would (5)_____ patted him on the back for trying, but his shirt was a mural (6)_____ sticky mud.

54. **heal** *v.* to cure
heel *n.* the back part of the foot

1. heel
2. heal
3. heel
4. heal
5. heal
6. heel
7. heel

■ The dog bit me, and I'm waiting now for my (1)_____ to (2)_____. The dog's owner felt like a (3)_____ but assured me that time will (4)_____ all wounds. After I (5)_____ my (6)_____ I may just plant the (7)_____ of my boot against the south end of that lousy hound.

55. **hear** *v.* to listen; perceive sounds by means of the ear
here *adv.* in this place

1. here
2. hear
3. here
4. Hear
5. hear
6. here

■ "Sit (1)_____ behind the post," said the usher. -- "But will I be able to (2)_____ from (3)_____?" I asked. -- "(4)_____, (5)_____!" came a voice from the next row. "Let's have some quiet in (6)_____."

56. **hoarse** *adj.* having a husky, grating voice
horse *n.* a large animal which may pull loads or carry riders

1. horse
2. hoarse
3. horse
4. hoarse
5. horse

■ "Don't (1)_____ around," growled the big cowboy in a (2)_____ voice. He grabbed Percy by the neck and added, "Sure, I painted your (3)_____ blue. What ya say to that?" -- In a soft voice, not (4)_____ at all, Percy said, "The first coat of paint on my (5)_____ is dry now."

57. **hole** *n.* a cavity; a pit
whole *adj.* entire; complete

1. whole
2. hole
3. hole
4. whole
5. whole
6. hole

■ We spent a (1)_____ day pushing our truck out of a (2)_____, an experience we needed like a (3)_____ in the head. Then I ate a (4)_____ pizza, and Laura ate a (5)_____ doughnut, all but the (6)_____.

page 107

58. **imply** *v.* to suggest; indicate
    infer *v.* to conclude; deduce

1. imply
2. infer
3. imply
4. infer
5. infer

■ The bloodstains (1) _____ that someone was hurt, and I (2) _____ that Nick was stabbed. Also, the empty jewel boxes (3) _____ that a robbery took place, and we may (4) _____ that Nick tried to prevent that robbery. What would Sherlock Holmes (5) _____ from these clues?

59. **incidence** *n.* the degree of occurrence
    incidents *n.* happenings; events

1. incidence
2. incidents
3. incidents
4. incidents
5. incidence

■ The high (1) _____ of crime in Pleasantville was impressed on me by several (2) _____. Five (3) _____ involved mugging, and three (4) _____ involved arson. Also our pleasant town had an unusual (5) _____ of wife-beating.

60. **ingenious** *adj.* clever; inventive; skillful
    ingenuous *adj.* innocent; frank; naive

1. ingenious
2. ingenious
3. ingenuous
4. ingenuous
5. ingenious

■ Although Joyce was a gifted and (1) _____ chess player and her brother was equally (2) _____, their remarks to the interviewer were simple and (3) _____; in fact, a child could not have been more (4) _____. Yet the pair had already patented an (5) _____ electric skateboard.

61. **later** *adv.* after some time
    latter *adj.* the last mentioned

1. later
2. latter
3. later
4. later
5. latter

■ The banquet ended (1) _____ than usual for Scott and Zelda. The former passed out at midnight and the (2) _____ a bit (3) _____. Parties and liquor!--the former attracted the Fitzgeralds and (4) _____ the (5) _____ killed them.

62. **lessen** *v.* to decrease; become less
    lesson *n.* a study assignment; an instructive experience

1. lesson
2. lessen
3. lessen
4. lesson
5. lesson
6. lessen
7. lesson

■ Toby's interest in her tuba (1) _____ began to (2) _____. Her funds also began to (3) _____, and therefore she had to choose between taking a music (4) _____ and a skating (5) _____. Without constant practice an ability will (6) _____; and I think there's a (7) _____ there for students of spelling, too.

63. **liable** *adj.* legally obligated *Informal*: likely
    libel *n.* writing that exposes a person to public
    ridicule *v.* to defame in writing

1. libel
2. liable
3. liable
4. libel
5. liable

■ Print those lies and it means a (1) _____
suit involving a million in damages, for which the editor
will be (2) _____. You'll also be held
(3) _____. I warn you: If you (4) _____
the actress in your article, she's (5) _____ to sue.

64. **loose** *adj.* not drawn tight; unfastened
    lose *v.* to mislay; fail to keep; fail to win

1. loose
2. lose
3. loose
4. loose
5. lose
6. lose

■ Buster's (1) _____ shoelace caused him to
(2) _____ the race. He tripped on the
(3) _____ lace and now he has a (4) _____
tooth which he may also (5) _____. "All this
bad luck will make me (6) _____ my mind," he
told his mother, and she said, "Small loss."

65. **mantel** *n.* the shelf above a fireplace
    mantle *n.* a cloak

1. mantle
2. mantel
3. mantle
4. mantle
5. mantel

■ The stranger wearing the green (1) _____
walked up to the (2) _____ above the blazing
hearth. The heat of the fireplace soon made him take off
his (3) _____, and a bit later he placed his
folded (4) _____ next to a cracked vase which
was standing on the (5) _____.

66. **marital** *adj.* pertaining to marriage
    martial *adj.* pertaining to war

1. martial
2. martial
3. marital
4. marital
5. martial

■ In the army band Jesse played (1) _____ music
and, incidentally, was awarded several (2) _____
ribbons. Later he got married, hoping for his fair quota
of (3) _____ bliss, but his (4) _____
life with Bertha was marked by pitched battles of a
(5) _____ nature.

67. **meat** *n.* animal flesh
    meet *v.* to encounter; come into contact with

1. meet
2. meat
3. meat
4. meat
5. meat
6. meet

■ Please (1) _____ Sam, our new (2) _____
salesman. If you want fresh poultry (3) _____,
lamb (4) _____, or rabbit (5) _____
(he'll split hares), you won't (6) _____ a better
butcher.

68. **medal** *n.* a decorative award for an outstanding act
    metal *n.* a substance such as iron, gold, or brass

1. medal
2. medal
3. metal
4. metal
5. medal

■ Herbert wears a (1) _____ or two on his suit lapel and another (2) _____ on his pajamas. Are they made of gold (3) _____ or some base (4) _____? Herbert should check that little detail whenever he buys a (5) _____ at the pawnshop.

69. **miner** *n.* somebody who works in a mine
    minor *adj.* of lesser importance *n.* a young person without full civil rights

1. minor
2. miner
3. minor
4. miner
5. minor

■ Mike was fifteen and the coal company couldn't hire a (1) _____ to be a (2) _____. However Mike made a (3) _____ change on his application form and he was a fully employed coal (4) _____ by the following Monday. Three years later he had a good salary and a somewhat (5) _____ lung problem.

70. **moral** (mor'əl) *adj.* pertaining to good conduct; virtuous; virtual [*a moral victory*] *n.* the lesson in a story
    morale (mə ral') *n.* state of mind with respect to confidence, enthusiasm, etc.

1. moral
2. morale
3. moral
4. morale
5. moral
6. moral

■ Our female athletes have excellent (1) _____ character and high (2) _____. It was your (3) _____ support that boosted their team (4) _____. And the (5) _____ of the story is that they have won, well, a (6) _____ victory.

71. **naval** *adj.* relating to a navy
    navel *n.* umbilicus; "belly button" [*navel orange*]

1. naval
2. navel
3. navel
4. naval
5. navel

■ On the deck some of the (1) _____ personnel were stripped to the (2) _____. One sailor was eating a (3) _____ orange; and another (4) _____ man was scratching his (5) _____.

72. **pail** *n.* a bucket
    pale *adj.* lacking color; feeble; ashen *n.* a boundary

1. pale
2. pale
3. pail
4. pale
5. pail

■ The victim's face was very (1) _____ and his hands were (2) _____. He must have lost a (3) _____ of blood. Apparently he had been riding his bicycle under the (4) _____ moon and had hit a (5) _____ of cement.

page 110

73. **peace** *n.* calm; the absence of war
    piece *n.* a small portion

1. piece
2. piece
3. peace
4. peace
4. peace
6. piece

    The Indian gave me a (1) _____ of venison, and I gave him a (2) _____ of cheese; then we smoked the (3) _____ pipe. "Me, paleface man," I said. "Me come in (4) _____. Me make-um end to fighting."— "Yes, you white hypocrites promise (5) _____," said the Indian, "but that's invariably a (6) _____ of baloney."

74. **peak** *n.* the summit of a mountain
    peek *v.* to look slyly

1. peek
2. peak
3. peak
4. peak
5. peak
6. peek

    ■ Take one (1) _____ at our mountain (2) _____ and climbing to the (3) _____ will become the (4) _____ of your ambition. Incidentally, if you fall off the (5) _____, take a quick (6) _____ toward the ocean: the view is fantastic.

75. **pedal** *n.* a foot-operated lever *v.* to work the pedals
    petal *n.* a flower leaf

1. petal
2. pedal
3. petal
4. petal
5. pedal

    ■ The little boy watched the artist, his little mouth like a rose (1) _____. The artist had taken her foot off the bicycle (2) _____ and begun to paint the garden scene: the (3) _____ of a daisy, a lotus (4) _____....Afterwards he saw her (5) _____ away.

Review those exercises in this chapter where you made errors. Then go on.

WORDS OFTEN CONFUSED (76-100)

14

DIRECTIONS: Study the following sets of words carefully. Note the differences in spelling and meaning. Then fill each blank with the word that fits the meaning.

COVER
THIS STRIP

---

76. personal *adj.* private
     personnel *n.* the persons employed in a business

1. personal	■ Nancy gets much (1) _____ satisfaction working
2. personnel	in the (2) _____ department. She says that the
3. personnel	(3) _____ manager, in her (4) _____
4. personal	opinion, is a real gentleman who takes a (5) _____
5. personal	interest in the company's (6) _____. Sometimes,
6. personnel	though, says Nancy, he gets too (7) _____.
7. personal	

77. picture *n.* a photograph, drawing, or other visual
       representation
     pitcher *n.* one who pitches in baseball; a container
       with a handle and spout

1. picture	■ Would you like to own a (1)_____ of your
2. pitcher	favorite baseball (2) _____? If so, send us three
3. picture	box tops showing the (3) _____ of Sugar Cruddies
4. picture	being shot out of a gun and you'll receive a (4) _____
5. pitcher	of a Yankee (5) _____ drinking victory champagne
6. pitcher	from a (6) _____.

78. **plain** *adj.* unadorned; homely *n.* a prairie
    plane *n.* an airplane; a flat level surface

1. plane
2. plain
3. plane
4. plain
5. plain

■ "If you're going to fly a (1) _____," advised my mother, "you should dress (2) _____. Your (3) _____ might hit a mountain or a grassy (4) _____, and the (5) _____ fact is that you don't want to ruin your good clothes."

79. **pole** *n.* a long slender piece of wood
    poll *n.* the voting at an election *v.* to take a sampling of the opinions of

1. pole
2. poll
3. poll
4. pole
5. poll

■ Abolitionist Henry D. Thoreau stood straight as a (1) _____ and refused to pay his (2) _____ tax. He felt that if he were to (3) _____ his neighbors, they also would be found opposed to supporting slavery, but being as unthinking as a fence (4) _____, they continued to pay the (5) _____ tax.

80. **pore** *n.* a tiny opening in the skin *v.* to read carefully
    pour *v.* to cause to flow; gush

1. pour
2. pore
3. pour
4. pour
5. pour
6. pore
7. pore

■ I see the perspiration (1) _____ from your every (2) _____, so (3) _____ yourself a drink. Meanwhile, commercials (4) _____ from the television set telling us to (5) _____ protein oil on every hair and facial (6) _____ --as though one could feed protein to hair or to a skin (7)_____ from the outside.

81. **presence** *n.* the condition of being there
    presents *n.* gifts

1. presents
2. presence
3. presence
4. presents
5. presents

   Don't discuss these Christmas (1) _____ in the (2) _____ of the children. Luckily, I had the (3) _____ of mind to hide Paul's (4) _____ as well as Wendy's (5) _____ in the broom closet, and they'll never go near a broom.

82. **principal** *adj.* most important *n.* a leader or chief person in a school, a trial, or a business; money that draws interest
    principle *n.* a general truth; rule of conduct

1. principal
2. principle
3. principal
4. principle
5. principal

■ Our high school (1) _____, a man of high (2) _____, told me that the (3) _____ cause of his financial success was this simple (4) _____: "Spend the interest on your savings but don't touch the (5) _____.

83. profit   *n.* financial gain
prophet   *n.* one who predicts future events; a divinely inspired religious leader

1. prophet
2. profit
3. prophet
4. profit
5. profit
6. prophet

■ A book by a Wall Street (1) _____ tells how investors can make a big (2) _____. But why would a (3) _____ sell his investment secrets for a small (4) _____ if he really knew how to make a big (5) _____? Could he be a phony (6) _____?

84. prophecy (-sē)   *n.* a prediction
prophesy (-sī')   *v.* to predict

1. prophesy
2. prophecy
3. prophecy
4. prophecy
5. prophesy
6. prophesy

■ For ten dollars Ezra would (1) _____ the sex of an unborn child, and he backed each (2) _____ with a money-back guarantee. "If my (3) _____ is wrong, I'll return your money," he promised. Obviously, Ezra's (4) _____ was often wrong, but half the time he would (5) _____ correctly and keep the money....Boy or girl? What would you (6) _____?

85. rapped   *v.* struck quick blows
wrapped   *v.* enclosed

1. rapped
2. rapped
3. wrapped
4. rapped
5. wrapped
6. wrapped

■ Somebody (1) _____ on my door and then (2) _____ again, a bit louder, but I was (3) _____ in thought. Had a raven (4) _____ at my chamber door? I finally (5) _____ a towel around my head and at the door I found an interesting gift: a fish (6) _____ in yesterday's newspaper.

86. respectfully   *adv.* with full respect; courteously
respectively   *adv.* in the order named

1. respectfully
2. respectively
3. respectively
4. respectfully
5. respectively

■ The photo shows Kay, May, and Fay listening (1) _____ to the mayor; they represent Lincoln, Grant, and Jefferson school (2) _____. The mayor awarded a gold and a silver medal to Jill and Phil (3) _____. You are (4) _____ invited to attend the banquet honoring Flo, Joe, and Shmoe, who won first, second, and third prizes (5) _____ in the poetry writing contest.

87. ring   *n.* a circular object   *v.* to cause a bell to sound
wring   *v.* to squeeze by twisting

1. wring
2. ring
3. ring
4. wring
5. ring
6. ring

■ Jane began to (1) _____ her hands while waiting for the telephone to (2) _____. "If that louse doesn't (3) _____ pretty soon," she muttered, "I'll (4) _____ his neck, the rat." She heard the doorbell (5) _____. -- Then: "Why, Jim," she said, "you've been buying me an engagement (6) _____, you darling!"

page 114

88. **road** *n.* a highway
     rode *v.* traveled on horseback, in a vehicle, etc.

1. rode
2. road
3. rode
4. rode
5. road
6. rode
7. road

■ Emily (1) _____ the gelding down the
(2) _____ and Tony (3) _____ the old
gray mare. A truck (4) _____ swiftly past the
dude ranch, forcing the horses off the (5) _____.
To impress Emily, Tony (6) _____ a bronco for
eight seconds, then landed on the (7) _____.

89. **role** *n.* a part taken by an actor
     roll *n.* a small cake of bread *v.* to revolve

1. role
2. role
3. roll
4. roll
5. role
6. roll

■ Linda, who plays the (1) _____ of heroine, and
Archie, who plays the (2) _____ of hero, are eating a
sweet (3) _____ in the stagecoach. Archie starts
singing, "Merrily we (4) _____ along!" Enter the
outlaw, a (5) _____ played by Jasper, and he wrestles
with Archie until they (6) _____ out of the
stagecoach door.

90. **sail** *n.* a piece of canvas attached to a vessel
          v. to travel by water
     sale *n.* the act of selling; selling at bargain prices

1. sale
2. sale
3. sail
4. sail
5. sale

■ My sister loves a discount (1) _____. In fact,
she met Dick at a garage (2) _____. Their friendship
began to (3) _____ along so smoothly that guess what:
The pair have set (4) _____ on a honeymoon trip to
Hawaii, where they'll soon be visiting a (5) _____
on coconuts.

91. **shone** *v., past tense of "shine"* was shining
     shown *v., pp. of "show"* displayed; demonstrated

1. shone
2. shown
3. shown
4. shone
5. shone
6. shown

■ Jane's eyes (1) _____ when she was (2) _____
the engagement ring. "It's the smallest diamond that I was
(3) _____," said Jim modestly, "but I liked the way
it (4) _____." As the evening sun (5) _____
over the incinerator, Jane whispered, "You've really
(6) _____ me true love, Jim."

92. **shudder** *n.* a convulsive shiver *v.* to tremble
     shutter *n.* a window screen; a device controlling a
          camera lens

1. shutter
2. shudder
3. shutter
4. shudder
5. shutter

■ The beauty queen pulled open the window (1) _____,
then began to (2) _____. Once more the nosy
cameraman on the lawn had begun to click his (3) _____.
"I (4) _____ to think what I'd do to that horrible
(5) _____ bug if I laid hands on him," she said.

93. **stake** *n.* a stick or post; something wagered
steak *n.* a slice of meat or fish

1. stake
2. stake
3. steak
4. steak
5. steak
6. stake

■ Tex stopped pounding the fence (1) _____ into the ground and said, "Ingrid, how'd you like to have me (2) _____ you to a sirloin (3) _____?" -- "But a (4) _____ is expensive," said Ingrid. "Can we afford a (5) _____?" -- "We can now, honey. My fence (6) _____ just struck oil."

94. **stationary** *adj.* not moving
stationery *n.* writing material

1. stationary
2. stationery
3. stationery
4. stationery
5. stationary
6. stationery

■ A clerk was standing (1) _____ behind the (2) _____ counter. I used your (3) _____ while riding the bus," I told her, "and believe me, a letter on your (4) _____ looks messy." -- Answered the clerk: "Be sure you're (5) _____ when you write on our (6) _____."

95. **steal** *v.* to take dishonestly; move secretly
steel *n.* an iron alloy

1. steel
2. steal
3. steel
4. steal
5. steel
6. steal

■ Because copper and (1) _____ have gone up in price, some rascals will (2) _____ the (3) _____ rails from under a trolley. One night they managed to (4) _____ my stainless (5) _____ sink and quietly (6) _____ away.

96. **summary** *n.* a condensation; a synopsis
summery *adj.* like summer

1. summery
2. summary
3. summery
4. summary
5. summary

■ It was a (1) _____ day, and I was writing a (2) _____ of Tolstoi's *War and Peace*. Edith was sitting in the (3) _____ shade of an oak tree, writing a (4) _____ of Hugo's *Les Misérables*. Anyhow, we decided that it's easier to write a (5) _____ than to write a fat novel.

97. **vain** *adj.* conceited; fruitless
vein *n.* a blood vessel

1. vain
2. vain
3. vein
4. vein
5. vain

■ Why is Horatio so (1) _____? Is he (2) _____ about his Puritan ancestry? Does his (3) _____ have bluer blood in it than my (4) _____? I keep asking these questions but in (5) _____.

98. **weak** *adj.* feeble
    week *n.* a seven-day period

1. week
2. weak
3. weak
4. weak
5. week
6. week

■ All (1) _____ Tom felt (2) _____.
His arms were (3) _____ and his legs were
(4) _____. He missed a whole (5) _____
of school. During the following (6) _____ he
got a sweet note from Mary; then he felt like Hercules.

99. **waist** *n.* the part of the body between chest and hips
    waste *n.* useless material *v.* to squander

■ Does Miss America have a twenty-six-inch (1) _____
or a forty-inch (2) _____? It's a sheer

1. waist
2. waist
3. waste
4. waist
5. waste
6. waste

(3) _____ of time to discuss the matter, says
Dr. Shlepp. The slenderest (4) _____ is a
complete (5) _____ unless a girl has
intelligence. "Get married in the evening," advises
Dr. Shlepp, "so if things don't work out, you don't
(6) _____ the whole day."

100. **waive** *v.* to give up a claim
     wave *n.* an upsurge of ocean water *v.* to move to
     and fro

1. wave
2. waive
3. waive
4. wave
5. wave
6. waive

■ The agent began to (1) _____ legal papers in Clem's
face. "To get our health insurance, Clem," he said, "you
must (2) _____ your right to a cataract operation.
Also you must (3) _____ your right to straightening
your nose." Clem felt a (4) _____ of dismay. "With
a (5) _____ of your hand," he said, "you make me
(6) _____ the privileges I came here for."

Review word sets 51-100, spelling and vocabulary, particularly where you may
have made errors. Then take the Chapters 13-14 Self-Test.

CHAPTERS 13-14: SELF-TEST

DIRECTIONS: Write the words in full. Complete this entire test before you
check and grade your answers.

_____ 1. The zebra looks like a [h-o-r-s-] in pajamas.
_____ 2. This is the store's third closing-out [s-a-l-].
_____ 3. They hanged the bandit to teach him a [l-e-s-n].
_____ 4. In preschool we learned how to [p-o-r-] sand.
_____ 5. The gopher dug a [-h-o-l-] that reached China.
_____ 6. We all retire, sooner or [l-a-t-r-].
_____ 7. Yehudi left us a gift, a [-r-i-n-g-] around the bathtub.
_____ 8. My tractor lurched [f-o-r-w-r-d-] into the canyon.
_____ 9. Did Eve, created from a rib, have a [n-a-v-l-]?
_____ 10. Teachers will [m-e-t] under the crabapple tree.
_____ 11. The doctor was held [l-i-b-l-] for malpractice.
_____ 12. You take the high [r-o-d-], and I'll take the bus.
_____ 13. Use good grammar in the [p-r-e-s-e-n-] of your boss.

_____ 14. The nurse's needle tapped a [v-n-], not an artery.
_____ 15. Television may be a [p-r-i-n-c-p-l-] cause of ignorance.
_____ 16. Junior drew this [p-i-c-r-] of a dog. Or is it a camel?
_____ 17. Inga was involved in both [i-n-c-i-d-e-n-].
_____ 18. The old [m-i-n-r-] couldn't find gold if he tripped on it.
_____ 19. A bill collector [-r-a-p-d] on my door.
_____ 20. The arrow hit Achilles in the [h-e-l-] of his foot.
_____ 21. From the orchid tree floated a flower [p-e-l-]
_____ 22. Life is a game, and we eventually [l-o-s-].
_____ 23. Alaska gets [s-u-m-r-y] weather in late July.
_____ 24. We came to [h-e-r-] a concert, not chatter.
_____ 25. On each wormy candied apple, the club made a big [p-r-o-t].
_____ 26. The judge wants the [p-l-a-n-] facts.
_____ 27. Chauncey's answers were childlike and [i-n-g-e-n-u-s].
_____ 28. The junkman buys iron, brass, and other [m-e-l].
_____ 29. The superannuated limburger had a [f-o-l] smell.
_____ 30. Tim's letter had a [p-e-r-s-n-l] touch, a plea for cash.
_____ 31. Franklin wrote memorable [m-o-r-l-] proverbs.
_____ 32. That's the ten-foot [p-o-l-] she won't touch him with.
_____ 33. What do these clues [i-p-y]?
_____ 34. I was [s-h-o-n-] a cottage that was more run down than I was.
_____ 35. The battle of the bulge is fought at the [w-a-s-t-].
_____ 36. Billy, let the nice dentist [p-e-k] at your toofie.
_____ 37. Long may our flag [w-a-v-] o'er the home of the brave.
_____ 38. Rusty's idea of exercise was to [r-o-l-] a pair of dice.
_____ 39. The world ended yesterday, according to one [p-r-o-p-h-y].
_____ 40. Your picture will always stand above the [m-a-n-t-l-].
_____ 41. "S," "O," and "B" stand for Sam, Ole, and Bill [r-s-p-c-t-y].
_____ 42. Mr. and Mrs. Rip Van Winkle had [m-a-r-t-l-] problems.
_____ 43. The cat stole your T-bone [s-t-a-k-].
_____ 44. The military guard stood as [s-t-a-t-n-r-y] as a hydrant.
_____ 45. A victim of shock usually looks [p-a-l-].
_____ 46. Hans fell into the molten [s-t-e-l]; now he's a VW bumper.
_____ 47. By Saturday the patient was very [w-e-k].
_____ 48. The cameraman clicked the [s-h-u-e-r], exposing the lens.
_____ 49. You should [- - -] studied.
_____ 50. _"Sleep in [p-e-c-e], and wake in joy"_ (Richard III,V,iii,155)

ANSWER KEY

Check your test answers by the following key. Deduct 2% per error from 100%.

1. horse	11. liable	21. petal	31. moral	41. respectively
2. sale	12. road	22. lose	32. pole	42. marital
3. lesson	13. presence	23. summery	33. imply	43. steak
4. pour	14. vein	24. hear	34. shown	44. stationary
5. hole	15. principal	25. profit	35. waist	45. pale
6. later	16. picture	26. plain	36. peek	46. steel
7. ring	17. incidents	27. ingenuous	37. wave	47. weak
8. forward	18. miner	28. metal	38. roll	48. shutter
9. navel	19. rapped	29. foul	39. prophecy	49. have
10. meet	20. heel	30. personal	40. mantel	50. _peace_

Score: _____ %

Your instructor will give you final tests on words 1-100 in Chapters 11-14.

ACTION WORDS: "ACHIEVE" TO "FASCINATE"

15

DIRECTIONS: Study the spelling of each word carefully, giving special attention to the trouble spots (underlined letters). Then write each word neatly three times.

1. ach<u>ie</u>ve   _____ _____ _____

2. a<u>c</u>knowle<u>d</u>ge _____ _____ _____

3. a<u>c</u>qu<u>a</u>inted _____ _____ _____

4. a<u>c</u>quire   _____ _____ _____

5. advert<u>is</u>e _____ _____ _____

6. an<u>a</u>l<u>y</u>ze   _____ _____ _____

7. apol<u>og</u>ize _____ _____ _____

8. appre<u>ci</u>ate _____ _____ _____

9. appro<u>a</u>ch   _____ _____ _____

10. as<u>su</u>re   _____ _____ _____

Review words 1-10 until you are sure you can spell them. Then go on and take the quiz.

COVER THIS STRIP	FILL THE BLANKS
	■ Electricians are _____ [a-q-a-n-t-d] with
acquainted	current affairs.
	■ You will better _____ [a-p-r-e-a-t-] this stew
appreciate analyze	if you don't _____ [a-n-l-z-] what's in it.
	■ To _____ [a-c-h-e-v-] respectable grades in
achieve acquire	college, first _____ [a-q-i-r-] mastery of spelling.
	■ Marvin started to _____ [a-p-l-g-z-] for
	dialing the wrong number and thus got _____
apologize acquainted	[a-q-a-n-t-d] with his future wife.
	■ Our pizza shop will have to _____ [a-d-v-r-t-i-]
advertise achieve acquire	if we expect to _____ [a-c-h-e-v-] our goal, which is to _____ [a-q-i-r-] a few bucks.
	■ I wish to _____ [a-p-l-g-z-] for denting your
apologize assure	new car and _____ [a-s-u-r-] you it won't happen again.
	■ Dingle decided to use the direct _____
approach appreciate acquainted	[a-p-r-o-c-h-] and said, "Rhoda, I'd really _____ [a-p-r-e-a-t-] getting _____ [a-q-a-n-t-d] with you."
	■ If you _____ [a-n-l-z-] this chess position, you
analyze acknowledge achieve	must _____ [a-k-n-o-l-g-] that Fischer will _____ [a-c-h-e-v-] checkmate in seven moves.
	■ We did _____ [a-d-v-r-t-i-] for a wine taster,
	and we _____ [a-p-r-e-a-t-] your extreme interest.
	This note is to _____ [a-k-n-o-l-g-] your
advertise appreciate acknowledge assure	application, as a reformed alcoholic, and to _____ [a-s-u-r-] you that your application will get all the consideration that it deserves.

approach
assure
acquire

■ As we _____ [a-p-r-o-c-h-] the baseball season,

the Bungville Bobcats want to _____ [a-s-u-r-]

our loyal fans that we'll soon _____ [a-q-i-r-]

a spitball pitcher.

■ I became _____ [a-q-a-n-t-d] with an amateur

psychologist who would _____ [a-n-l-z-] my every

acquainted
analyze
apologize

word and nod until I would _____ [a-p-l-g-z-]

to him for living.

■ I didn't notice the stealthy _____ [a-p-r-o-c-h-]

approach
acknowledge
advertise

of the mugger, since one must _____ [a-k-n-o-l-g-]

that such people don't _____ [a-d-v-r-t-i-].

■ *"Some are born great, some _____ [a-c-h-e-v-]*
greatness, and some have greatness thrust upon them."
(Twelfth Night, II, v, 158)

achieve

DIRECTIONS: Continue as before. Study the spelling carefully. Write each word three times.

11. atta<u>c</u>ked _____ _____ _____

12. ben<u>e</u>fi<u>te</u>d _____ _____ _____

13. <u>c</u>el<u>e</u>b<u>r</u>ate _____ _____ _____

14. comp<u>a</u>re _____ _____ _____

15. conde<u>mn</u> _____ _____ _____

16. criti<u>ci</u>ze _____ _____ _____

17. dam<u>a</u>ge _____ _____ _____

18. dec<u>ei</u>ve _____ _____ _____

19. develo<u>p</u> _____ _____ _____

20. di<u>sa</u>gree _____ _____ _____

Review words 11-20. Then take the quiz.

COVER THIS STRIP	FILL THE BLANKS

compare
deceive

■ Those who _____ [c-o-m-p-r-] themselves to

saints will _____ [d-e-c-e-v-] you in other ways, too.

criticize
develop

■ Never _____ [c-r-i-t-z-] the photographs until

you _____ [d-e-v-l-p-] the film.

celebrate
disagree

■ The old couple want to _____ [c-e-l-b-r-t-]

their happy anniversary but they _____ [d-i-s-g-r-e-]

angrily about what to do.

condemn

■ A consumers' group voted to _____ [c-n-d-e-m-]

the electric chair because it is unsafe.

benefited
celebrate

■ We were _____ [b-e-n-f-t-d] by a ten-dollar

raise, so we began to _____ [c-e-l-b-r-t-] by

spending fifty.

attacked
damage
benefited

■ "Do you really believe the smog has _____

[a-t-a-k-d] and done _____ [d-a-m-g-] to your

lungs?" asked the refinery manager, and I answered, "Well,

sir--hak, hak!--I don't think that the smog--hak!--has

_____ [b-e-n-f-t-d] them."

criticize
celebrate

■ It's unfair to _____ [c-r-i-t-z-] religious

sects that _____ [c-e-l-b-r-t-] holidays different

from our own.

disagree
condemn
attacked

■ I _____ [d-i-s-g-r-e-] with your beliefs, but

strongly _____ [c-n-d-e-m-] those who have

_____ [a-t-a-k-d] your right to express yourself.

deceive
develop
damage

■ If you continue to _____ [d-e-c-e-v-] your

child, she will _____ [d-e-v-l-p-] a distrust that

will _____ [d-a-m-g-] her little psyche.

page 122

compare
deceive

develop
disagree

criticize
condemn
compare

benefited
attacked
damage

compare

■ A poet would _____ [c-o-m-p-r-] you to a

lovely flower, Alice. But don't let him _____

[d-e-c-e-v-] you.

■ Strong love cannot _____ [d-e-v-l-p-] between

two people who constantly _____ [d-i-s-g-r-e-].

■ Before we _____ [c-r-i-t-z-] or _____

[c-n-d-e-m-] these drifters, we should _____

[c-o-m-p-r-] our own early advantages with theirs.

■ Al's mood was not _____ [b-e-n-f-t-d] when he

was _____ [a-t-a-k-d] by a Doberman which

inflicted _____ [d-a-m-g-] to his rented tuxedo.

■ *"To what, my love, shall I* _____ *[c-o-m-p-r-]*
thine eyes?"   (*Midsummer Night's Dream, III, ii, 138*)

DIRECTIONS: Continue as before. Study the spelling carefully. Write each word three times.

21. disappear _____ _____ _____

22. disappoint _____ _____ _____

23. disguise _____ _____ _____

24. distinguish _____ _____ _____

25. educate _____ _____ _____

26. embarrass _____ _____ _____

27. equipped _____ _____ _____

28. exaggerate _____ _____ _____

29. examine _____ _____ _____

30. fascinate _____ _____ _____

Review words 21-30. Then take the quiz.

COVER
THIS STRIP

FILL THE BLANKS

disguise
educate

■ You can _____ [d-s-g-i-s-] a donkey to look

like a philosopher, but you can't _____

[e-u-c-a-t-] him.

examine
fascinate
disappoint

■ Let's _____ [e-x-m-n-] the sources of our

ideas. What we discover will _____ [f-a-c-n-a-t-]

and possibly _____ [d-s-p-o-n-t-] us.

educate
equipped
distinguish

■ If you _____ [e-u-c-a-t-] your mind, you will

be well _____ [e-q-i-p-d] to _____

[d-s-t-n-g-s-h] yourself.

embarrass

■ Igor's loose suspenders often _____

[e-m-b-r-a-s] him in a fast-rising elevator.

examine
exaggerate

■ When you _____ [e-x-m-n-] a dental cavity,

it feels a mile deep. That's because your tongue has a

tendency to _____ [e-a-g-r-a-t-e].

equipped
educate
embarrass
disappear

■ A man who is not _____ [e-q-i-p-d] to use good

grammar should _____ [e-u-c-a-t-] himself or he

will _____ [e-m-b-r-a-s] his wife in company and

make her want to _____ [d-s-a-p-e-r] in shame.

distinguish
fascinate

■ At the zoo I can hardly _____ [d-s-t-n-g-s-h]

a moose from a mouse, but the chimps are comedians and they

_____ [f-a-c-n-a-t-] me.

disappear
disappoint

■ If you want food to _____ [d-s-a-p-e-r], just

invite "Tiny" Tony. He won't _____ [d-s-p-o-n-t] you.

disguise
exaggerate
disappoint

■ Put on the Charlie Chaplin _____ [d-s-g-i-s-],

but don't _____ [e-a-g-r-a-t-e] his walk or you

will _____ [d-s-p-o-n-t] me.

examine

embarrass
distinguish

equipped
disguise
fascinate

disappear
disappoint
exaggerate

disguise

- Don't _____ [e-x-m-n-] a gift horse in the teeth.

- Do nothing that will _____ [e-m-b-r-a-s] your parents. That alone will _____ [d-s-t-n-g-s-h] you in this generation.

- Detective Shomes is _____ [e-q-i-p-d] with a potato-nose _____ [d-s-g-i-s-] that would fool his mother. It will _____ [f-a-c-n-a-t-] you.

- Our money will _____ [d-s-a-p-e-r] and our friends will _____ [d-s-p-o-n-t] us, but let us not _____ [e-a-g-r-a-t-e]--things may get much worse.

- *"We must _____ [d-s-g-i-s-] ourselves."*
  (Winter's Tale, IV, ii, 61)

16

BI: TWO

31. bicameral   (bi kam'ər əl)   *adj.* having two legislative chambers

      Congress is *bicameral*; it consists of a House and a Senate.
      Most states operate under a *bicameral* system of lawmaking.

<u>bicameral legislature</u>   _____   _____
     (copy twice)

32. biceps   (bī'seps)   *n.* a muscle having two points of origin

      The bulging muscle in your upper arm is your *biceps.*
      A *biceps* is also located at the back of the thigh.

<u>strong biceps</u>   _____   _____

33. bifocals   (bī'fō kəlz)   *n.* a pair of glasses with lenses ground for
close focus and for distant focus

      Grandma squinted and adjusted her *bifocals.*
      Use the lower part of your *bifocals* for reading.

<u>pair of bifocals</u>   _____   _____

34. **bigamy** (big'ə mē) *n.* being married to two people at the same time

A cynic has said that *bigamy* is its own punishment.
Two wives? Then he's a *bigamist*.

guilty of bigamy   _____   _____

35. **bilingual** (bī ling'gwəl) *adj.* able to speak two languages; spoken or written in two languages

Bilingual sales clerks are in demand.
Many Swiss are *bilingual*.

bilingual education   _____   _____

36. **bipartisan** (bī pär'ti zən) *adj.* representing two parties

Appoint a *bipartisan* committee.
The proposed law has *bipartisan* support.

bipartisan policy   _____   _____

37. **bisect** (bī'sekt) *v.* to cut in two

We will now *bisect* the line AB.
The log was *bisected* by a circular saw.

bisect angles   _____   _____

38. **biracial** (bī rā'shəl) *adj.* involving two races, such as black and white

Job competition often causes *biracial* friction.
Let's work for *biracial* harmony.

biracial society   _____   _____

Review words 31-38. Then go on.

QUIZ

DIRECTIONS: Fill the blanks with words we studied that are derived from the Latin prefix BI (two). Be sure you spell the words correctly.

COVER
THIS STRIP

| biracial | ■ Many schools are _____ [b-r-a-c-l] but few |
| bilingual | are _____ [b-l-n-g-l]. |

bifocals
biceps

bisect

■ The hoodlum found out that the old man may be wearing

_____ [b-f-c-s] but that he has very powerful

_____ [b-c-p-].

■ The new freeway will _____ [b-s-c-] our city.

■ The _____ [b-c-m-r-] legislature is part of our

bicameral

system of checks and balances.

■ Republicans and Democrats got together to pass a

_____ [b-p-t-s-n] bill that will promote

bipartisan
bilingual
biracial

_____ [b-1-n-g-1] education and _____

[b-r-a-c-1] harmony.

■ A preacher wearing _____ [b-f-c-s] told me that

the Bible forbids _____ [b-g-m-y]: "No man can

bifocals
bigamy

serve two masters."

■ You don't need big _____ [b-c-p-] to

biceps
bisect

_____ [b-s-c-] the base of a triangle.

■ Unless my _____ [b-f-c-s] deceive me, our

_____ [b-c-m-r-] legislature has just passed a

bifocals
bicameral
bipartisan
bigamy

_____ [b-p-t-s-n] bill that will increase the

prison sentence for _____ [b-g-m-y].

■ Sailor Sam, who is _____ [b-1-n-g-1], is wanted

bilingual
bigamy

in London and Naples on a charge of _____ [b-g-m-y].

■ Parliament, with its House of Commons and House of Lords,

bicameral
biracial

is _____ [b-c-m-r-] but not _____[b-r-a-c-1].

■ I knew Blinky when he had skinny _____ [b-c-p-]

and didn't know how to _____ [b-s-c-] an angle,

biceps
bisect
bipartisan

yet now he's chairman of a powerful _____

[b-p-t-s-n] committee in Washington.

■ *"Seduced the pitch and height of all his thoughts*
To base declension and loathed _____ *[b-g-m-y]."*
(Richard III, III, vii, 189)

bigamy

page 128

OTHER DERIVATIVES OF BI (TWO):

biangular (bī ang'gyə lər) *adj.* having two angles or corners

biannual (bī an'yoo əl) *adj.* coming twice a year

bicentennial (bī'sen ten'ē əl) *adj.* happening every 200 years [*a bicentennial exposition*] *n.* a 200th anniversary

bichloride (bī klōr'īd) *n.* a compound having two atoms of chlorine [*bichloride of mercury*]

bicultural (bī kul'chər əl) *adj.* combining two cultures in one area [*a bicultural neighborhood*]

bicuspid (bī kus'pid) *n.* a tooth having a two-pointed crown; a premolar, located between the cuspids and the molar teeth

biennial (bī en'ē əl) *adj.* happening every two years *n.* a two-year plant [*a biennial session of Congress*]

bifocals (bī fō'kəlz) *n.pl.* a pair of glass with the lens ground for close vision and for distant vision

bilateral (bī lat'ər əl) *adj.* involving two sides; reciprocal [*a bilateral agreement*]

billion (bil'yən) *adj.*, *n.* a thousand million

bimetallism (bī met'ə liz əm) *n.* the use of two metals, such as gold and silver, as a monetary standard, at a fixed relative value

bimonthly (bī munth'lē) *adj.* once every two months [*a bimonthly magazine*]

binary (bī'nər ē) *adj.* two-fold; double [*binary star*]; pertaining to a number system to the base two

binaural (bī nôr'əl) *adj.* involving both ears

binoculars (bī nok'yə lərz) *n.* an optical device, such as field glasses, for both eyes

binomial (bī nō'mē əl) *n.* a two-term mathematical expression such as 3X − 7

biplane (bi'plān') *n.* an airplane having two sets of wings, one above the other

bipolar (bī pō'lər) *adj.* having two poles, as the earth

biquarterly (bī kwôr'tər lē) *adj.* happening twice in each three-month period

bisexual (bī sek'shoo wəl) *adj.* sexually attracted to both sexes *n.* a person sexually responsive to both sexes

39. **intercede** (in'tər sed') *v.* to mediate; plead in behalf of others

    Our nation *interceded* in the Near East dispute.
    The strikers welcomed the *intercession* by the governor.

    intercede for me _____ _____
    (copy twice)

40. **intercept** (in'tər sept') *v.* to stop on the way; cut off

    The coast guard must *intercept* the smuggled cargo.
    The teacher *intercepted* my note to Dolly.

    intercept the pass _____ _____

41. **interfaith** (in'tər fāth') *adj.* between different religious groups

    Interfaith meetings promote understanding.
    A fight broke out at the *interfaith* conference.

    interfaith alliance _____ _____

42. **interim** (in'tər im) *adj.* temporary [*an interim committee*] *n.* the period of time in between; meantime

    Her concert was delayed, and in the *interim* she composed music.
    Linda served on the *interim* council.

43. **intermittent** (in'tər mit'ənt) *adj.* stopping and starting at intervals; periodic

    We heard the *intermittent* roar of cannon.
    An *intermittent* rain dampened the garden wedding.

    intermittent pains _____ _____

44. **interpret** (in tûr'prit) *v.* to bring out the meaning of; explain; translate

    The minister *interpreted* the Scriptural passage.
    We applauded her *interpretation* of Cleopatra.

    interpret the poem _____ _____

45. **interrogate** (in ter'ə gāt') *v.* to ask questions

> The officer *interrogated* a bystander.
> The attorney continued his *interrogation.*

interrogate the witness _____ _____

46. **interurban** (in'tər ur'bən) *adj.* between cities *n.* a train operating between cities

> Cindy caught the six o'clock *interurban.*
> The *interurban* train connects Washington and New York.

interurban passengers _____ _____

Review words 39–46. Then go on.

QUIZ

DIRECTIONS: Fill the blanks with words we studied that are derived from the Latin prefix INTER (between). Be sure you spell the words correctly.

COVER
THIS STRIP
_____

intercept	■ For a billion dollars we'll build a rocket that might _____ [i-n-c-p-t] one of the enemy rockets.
interurban interpret	■ Next to me on the _____ [i-n-r-b-n] train sat a student trying to _____ [i-n-p-r-t] a poem.
interrogate intercede	■ The mayor began to _____ [i-n-g-a-t-] the farm woman who had asked him to _____ [i-n-t-c-e-d-] for her son who had stolen a pig.
intermittent interpret	■ Homer heard _____ [i-n-t-m-t-t] dots and dashes from the *Titanic* but didn't bother to _____ [i-n-t-p-r-t] it because the message was probably boring.
intercept interrogate interpret	■ If enemy forces _____ [i-n-c-p-t] the coded note on Rover's leg, they will _____ [i-n-g-a-t-] our dog in an effort to _____ [i-n-t-p-r-t] the message--so bowwow for them!

■ The _____ [i-n-r-b-n] railway workers are on

strike, so please ride bicycles to meetings of the

_____ [i-n-f-t-h] congress in the _____

[i-n-t-m-].

interurban
interfaith
interim

■ The doctor told me to watch my food, and in the

interim

_____ [i-n-t-m] somebody stole my coat.

■ My sleep was enriched by the _____

[i-n-t-m-t-t] visit of _____ [i-n-r-b-n] trains

intermittent
interurban

which roared past my bedroom.

■ Catholics, Protestants, and Jews at the _____

[i-n-f-t-h] congress decided to _____ [i-n-t-c-e-d-]

interfaith
intercede

for the blacks of South Africa.

■ Mr. Peepers now made _____ [i-n-t-m-t-t]

efforts to _____ [i-n-g-a-t-] his daughter about

her secret lover; and, in the _____ [i-n-t-m] he

intermittent
interrogate
interim
intercept

tried to _____ [i-n-c-p-t] the mash notes

addressed to her.

■ At the _____ [i-n-f-t-h] meeting, a widow was

interfaith
intercede

praying that St. Jude _____ [i-n-t-c-e-d-] for her.

■ *"I will in the _____ [i-n-t-m] undertake one
of Hercules' labors"*

interim

(Much Ado About Nothing, II, i, 380)

Non-test examples

OTHER DERIVATIVES OF INTER (BETWEEN):

interact (in tər akt') *v.* to act on one another

intercom (in'tər kom') *n.* a system of communication between rooms,
planes, police cars, etc.

intercourse (in'tər kōrs') *n.* dealings between people or nations;
communication; sexual joining of two individuals

intercrop (in'tər krop') *v.* to grow one crop between the rows of
another, for example, carrots between rows of corn

intercut (in′tər kut′) *v.* to cut from one type of film shot to another, as from a close-up to a long shot

interdental (in′tər den′təl) *adj.* between the teeth [*interdental plaque*]

interdependent (in′tər di pen′dənt) *adj.* dependent on each other

interdict (in′tər dikt′) *v.* to forbid with authority; prohibit

interferon (in′tər fēr′on) *n.* a cellular protein that fights virus infection

intergalactic (in′tər gə lak′tik) *adj.* between galaxies [*intergalactic rockets*]

interject (in′tər jekt′) *v.* to throw in between; insert; interrupt with [*Listeners interjected an occasional "By golly" or a "Judas Priest!"*]

interlace (in′tər lās′) *v.* to weave together; blend [*the interlaced branches*]

interlard (in′tər lärd′) *v.* to mix together; diversify [*a sermon interlarded with Bartlett's quotations*]

interlinear (in′tər lin′ē ər) *adj.* inserted between lines [*an interlinear translation*]

interlocutory (in′tər lok′yə tōr′ē) *adj. Law.* of a court decision that is not yet final [*an interlocutory divorce*]

interlude (in′tər lōōd′) *n.* anything such as music that fills time between two events; time between events

interlunar (in′tər lōō′nər) *adj.* of the four-day period each month between old and new moon when the moon is invisible

intermezzo (in′tər met′sō) *n.* a short musical or other entertainment between the main divisions of an opera or other program

intermural (in′tər myōōr′əl) *adj.* taking place between two institutions [*an intermural football game*]

internecine (in′tər nē′sin) *adj.* of a deadly conflict within a group, as in a civil war; mutually destructive [*internecine slaughter*]

interpolate (in′tûr′pə lāt′) *v.* to insert between other things [*Words were interpolated into the original text.*]

interpose (in′tər pōz′) *v.* to put between; interrupt with a remark [*May I interpose a comment?*]

interregnum (in′tər reg′nəm) *n.* a period during which a country has no ruler; a period between kings; a break in continuity [*Assassination of the dictator was followed by a brief interregnum.*]

intersect (in'tər sekt') *v.* to cross each other; cut by passing across [*The two main streets intersect at the lard factory.*]

intersperse (in'tər spûrs') *v.* to scatter here and there [*Picket signs were interspersed among the crowd.*]

interstellar (in'tər stel'ər) *adj.* between the stars [*interstellar space*]

intervene (in'tər vēn') *v.* to come between things; interfere with a threat of force [*Teddy Roosevelt intervened in Cuba.*]

The meanings of the following words, derived from INTER (between), are quite obvious:

interacademic	intergovernmental	interracial
inter-American	intergroup	interrelated
interatomic	interlibrary	interreligious
interchangeable	interlock	interruption
intercity	intermarriage	interscholastic
intercollegiate	intermediate	intersection
intercontinental	intermingle	interstate
intercounty	intermission	intertribal
interdenominational	international	intertwine
interdistrict	interpersonal	interval
interfere	interplanetary	interview

MULTI: MANY

47. **multicolored** (mul'ti kul'ərd) *adj.* of many colors

> *Multicolored* flags fluttered in the breeze.
> The native wore *multicolored* robes.

multicolored flowers _____ _____
    (copy twice)

48. **multilingual** (mul'ti ling'gwəl) *adj.* able to speak more than two languages; spoken or written in more than two languages

> This movie is produced in *multilingual* versions.
> Our tourist guide is *multilingual*.

multilingual crowds _____ _____

49. multiple (mul'tə pəl) *adj.* involving many parts; manifold

> Milton suffered *multiple* injuries.
> Bugsy was convicted on *multiple* counts of burglary.

multiple sclerosis _____ _____

50. multitude (mul'ti tood') *n.* a throng; a great number of persons or things

> In Arlington Cemetery lie a *multitude* of heroes.
> The old man fed a *multitude* of pigeons.

huge multitude _____ _____

Review words 47–50. Then go on.

QUIZ

DIRECTIONS: Fill the blanks with words we studied that are derived from the Latin prefix MULTI (many). Be sure you spell the words correctly.

COVER
THIS STRIP

multitude multiple	■ We must help the _____ [m-1-t-d-] of victims of _____ [m-p-1-] sclerosis.
	■ In a battle with the cat, our mynah bird suffered _____ [m-p-1-] bites and scratches; and, being
multiple multilingual	_____ [m-1-g-1], the mynah swore at the cat in three languages.
	■ I handed the gas-filled, _____ [m-c-1-r-d]
multicolored	balloons to the tiny girl, and she floated away.
	■ At the county fair we met a _____ [m-1-t-d-]
multitude multicolored	of children licking _____ [m-c-1-r-d] popsicles.
	■ The _____ [m-1-t-d-] of Olympic spectators
	were waving _____ [m-c-1-r-d] pennants and
multitude multicolored multilingual	shouting _____ [m-1-g-1] phrases of encouragement.

page 135

multiple multilingual *multitude*	■ Monica took a _____ [m-p-l-] choice test in German and French and proved that she is truly _____ [m-l-g-l]. ■ *"He's loved of the distracted _____ [m-l-t-d-], Who like not in their judgment, but their eyes."* *(Hamlet, IV, iii, 4)*

Non-test examples

OTHER DERIVATIVES OF MULTI (MANY):

multifaceted (mul′tē fas′i tid) *adj.* having many facets or aspects [*a multifaceted personality*]

multiflora (mul′ti flōr′ə) *adj.* having clusters of small flowers [*a multiflora rose*]

multimillionaire (mul′tē mil′yə när′) *n.* a person who has several million dollars, pounds, or francs

multiplex (mul′tə pleks′) *adj.* a system whereby several signals or messages can be carried on the same circuit at the same time

multiplicand (mul′tə pli kand′) *n.* a number which is to be multiplied by another number

multistage (mul′ti stāj′) *adj.* of a rocket that has more than one stage [*a successful multistage launching*]

The meanings of the following words, derived from MULTI (many), are quite obvious:

multiangular	multifocal	multiphase
multibirth	multiform	multipropellant
multibladed	multihued	multipurpose
multibranched	multi-infection	multiracial
multicellular	multijet	multirooted
multichanneled	multimedia	multitoed
multicircuit	multimegaton	multitoned
multicoil	multimolecular	multisegmented
multidirectional	multimotor	multivitamin
multiengined	multinational	multivoiced

Review words 1-50, spelling and vocabulary. Then take the Chapters 15-16 Self-Test.

CHAPTERS 15-16: SELF-TEST

DIRECTION: Write the words in full. Complete this entire test before you check and grade your answers.

_____ 1. My suit is [e-q-i-p-d] with moth holes for ventilation.
_____ 2. Reporters have been known to [e-a-g-e-r-a-t-] the facts.
_____ 3. My parents got [a-q-a-n-t-d] in a bomb shelter.
_____ 4. David was [a-t-a-k-d] by an anti-Semitic bumblebee.
_____ 5. The optometrist began to [e-x-m-n-] my retinas.
_____ 6. A bomb hit our farmhouse and did six dollars [d-a-m-g-].
_____ 7. Hiram vowed to [a-c-h-e-v-] health if it killed him.
_____ 8. Fish didn't bite but I [a-s-u-r-] you the mosquitoes did.
_____ 9. The carnival sideshows will [f-a-c-n-a-t-] you.
_____ 10. A bride should [a-k-n-o-l-g-] gifts, even lousy ones.
_____ 11. My cold began to [d-s-p-e-r-]; it turned into pneumonia.
_____ 12. Schools can [e-u-c-a-t-e] you only if you cooperate.
_____ 13. The fog began to [a-p-r-o-c-h-] on little cat feet.
_____ 14. This judge will [c-n-d-e-m-] Tex to a shocking fate.
_____ 15. The prolonged strikes [b-e-n-f-t-d] no one.
_____ 16. Howling babies can [e-m-b-r-a-s] their mothers.
_____ 17. The beggar said he'd [a-p-r-e-c-a-t-] ten dollars for coffee.
_____ 18. Swindlers love to [d-e-c-e-v-] a country bumpkin.
_____ 19. Roosters believe that it pays to [a-d-v-r-t-i-].
_____ 20. Never [c-m-p-r-] your wife's cooking with your mother's.
_____ 21. Identical twins aren't easy to [d-s-t-n-g-s-h].
_____ 22. He ran over my dog and came to [a-p-o-l-g-z-].
_____ 23. Short talks rarely [d-i-s-a-p-o-n-t-] an audience.
_____ 24. Babies cry when they [a-q-i-r-] a new tooth.
_____ 25. Even Hercules once had to [d-e-v-l-p-] his muscles.
_____ 26. Don't [c-r-i-t-z-e] this dull, witless, badly acted movie.
_____ 27. At Halloween I didn't have to wear a [d-i-s-g-i-].
_____ 28. Your nineteenth birthday? Let's [-e-l-e-b-r-t-]!
_____ 29. The doctor wants to [a-n-l-z-] your blood, if you have any.
_____ 30. Dictators rub out those who [d-i-s-g-r-e-] with them.

Write correctly the words we studied that are derived from the Latin prefixes BI, INTER, and MULTI:

_____ 31. Grandma peered at me over her [b-i-f-c-l-].
_____ 32. The next town? Take the [i-t-r-u-b-n-] train.
_____ 33. When the president speaks, a [m-l-t-d-] listen.
_____ 34. The sheriff began to [i-n-t-r-g-a-t-] the hobo in the Rolls.
_____ 35. Corruption was sniffed out by the [b-i-p-r-t-s-n] committee.
_____ 36. A personal computer has [m-l-t-p-l-] uses.
_____ 37. Sandy leapt to [i-t-r-e-p-t-] the basketball.
_____ 38. Learn French, and you'll be [b-1-n-g-l-].
_____ 39. She's married to two military draftees? That's [b-g-m-]!
_____ 40. The lifeguard sat around, displaying his [b-i-e-p-s-].

Write the letter that indicates the best definition.

( ) 41. bicameral   a. speaking many languages
( ) 42. bisect   b. to plead for others
( ) 43. biracial   c. the time in between
( ) 44. intercede   d. having many colors
( ) 45. interfaith   e. cut in half
( ) 46. interim   f. periodic; off and on
( ) 47. intermittent   g. having two lawmaking bodies
( ) 48. interpret   h. between religious groups
( ) 49. multicolored   i. having two racial groups
( ) 50. multilingual   j. to explain or translate

ANSWER KEY

Check your test answers by the following key. Deduct 2% per error from 100%.

1. equipped	11. disappear	21. distinguish	31. bifocals	41. g
2. exaggerate	12. educate	22. apologize	32. interurban	42. e
3. acquainted	13. approach	23. disappoint	33. multitude	43. i
4. attacked	14. condemn	24. acquire	34. interrogate	44. b
5. examine	15. benefited	25. develop	35. bipartisan	45. h
6. damage	16. embarrass	26. criticize	36. multiple	46. c
7. achieve	17. appreciate	27. disguise	37. intercept	47. f
8. assure	18. deceive	28. celebrate	38. bilingual	48. j
9. fascinate	19. advertise	29. analyze	39. bigamy	49. d
10. acknowledge	20. compare	30. disagree	40. biceps	50. a

Score: _____%

Review carefully any words which you have missed in the foregoing Self-Test.

Your instructor will give you a final test on words 1-50 in Chapters 15 and 16.

ACTION WORDS: "GUARANTEE" TO "WHISPER"

17

DIRECTIONS: Study the spelling of each word carefully, giving special attention to the trouble spots (underlined letters). Then write each word neatly three times.

1. g<u>ua</u>rantee _____ _____ _____

2. imag<u>i</u>ne _____ _____ _____

3. in<u>tr</u>oduce _____ _____ _____

4. man<u>a</u>ge _____ _____ _____

5. me<u>a</u>sure _____ _____ _____

6. mi<u>ss</u>pell _____ _____ _____

7. m<u>u</u>rder _____ _____ _____

8. ob<u>ey</u> _____ _____ _____

9. obl<u>ig</u>ed _____ _____ _____

10. occur<u>r</u>ed _____ _____ _____

Review words 1-10 until you are sure you can spell them. Then go on and take the quiz.

QUIZ

COVER THIS STRIP	FILL THE BLANKS

COVER THIS STRIP | FILL THE BLANKS

measure
manage

■ A waltz has three beats to the _____ [m-e-s-r-], but sometimes I _____ [m-a-n-g-] to put in four.

imagine

■ The florist is ill, and I can't _____ [i-m-a-g-n-] what gift to send a florist.

obliged
introduce

■ We are _____ [o-b-l-g-] to interrupt this TV drama to _____ [i-n-t-r-d-c-] you to a new coffee.

guarantee
manage
murder
occurred

■ I _____ [g-a-r-n-t-e-] that Hercule Poirot will _____ [m-a-n-g-] to solve the mystery of the _____ [m-r-d-r] that has _____ [o-c-u-r-d].

introduce
imagine
obey
misspell

■ Let me _____ [i-n-t-r-d-c-] you to a rule that I _____ [i-m-a-g-n-] you will _____ [o-b-y]: Please _____ [m-i-s-p-l-] as few words as possible.

obliged
manage

■ The judge said he'd feel _____[o-b-l-g-] to me if I'd _____ [m-a-n-g-] to keep my mouth shut.

misspell
murder

■ Any time we _____ [m-i-s-p-l-] a word, we _____ [m-r-d-r] a bit of our beautiful language.

obliged
murder
occurred

■ Pardon me, sir, but I feel _____ [o-b-l-g-] to report that a _____ [m-r-d-r] seems to have _____ [o-c-u-r-d] in the kitchen.

measure
introduce

■ The pianist played a _____ [m-e-s-r-] or two to _____ [i-n-t-r-d-c-] Buster's bass drum solo.

obliged
obey
imagine

■ I feel _____ [o-b-l-g-] to _____ [o-b-y] my doctor, and eating these two pizzas will, I _____, [i-m-a-g n-], interfere with my diet.

measure

■ The shoe clerk began looking for a yardstick so he could _____ [m-e-s-r-] my feet.

page 140

occurred guarantee	■ Our policies paid promptly when accidents _____ [o-c-u-r-d]. Bump your head and you'll get a lump sum; we _____ [g-a-r-n-t-e-] that.
	■ "Consult my book and I _____ [g-a-r-n-t-e-] that you'll never _____ [m-i-s-p-1-] another word," said Mr. Webster.
guarantee misspell	
obey	■ The bride promised to love and honor, but not to _____ [o-b-y].
murder	■ *"O wondrous thing! How easily* _____ *[m-r-d-r] is discovered!"* (Titus Andronicus, II, iii, 287)

DIRECTIONS: Continue as before. Study the spelling carefully. Write each word three times.

11. omi<u>tt</u>ed _____ _____ _____

12. op<u>e</u>rate _____ _____ _____

13. par<u>a</u>lyze _____ _____ _____

14. p<u>e</u>rspire _____ _____ _____

15. practi<u>c</u>e _____ _____ _____

16. prefer<u>r</u>ed _____ _____ _____

17. pr<u>o</u>ve _____ _____ _____

18. p<u>u</u>rsue _____ _____ _____

19. reco<u>g</u>nize _____ _____ _____

20. reco<u>m</u>mend _____ _____ _____

Review words 11-20. Then take the quiz.

QUIZ

COVER THIS STRIP	FILL THE BLANKS
omitted perspire	■ When Gus saw his name was _____ [o-m-i-t-d] from the graduation list, he began to _____ [p-s-p-i-r-].

■ The young surgeon offered to _____ [o-p-r-a-t-]

operate
practice

on my heart or brain for nothing, just for _____ [p-r-a-t-i-c-].

■ Uncle Joe _____ [p-r-f-r-d] to _____

preferred
pursue

[p-r-s-u-] his favorite hobby: girl watching.

■ The football star said that for cash he'll say that he

preferred
recommend

_____ [p-r-f-r-d] Honey Cruddies for breakfast,

and he will _____ [r-e-c-m-n-d] them highly.

■ We _____ [r-e-c-m-n-d] the gold-inlay job but

recommend
recognize
paralyze

_____ [r-e-g-n-i-z-] that the dental costs may

_____ [p-r-l-z-e] you.

■ The coach said, "I want you to _____ [p-r-s-u-]

pursue
prove
perspire

that basketball until you _____ [p-r-o-v-] you can

really _____ [p-s-p-i-r-]"; and I said, "No sweat."

■ We hope you _____ [r-e-g-n-z-] these bracketed

recognize
omitted

words, even though a few letters are _____ [o-m-i-t-d].

■ The karate expert wanted to _____ [p-r-o-v-]

that he could _____ [p-r-l-z-e] me with one blow;

prove
paralyze
pursue
omitted

but I didn't wish to _____ [p-r-s-u-] the matter

further, so we _____ [o-m-i-t-d] that experiment.

■ Cotton athletic suits are _____ [p-r-f-r-d],

preferred
recommend
perspire

and we _____ [r-e-c-m-n-d] them to joggers who

intend to _____ [p-s-p-i-r-].

■ The doctors _____ [r-e-g-n-z-] that, without

insurance, their medical _____ [p-r-a-t-i-c-] may

practice
operate
paralyze

suffer if they _____ [o-p-r-a-t-] on a boil and

_____ [p-r-l-z-e] a patient.

prove

■ To love is to _____ [p-r-o-v-] that life is good.

operate
practice

■ The late Mr. Jiggs was hoping to _____ [o-p-r-a-t-]

an airplane without any flying _____ [p-r-a-t-i-c-].

■ *"O, swear not by the moon, th' inconstant moon,...*
Lest that thy love _____ [p-r-o-v-] *likewise*
variable." (Romeo and Juliet, II, ii, 111)

prove

DIRECTIONS: Continue as before. Study the spelling carefully. Write each word three times.

21. sacrifice   _____   _____   _____

22. seize   _____   _____   _____

23. shining   _____   _____   _____

24. speak   _____   _____   _____

25. stopped   _____   _____   _____

26. succeed   _____   _____   _____

27. transferred   _____   _____   _____

28. translate   _____   _____   _____

29. using   _____   _____   _____

30. whisper   _____   _____   _____

Review words 21-30. Then take the quiz.

QUIZ

COVER
THIS STRIP   FILL THE BLANKS

transferred

■ The deaf clerk has been _____ [t-r-a-s-f-r-d]

to the complaints department.

■ The librarian used to _____ [s-e-z-e] me by the

seize
speak
whisper

ear when I'd _____ [s-p-e-k-] above a

_____ [w-s-p-r-].

■ Orville lost the _____ [s-a-c-r-f-i-] fly in

sacrifice
shining
stopped

the _____ [s-h-i-n-i-g] sun, so he _____

[s-t-o-p-d] the baseball with his nose.

translate

■ The watchdog says "Woof," which I _____ [t-r-n-l-a-t-] to mean "scram!"

transferred
seize
sacrifice

■ Since we're being _____ [t-r-a-s-f-r-d] to the Alaska office, we _____ [s-e-z-e] this opportunity to sell you this freezer at a _____ [s-a-c-r-f-i-].

sacrifice
shining
whisper

■ Her eyes were _____ [s-h-i-n-i-g] as she began to _____ [w-s-p-r] three little words: "The cat died."

■ Men who _____ [s-p-e-k-] loudly when they

speak
succeed
whisper

_____ [s-u-c-e-d-] usually _____ [w-s-p-r] when they fail.

■ If you can _____ [t-r-n-l-a-t-] a few languages,

translate
succeed
transferred

you will _____ [s-u-c-e-d-] abroad wherever you are _____ [t-r-a-s-f-r-d].

■ Junior is making his _____ [s-a-c-r-f-i-] for our country: he's _____ [u-s-n-g] no unnecessary

sacrifice
using

energy.

■ Some students _____ [s-u-c-e-d-] in Latin class

succeed
using
translate

without _____ [u-s-n-g] a "pony" to help them _____ [t-r-n-l-a-t-].

■ I'd like to _____ [s-e-z-e] the carnival hawker

seize
stopped
speak

who sold me this watch which has _____ [s-t-o-p-d] and this radio which will not _____ [s-p-e-k-].

■ Now that we're _____ [u-s-n-g] a solar heater,

using
stopped
shining

the sun has _____ [s-t-o-p-d] _____ [s-h-i-n-i-g].

■ *"Then the whining schoolboy, with his satchel*
  And _____ [s-h-i-n-i-g] morning face, creeping like snail
    Unwillingly to school."
                              (As You Like It, II, vii, 146)

shining

page 144

LATIN PREFIXES: "POST" TO "TRANS"

18

POST: AFTER

31. posterior (po stēr'ē ər) *adj*. toward the rear; behind *n*. the buttocks

    The castle has anterior and *posterior* gardens.
    Pete was badly sunburned on his legs and *posterior*.

    posterior side _____ _____
    (copy twice)

32. posterity (po ster'i tē) *n*. all our descendants; future generations

    Our national debt is a threat to *posterity*.
    Will *posterity* know blue skies and clear water?

    our posterity _____ _____

33. postgraduate (pōst graj'oo it) *adj*. pertaining to courses taken after graduation *n*. a student taking advanced work after graduation

    Many alumni return to take *postgraduate* courses.
    Harvard offers many *postgraduate* programs.

    postgraduate work _____ _____

34. posthumous (pos'chə məs) *adj*. published after the death of an author; born after the father's death; occurring after one's death

    Mark Twain's *The Mysterious Stranger* was published *posthumously*.
    Emily Dickinson has won *posthumous* praise.

    posthumous child _____ _____

page 145

35. postpone (pōst pōn') *v.* to put off to a later time; defer; delay

>We're *postponing* the game because of smog.
>The salesman disappeared, so the wedding was *postponed*.

postpone meetings _____ _____

Review words 31-35. Then go on.

QUIZ

DIRECTIONS: Fill the blanks with words we studied that are derived from the Latin prefix POST (after). Be sure you spell the words correctly.

COVER
THIS STRIP

posterior	■ The front of the tenement has been painted, but the _____ [p-s-t-e-r-] is a shambles.
posthumous	■ Private Diamond died three months before the birth of his _____ [p-s-t-h-m-s] child.
posterior postpone postgraduate	■ My mountain-climbing friend fell on his _____ [p-s-t-e-r-] and will have to _____ [p-t-p-o-n-] taking his _____ [p-t-g-r-a-d-] courses.
postpone posterity	■ If we _____ [p-t-p-o-n-] payment of our debts, _____ [p-t-r-y] will have to pay the bill.
postgraduate posterity	■ Our _____ [p-t-g-r-a-d-] seminar noted that the American colonists fought for "ourselves and our _____ [p-t-r-y]."
postpone posterior	■ I'll brush our horse's mane now and will _____ [p-t-p-o-n-] brushing his _____ [p-s-t-e-r-] until later.
posthumous posterity	■ Nathan Hale could not foresee what _____ [p-s-t-h-m-s] honor would be accorded him by _____ [p-t-r-y].

<table>
<tr><td>postgraduate
posthumous</td><td>■ As a _____ [p-t-g-r-a-d-], Laura was

fascinated by Thomas Wolfe's _____ [p-s-t-h-m-s]

novels.</td></tr>
<tr><td>posterior</td><td>■ "The _____ [p-s-t-e-r-] of the day, most
generous sir, is...the afternoon."
(Love's Labour's Lost, V, i, 96)</td></tr>
</table>

OTHER DERIVATIVES OF POST (AFTER):

Non-test examples

postbellum (pōst bel'əm) *adj.* occurring after the war; after the Civil War [*postbellum era*]

postdate (pōst dāt') *v.* to give a later date than the true date; follow in time

postdiluvian (pōst'də loo'vē ən) *adj.* after the flood *n.* a person who lived after the flood

postdoctoral (pōst dok'tər əl) *adj.* after the doctorate [*postdoctoral research*]

postern (pōs'tərn) *n.* a rear or side door [*the postern gate*]

posthypnotic (pōst'hip not'ik) *adj.* pertaining to the period after a hypnotic trance [*posthypnotic suggestion*]

postlude (pōst'lood') *n.* organ music played after a church service

postmeridian (pōst'mə rid'ē ən) *adj.* in the afternoon [*the postmeridian heat*]

postnatal (pōst nāt'əl) *adj.* after birth [*postnatal care*]

postnuptial (pōst nup'shəl) *adj.* after marriage [*postnuptial bliss*]

postoperative (pōst op'ər ə tiv) *adj.* after a surgical operation [*postoperative diet*]

postpartum (pōst par'təm) *adj.* after childbirth [*postpartum exhaustion*]

postprandial (pōst pran'dē əl) *adj.* after a meal [*postprandial conversation*]

Several hundred additional words are derived from POST (after). Many of the terms relate to medicine or to history. Examples are given:

postanesthetic	post-Caesarean	post-classical
postarmistice	post-Chaucerian	postconfinement
postbreakfast	post-Christmas	post-Darwinian

postdigestive	postinfluenzal	post-Newtonian
post-Easter	post-Kantian	postpuberty
postelection	post-Lent	post-Revolutionary
postelementary	postmalarial	postseason
post-Elizabethan	postmarital	post-Shakespearean
posteruptive	post-Marxian	post-Socratic
postglacial	postmedieval	postsyphilitic
post-Homeric	postmenopausal	posttraumatic
post-Ibsen	postmenstrual	posttubercular

SUB: UNDER

36. **subconscious** (sub kon′shəs) *adj.* existing in the mind beneath awareness

>   We are ruled by *subconscious* motivations.
>   She felt a *subconscious* distrust.

subconscious desire _____   _____
   (copy twice)

37. **subdue** (sub do͞o′) *v.* to conquer; overcome

>   Try to *subdue* your passion, Romeo.
>   You can't *subdue* a tiger with a slingshot.

subdued voices _____   _____

38. **subjective** (səb jek′tiv) *adj.* existing in the mind; personal; emphasizing one's opinions

>   *Subjective* evaluations of a movie vary widely.
>   Do you prefer an objective or a *subjective* test?

subjective judgments _____   _____

39. **submarginal** (sub mär′ji nəl) *adj.* below minimum standards

>   The housing area is decayed and *submarginal*.
>   The buses have a *submarginal* safety record.

submarginal land _____   _____

40. subpoena (sə pē'nə) *n.* a legal order to appear in court *v.* to order a person to appear in court, possibly with certain documents, etc.

> I was *subpoenaed* to appear as a witness.
> The messenger pushed the *subpoena* into Harold's hand.

serve a subpoena   _____ _____

41. subsequent (sub'sə kwent') *adj.* occurring later; following in time order

> The love affair gave them *subsequent* problems.
> Alexander Hamilton was *subsequently* killed in a duel.

subsequent events   _____ _____

42. subterfuge (sub'tər fyōōj') *n.* a plan or trick to hide one's real objective or to evade a bad situation; a stratagem to deceive others or to gain some end

> Ulysses resorted to *subterfuge* to escape the Cyclops.
> Who knows what *subterfuge* the smugglers will use next?

a clever subterfuge   _____ _____

43. subtle (sut'l) *adj.* delicate; able to make fine distinctions; delicately skillful; ingenious; sly; cunning

> Flo and Moe exchanged a *subtle* glance.
> The artist added a few final *subtleties* to the portrait.

subtle remarks   _____ _____

44. suburban (su bûr'bən) *adj.* pertaining to the residential community just outside the city

> Kate commutes to her *suburban* home.
> *Suburbia* is the happy land of lawn mowers and swimming pools.

suburban train   _____ _____

45. subversive (sub vûr'siv) *adj.* tendency to overthrow a government or institution *n.* a person who seeks to overthrow the establishment

> Criticism of the war was considered *subversive*.
> Joe McCarthy saw *subversives* behind every bush.

subversive activity   _____ _____

Review words 36-45. Then go on.

QUIZ

DIRECTIONS: Fill the blanks with words we studied that are derived from the Latin prefix SUB (under). Be sure you spell the words correctly.

COVER
THIS STRIP

subtle
subterfuge

subjective
subconscious
subversive

subdue
subpoena

submarginal
subjective
subsequent

subterfuge
subsequent
subtle

subconscious
subdue

suburban
subversive
subpoena

- Prisoner 24813 was as _____ [s-t-l-] as a fox and managed, by some _____ [s-t-f-u-g-], to escape in a laundry bag.

- The psychiatrist gave Bertha some _____ [s-j-c-t-v-] tests and decided that Bertha's _____ [s-c-o-n-u-s] mind was swarming with _____ [s-v-r-s-v-] elements.

- The process server had to _____ [s-d-u-] the seeing eye dog before he could _____ [s-p-e-n-a-] the blind man.

- The farmer's opinion that this is _____ [s-m-g-n-l-] land was purely _____ [s-j-c-t-v-], for in _____ [s-s-q-n-t] seasons it has produced quite edible turnips.

- Mark Antony's initial praise of Brutus is a _____ [s-t-f-u-g-]. His _____ [s-s-q-n-t] remarks, in _____ [s-t-l-] fashion, inflame the rabble against Brutus and his comrades.

- Freud believed that we all have naughty _____ [s-c-o-n-u-s] urges that we have been taught to _____ [s-d-u-].

- Convinced that one of our _____ [s-b-b-n] residents was a _____ [s-v-r-s-v-], we served her a gift-wrapped _____ [s-p-e-n-a-].

subjective submarginal	■ "Theme grades are somewhat _____ [s-j-c-t-v-]," said the English teacher, "but this theme is definitely _____ [s-m-g-n-1-]."
suburban subsequent subdue	■ Retired people buy a _____ [s-b-b-n] home and spend the _____ [s-s-q-n-t] years of their life trying to _____ [s-d-u-] the weeds on the lawn.
subpoena subtle	■ To serve a _____ [s-p-e-n-a-] to Bugsy required _____ [s-t-1-] tricks--and courage.
submarginal suburban	■ Ms. Sharp bought some _____ [s-m-g-n-1-] land for a song; then put up a _____ [s-b-b-n] tract that netted her a few barrels of cash.
subconscious	■ Our instinctive drives, we are told, are rooted in our _____ [s-c-o-n-u-s] mind.
subversive subterfuge	■ A genuine _____ [s-v-r-s-v-] will use any _____ [s-t-f-u-g-] to learn military secrets.
subtle	■ *"I feel this youth's perfections* *With an invisible and* _____ *[s-t-1-] stealth* *To creep in at my eyes."* *(Twelfth Night, I, v, 316)*

OTHER DERIVATIVES OF SUB (UNDER): *Non-test examples*

subclinical (sub klin'i kəl) *adj.* of disease symptoms too mild to be noticed in clinical tests [*the subclinical stage*]

subculture (sub'kul'chər) *n.* the behavioral patterns of a distinctive social group [*the hippie subculture*]

subcutaneous (sub kyoo tā'nē əs) *adj.* under the skin [*subcutaneous injections*]

subjectivism (səb jek'ti viz əm) *n.* the theory that knowledge is subjective and relative, not objective

subjugate (sub'jə gāt') *v.* to bring under control; conquer [*to subjugate the natives*]

subjunctive (səb junk'tiv) *adj.* of that mood of a verb used to express a condition contrary to fact, as in "If I were king."

subliminal (sub lim′ə nəl) *adj.* below the threshold of consciousness [*subliminal advertising*]

submerge (səb mûrj′) *v.* to sink under water or the like; cover over [*The whales emerge, then submerge.*]

submersible (səb mûr′sə bəl) *adj.* able to function under water
n. a submarine

submissive (səb mis′iv) *adj.* tame; unresisting; humbly obedient [*submissive children*]

submit (səb mit′) *v.* to yield to the control of others; give in; suggest; present for approval [*submit a plan*]

subordinate (sə bor′də nit) *adj.* below another in rank [*subordinate clause*]; (sə bôr′də nāt′) *v.* to treat as inferior; control; subdue

suborn (sə bôrn′) *v.* to induce someone to give false testimony or commit some other crime [*suborn a witness*]

subrogate (sub′rə gāt′) *v.* to substitute one person, such as a creditor, for another

sub rosa (sub rō′zə) secretly; confidentially [*The council met sub rosa.*]

subscribe (səb skrīb′) *v.* to pay a sum for issues of a periodical; agree to pay money for a special purpose; support [*subscribe to women's rights*]

subservient (səb sur′vē ənt) *adj.* helpful or of service in a subordinate capacity [*a subservient housekeeper*]

subside (səb sīd′) *v.* to sink to a lower level; abate; settle; become less active [*The waves subsided.*]

subsidy (sub′sə dē) *n.* a grant of money by the government to aid a private enterprise or a charitable organization [*a farm subsidy*]

subsistence (səb sis′təns) *n.* means of support sufficient to sustain life; existence [*a bare subsistence*]

subsonic (sub son′ik) *adj.* pertaining to speed that is less than that of sound [*The plane slowed to subsonic levels.*]

substantiate (səb stan′shē āt′) *v.* to confirm by giving evidence [*to substantiate Einstein's theory*]

subterranean (sub′tə rā′nē ən) *adj.* underground [*subterranean tunnels*]

subtrahend (sub′trə hend) *n.* Math. a number that is subtracted from another number

subversive (səb vûr′siv) *adj.* tending to cause the downfall or the ruin of; undermining the principles of [*subversive elements in our society*]

The prefix SUB is extremely common in our language. Its various shades of meaning include *under; below; lower in importance; slightly.* Examples:

subacid	subdivision	suboceanic
subacute	subeditor	subregion
subaffluent	subentry	subsample
subagent	subfamily	subsection
subaqueous	subfloor	subsoil
subarid	subfreezing	subsolar
subatomic	subgenus	subspecies
subbasement	subgroup	substandard
subbranch	subhead	substation
subcaliber	subhuman	substitute
subcaptain	subintention	substratum
subcashier	subkingdom	substructure
subcelestial	sublease	subsurface
subcommittee	sublet	subsystem
subcompact	sublethal	subtemperate
subcontinent	sublibrarian	subtenant
subcontractor	sublieutenant	subtopic
subcouncil	submarine	subtotal
subdeb	subminiature	subtract
subdialect	subnormal	subtropical
subdistrict	subnuclear	subway

TRANS: ACROSS

46. transact (tran sakt′) *v.* to conduct; carry on; negotiate (business)

> The diplomats have *transacted* an agreement.
> Vivian masterminded the real estate *transaction.*

transact business _____ _____
  (copy twice)

47. **transgress** (trans gres′) *v.* to pass over (a limit or boundary); sin; break a law or commandment

>   Poor Lem! He *transgressed* the code of the hills.
>   Forgive us our *transgressions*.

transgress the law _____   _____

48. **transition** (tran zish′ən) *n.* a passing from one condition or stage to another

>   The *transition* to winter came quickly.
>   Words like "however," "thus," and "later" are *transitional*.

smooth transition _____   _____

49. **transitory** (tran′sə tôr′ē) *adj.* temporary; fleeting; not permanent

>   Life is *transitory*.
>   He could find only *transitory* employment.

transitory fame _____   _____

50. **translucent** (trans lōō′sənt) *adj.* letting light through but diffusing it so that objects on the opposite side are not clearly visible

>   The shower door is *translucent*.
>   What a clear explanation!--quite *translucent*.

translucent bulb _____   _____

Review words 46-50. Then go on.

QUIZ

DIRECTIONS: Fill the blanks with words we studied that are derived from the Latin prefix TRANS (across). Be sure you spell the words correctly.

COVER
THIS STRIP
_____

	■ The Puritans preached that if you _____
transgress	[t-r-g-s] the will of the Almighty, your pleasures will be
transitory	_____ [t-r-t-r-y].
	■ Most students thoroughly enjoy the _____
transition	[t-r-t-n] from high school to college.

page 154

transact	■ Pawnbrokers _____ [t-r-s-c-] many a sad business deal.
translucent transact	■ The casino had _____ [t-r-l-t] windows so that the gamblers could _____ [t-r-s-c-] their affairs in privacy.
transgress transitory	■ If some Americans can _____ [t-r-g-s] the law without fear of punishment, our democracy will prove to be _____ [t-r-t-r-y].
translucent transition	■ Oswald loved playing with his _____ [t-r-l-t] marbles, and for him the _____ [t-r-t-n] to kindergarten came all too quickly.
translucent transact transgress	■ The mobsters gathered under one small _____ [t-r-l-t] bulb to _____ [t-r-s-c-] their secret business and to plot nasty ways to _____ [t-r-g-s] the law.
transitory transition transgressed	■ Life is _____ [t-r-t-r-y], and the _____ [t-r-t-n] from infancy to old age is like the blink of an eye.
	■ *"I would not marry her, though she were endowed with all that Adam had left him before he* [t-n-g-d].* (Much Ado About Nothing, II, i, 260)*

Non-test examples

OTHER DERIVATIVES OF TRANS (ACROSS):

transceiver (tran sē' vər) *n.* an apparatus that can both transmit and receive radio signals

transcend (tran send') *v.* to surpass; excel; go beyond the limits of [*She transcended all previous efforts.*]

transducer (trans dōōs'ər) *n.* a device that transmits energy from one system to another

transept (tran'sept) *n.* an arm of a cross-shaped church which is at right angles to the long central section

transfigure (trans fig'yər) *v.* to change the outward appearance so as to glorify [*Her face was transfigured.*]

transfinite (trans fī'nīt) *adj.* beyond any finite amount

transfix (trans fix') *v.* to make motionless as though pierced through; impale [*transfixed with fear*]

transfusion (trans fyōō'zhən) *n.* the transferring of blood, blood plasma, etc., into a blood vessel

transient (tran'shənt) *adj.* temporary [*the transient seasons*] *n.* a person who stays for a short time [*a jobless transient*]

transistor (tran sis'tər) *n.* a solid-state electronic device that controls the flow of current, doing the work of a vacuum tube

transit (tran'sit) *n.* a passage across; a system of public transportation; passage of a heavenly body across a space *v.* to make a passage

transitive (tran'sətiv) *adj.* involving an action that passes over and takes effect on an object; taking a direct object [*a transitive verb*]

transparent (trans par'ənt) *adj.* easily seen through

transmit (trans mit') *v.* to send from one place to another; pass along; send out radio or television signals [*We transmitted an SOS.*]

transmogrify (trans mog'rə fī') *v.* to change or transform in grotesque fashion [*Tar and feathers had transmogrified him.*]

transmutation (trans'myōō tā'shən) *n.* a change of one thing into another, as lead into gold

transpire (tran spīr') *v.* to give off moisture, as through the skin; leak out and become known [*It transpired that he was an alcoholic.*]

transpose (trans pōz') *v.* to shift position; interchange; play music in a different key [*The pianist transposed to the key of G.*]

transversal (trans vur'səl) *n.* a line that crosses two or more lines

transvestite (trans ves'tīt) *n.* one who gets sexual pleasure from wearing clothes of the opposite sex

The prefix TRANS (across) is extremely common. Its shades of meaning include *across, beyond, through.* Examples:

trans-Asiatic	transfer	transmigration	transpacific
transatlantic	transform	trans-Mississippi	transpeninsular
trans-Canadian	transfrontier	transnational	transparish
transcription	translate	transoceanic	transplant
transdesert	transmarine	transom	transpolar
transequatorial	trans-Mediterranean	transorbital	transportation

Review words 1-50, spelling and vocabulary. Then take the Chapters 17-18 Self-Test.

CHAPTERS 17-18: SELF-TEST

DIRECTIONS: Write the words in full. Complete this entire test before you check and grade your answers.

1. Barnum [p-r-f-r-d] to fool all the people all the time.
2. When we sing, nobody can [r-e-g-n-i-z-] the tune.
3. I'll [s-u-c-e-d] as a bone specialist. I have the head for it.
4. That lawyer could [p-r-o-v-] that Lincoln shot Booth.
5. The tiger's eyes were [s-h-i-n-i-g-]--so I left.
6. After twenty miles, the jogger was [o-b-l-i-g-d] to rest.
7. You are more beautiful than I could [i-m-a-g-n-].
8. If I [m-i-s-p-e-l-] a word, I'll drill until I master it.
9. Grandpa told me to [w-i-s-p-r] in his good ear.
10. I [r-e-c-m-n-d] the Army for early risers.
11. A soldier must [o-b-y] orders, even if they sound stupid.
12. Finding a leg, the sheriff suspected [m-r-d-r].
13. It's easy to [s-p-e-k] up in class if you know the answer.
14. Never [p-r-s-u-] a butterfly over a cliff.
15. They [g-a-r-n-t-e-] this tire for the life of the tire.
16. Mother was [u-s-n-g] Dad's razor to cut linoleum.
17. The bass drummer gets a bang out of band [p-r-a-t-i-c-].
18. Butch should [s-e-z-e] opportunities, not girls.
19. I wish the buck [s-t-o-p-d] at my desk.
20. A funny thing [o-c-u-r-d] on the way to the hospital.
21. A healthy youngster is rich beyond [m-e-s-r-].
22. Grandma said that boys sweat but girls [p-s-p-i-r-].
23. My luggage was [t-r-a-s-f-r-d] to Dover instead of Denver.
24. The boss fired Kay because she [o-m-i-t-d] a comma.
25. Our left fielder fumbled the [s-a-c-r-f-c-] fly.
26. The CIA needs people who can [t-r-a-n-l-a-t-] Russian.
27. How do prizefighters [m-a-n-g-e] on a mere million dollars?
28. Teacher will [i-n-t-r-d-u-] you to some Greek derivatives.
29. Snakebites could [p-r-l-z-e] a pioneer; so could whiskey.
30. The doctor is ready now to [o-p-r-a-t-] on your liver.

Write correctly the words we studied that are derived from the Latin prefixes POST, SUB, and TRANS:

31. Judgment of modern art is quite [s-b-j-t-v-].
32. The actor described his marriage and [s-b-s-q-n-t] divorce.
33. Aaron does nothing that he can [p-s-t-p-n-].
34. The burglar used the [s-b-t-r-f-g-] of dressing like Santa.
35. This lamp needs a [t-r-n-l-u-n-t] light bulb.
36. Weep for the victims of those who [t-r-a-g-r-s] the law.
37. Some day you freshmen will take [p-s-t-g-r-a-d-] courses.
38. John D. Rockefeller left some oil wells to his [p-t-r-t-y].
39. City people dream of owning a [s-u-b-r-b-] home.
40. The court will [s-b-p-n-] "Nails" McGurk as a material witness.

Write the letter that indicates the best definition.

( ) 41. posterior   a. to sin
( ) 42. posthumous   b. delicate; cunning
( ) 43. subconscious   c. below standard
( ) 44. subdue   d. undermining the government
( ) 45. submarginal   e. occurring after death
( ) 46. subpoena   f. below the level of self-awareness
( ) 47. subtle   g. going from one condition to another
( ) 48. subversive   h. toward the back side
( ) 49. transgress   i. to conquer
( ) 50. transition   j. an order to appear in court

ANSWER KEY

Check your test answers by the following key. Deduct 2% per error from 100%.

1. preferred	11. obey	21. measure	31. subjective	41. h
2. recognize	12. murder	22. perspire	32. subsequent	42. e
3. succeed	13. speak	23. transferred	33. postpone	43. f
4. prove	14. pursue	24. omitted	34. subterfuge	44. i
5. shining	15. guarantee	25. sacrifice	35. translucent	45. c
6. obliged	16. using	26. translate	36. transgress	46. j
7. imagine	17. practice	27. manage	37. postgraduate	47. b
8. misspell	18. seize	28. introduce	38. posterity	48. d
9. whisper	19. stopped	29. paralyze	39. suburban	49. a
10. recommend	20. occurred	30. operate	40. subpoena	50. g

Score: _____%

Review carefully any words which you have missed in the foregoing Self-Test.

Your instructor will give you a final test on words 1-50 in Chapters 17 and 18.

SUPPLEMENTARY LATIN DERIVATIVES

DIRECTIONS: Study the meaning of each Latin prefix and root. One English derivative is given. Fill the blanks at the right with two more derivatives. If in doubt about a word, check its sources in the dictionary.

PREFIX	MEANING	DERIVATIVES		
1. ANTE	before	*antedate*	_____	_____
2. CIRCUM	around	*circle*	_____	_____
3. CONTRA, COUNTER	against	*contradict*	_____	_____
4. DE	away; down	*defame*	_____	_____
5. INTRA, INTRO	within	*intrastate*	_____	_____
6. PRE	before	*prejudice*	_____	_____
7. RETRO	back	*retrogress*	_____	_____
8. SEMI	half	*semilunar*	_____	_____
9. SUPER	above	*superior*	_____	_____
10. UNI	one	*unicorn*	_____	_____

ROOT	MEANING	DERIVATIVES		
11. AC, ACR	sharp	*acrimony*	_____	_____
12. AER	air	*aerial*	_____	_____
13. AGR	field	*agrarian*	_____	_____
14. ALI	another	*alias*	_____	_____
15. ANIM	spirit; life	*animation*	_____	_____
16. APT, EPT	adjust	*aptitude*	_____	_____
17. ART	art; craft	*artificial*	_____	_____
18. AVI	bird	*aviary*	_____	_____
19. BEL, BELL	war	*rebel*	_____	_____
20. BREV	short	*abbreviate*	_____	_____

ROOT	MEANING	DERIVATIVES		
21. CAP, CAPT	take; seize	*captivate*	_____	_____
22. CAPIT	head	*capitol*	_____	_____
23. CARN	flesh	*carnivorous*	_____	_____
24. CID, CIS	kill; cut	*incision*	_____	_____
25. CIV	citizen	*civil*	_____	_____
26. CLAM	shout	*clamor*	_____	_____
27. CORD	heart	*cordial*	_____	_____
28. CORP	body	*corpulent*	_____	_____
29. CRED, CREDIT	believe, trust	*credo*	_____	_____
30. CRUC	cross	*excruciating*	_____	_____
31. DENT	tooth	*indent*	_____	_____
32. DIGN	worthy	*dignity*	_____	_____
33. DOC, DOCT	teach; prove	*doctrine*	_____	_____
34. DOM	master	*domineer*	_____	_____
35. DON	bestow	*donor*	_____	_____
36. DU	two	*duet*	_____	_____
37. DUC, DUCT	lead	*abduct*	_____	_____
38. EGO	I	*egomania*	_____	_____
39. ERR	wander	*error*	_____	_____
40. FIN	end; limit	*define*	_____	_____
41. FORT	strong	*fortitude*	_____	_____
42. FRAG, FRACT	break	*fragile*	_____	_____
43. FRATER	brother	*fraternal*	_____	_____
44. FUS	pour	*effusive*	_____	_____
45. GEN	birth; race	*progeny*	_____	_____
46. GRAT	please; favor	*gratify*	_____	_____
47. GRAV	heavy	*gravity*	_____	_____

ROOT	MEANING	DERIVATIVES		
48. JAC, JACT, JEC	throw	*dejected*	_____	_____
49. JUNCT	join	*adjunct*	_____	_____
50. LABOR	work	*elaborate*	_____	_____
51. LEG	law	*legal*	_____	_____
52. LEV	light; rise	*elevator*	_____	_____
53. LIB	book	*libel*	_____	_____
54. LOC	place	*location*	_____	_____
55. LOQU, LOCUT	talk	*loquacious*	_____	_____
56. LUC	light	*elucidate*	_____	_____
57. MAGN	large	*magnitude*	_____	_____
58. MAN	hand	*manual*	_____	_____
59. MAR	sea	*mariner*	_____	_____
60. MATER, MATR	mother	*maternal*	_____	_____
61. MEDI	middle	*medium*	_____	_____
62. MIN	little; less	*minute*	_____	_____
63. MIT, MISS	send	*missive*	_____	_____
64. MON, MONIT	warn	*premonition*	_____	_____
65. MOR	custom	*morals*	_____	_____
66. MOV, MOT, MOB	move	*motivate*	_____	_____
67. MUT	change	*commute*	_____	_____
68. NAV	ship	*navigate*	_____	_____
69. NOMEN, NOMIN	name	*nominee*	_____	_____
70. NOV	new	*novice*	_____	_____
71. OCUL	eye	*monocle*	_____	_____
72. PAR	equal	*parity*	_____	_____
73. PATER, PATR	father	*patricide*	_____	_____
74. PEND	hang	*pendulum*	_____	_____

ROOT	MEANING	DERIVATIVES		
75. PON, POSIT	place	*deposit*	_____	_____
76. PORT, PORTAT	carry	*imported*	_____	_____
77. PRIM	first	*primitive*	_____	_____
78. RAT, RATION	reason	*irrational*	_____	_____
79. RUPT	break	*erupt*	_____	_____
80. SANCT	holy	*sanction*	_____	_____
81. SEG, SECT	cut	*dissect*	_____	_____
82. SEQU, SECUT	follow	*sequel*	_____	_____
83. SIGN	sign	*resign*	_____	_____
84. SIMIL	like	*simile*	_____	_____
85. SOL	alone	*soliloquy*	_____	_____
86. SON	sound	*resonant*	_____	_____
87. SPIR, SPIRIT	breathe	*inspire*	_____	_____
88. STRUCT	build	*construct*	_____	_____
89. TEN	hold	*tenacious*	_____	_____
90. TERRA	earth	*terrain*	_____	_____
91. TRACT	draw; pull	*extract*	_____	_____
92. TURB	agitate	*turbulent*	_____	_____
93. URB	city	*urban*	_____	_____
94. VAC	empty	*vacant*	_____	_____
95. VERT, VERS	turn	*divert*	_____	_____
96. VID, VIS	see	*visual*	_____	_____
97. VINC, VICT	conquer	*invincible*	_____	_____
98. VIT	life	*vital*	_____	_____
99. VIV	life	*revive*	_____	_____
100. VULG	common	*vulgate*	_____	_____

DESCRIPTIVE WORDS: "ABSOLUTELY" TO "GENUINE"

19

DIRECTIONS: Study the spelling of each word carefully, giving special attention to the trouble spots (underlined letters). Then write each word neatly three times.

1. absolut<u>e</u>ly _____ _____ _____

2. accident<u>al</u>ly _____ _____ _____

3. acc<u>u</u>rate _____ _____ _____

4. ad<u>e</u>quate _____ _____ _____

5. ambi<u>ti</u>ous _____ _____ _____

6. an<u>ci</u>ent _____ _____ _____

7. appar<u>e</u>ntly _____ _____ _____

8. a<u>w</u>kward _____ _____ _____

9. brill<u>ia</u>nt _____ _____ _____

10. cert<u>ai</u>nly _____ _____ _____

Review words 1-10 until you are sure you can spell them. Then go on and take the quiz.

COVER
THIS STRIP   FILL THE BLANKS

■ Harvey was an _____ [a-k-w-r-d] dancer, and

awkward
absolutely   Doris was _____ [a-b-s-l-t-l-y] not amused when he
accidentally

_____ [a-c-d-n-t-l-y] landed on her bunions.

■ The _____ [a-n-c-e-n-t] Greeks, despite their

ancient
apparently   sins, were _____ [a-p-r-n-t-l-y] extremely
brilliant

_____ [b-r-i-l-n-t] architects.

■ A hiker in Death Valley must be _____

[a-b-s-l-t-l-y] sure he has an _____ [a-d-q-t-e]

absolutely
adequate   supply of water, or he will _____ [c-r-t-n-l-y]
certainly
ambitious   become a dinner for the _____ [a-m-b-i-u-s] vultures.

■ Although Joe Stumble is an _____ [a-k-w-r-d]

tennis player and not very _____ [a-c-r-a-t-], he

awkward
accurate   did make one _____ [b-r-i-l-n-t] return that hit
brilliant

the champion in the groin.

■ My little brother was not _____ [a-m-b-i-u-s],

and ten minutes of mauling the violin each day seemed

ambitious
adequate   _____ [a-d-q-t-e].

■ William Tell was an _____ [a-c-r-a-t-]

marksman, and so he hit the apple--a pippin of a shot!--but

accurate
awkward   if he had been _____ [a-k-w-r-d], he might have
accidentally

_____ [a-c-d-n-t-l-y] pronged his son in the ear.

■ My watch, which was less than _____ [a-c-r-a-t-],

_____ [a-p-r-n-t-l-y] lost ten minutes a day,

accurate
apparently   but in our slow-moving village I felt that my timepiece was
certainly
adequate   _____ [c-r-t-n-l-y] _____ [a-d-q-t-e].

- Julius Caesar _____ [a-p-r-n-t-l-y] was

_____ [a-m-b-i-u-s]; and so, for the sake of Rome,

apparently
ambitious
absolutely

friend Brutus felt _____ [a-b-s-l-t-l-y] justified

in ventilating Caesar with a dagger.

- The geologist _____ [a-c-d-n-t-l-y] dug up the

shinbone of an _____ [a-n-c-e-n-t] mastodon. It

accidentally
ancient
certainly
brilliant

_____ [c-r-t-n-l-y] was a _____ [b-r-i-l-n-t]

discovery....No, Sam, the meat was not fresh.

- The _____ [a-n-c-e-n-t] mariner stopped me and

ancient

held me with his glittering eye.

- "The noble Brutus
Hath told you Caesar was _____ [a-m-b-i-u-s]."
(Julius Caesar, III, ii, 83)

ambitious

DIRECTIONS: Continue as before. Study the spelling carefully. Write each
word three times.

11. changeable _____ _____ _____

12. complete _____ _____ _____

13. conscious _____ _____ _____

14. convenient _____ _____ _____

15. dangerous _____ _____ _____

16. delicious _____ _____ _____

17. desirable _____ _____ _____

18. desperate _____ _____ _____

19. disastrous _____ _____ _____

20. divine _____ _____ _____

Review words 11-20. Then take the quiz.

QUIZ

COVER THIS STRIP	FILL THE BLANKS
	■ Those who tried to _____ [c-m-p-l-e-t-] the
	Panama Canal learned that malaria can be _____
complete disastrous	[d-s-a-s-t-r-s].
	■ Serious students find that owning the _____
complete desirable convenient	[c-m-p-l-e-t-] works of Shakespeare is both _____
	[d-s-i-r-b-l-] and _____ [c-o-n-v-e-n-t].
	■ The sailor was _____ [c-o-n-s-u-s] of the
	_____ [c-h-a-n-g-b-l-] winds and felt that an
conscious changeable dangerous desirable	encounter with the _____ [d-a-n-g-r-s-]
	typhoons was hardly _____ [d-s-i-r-b-l-].
	■ At every _____ [c-o-n-v-e-n-t] opportunity
convenient divine desperate	Harold told Alma that she was _____ [d-v-i-n-]
	and that he was _____ [d-e-s-p-r-t-] to marry her.
	■ Junk foods are _____ [d-e-l-i-u-s], but their
delicious disastrous	effect on the human body can be _____ [d-s-a-s-t-r-s].
	■ Although their fortunes were _____ [c-h-a-n-g-b-l-],
changeable conscious divine	the Puritans were always _____ [c-o-n-s-u-s] of a
	_____ [d-v-i-n-] power that could help them.
	■ Sprayed vegetables are _____ [c-o-n-v-e-n-t]
convenient delicious dangerous	and _____ [d-e-l-i-u-s], yet they can be
	_____ [d-a-n-g-r-s].
	■ A writer's mind is _____ [c-h-a-n-g-b-l-], and
changeable desirable	he finds an eraser rather _____ [d-s-i-r-b-l-].
	■ The fullback ate two _____ [c-m-p-l-e-t-]
complete delicious	snake steaks and said that they were _____ [d-e-l-i-u-s], a rattling good meal.

conscious
divine
desperate

■ The crash victim was barely _____ [c-o-n-s-u-s],

and it seemed that only _____ [d-v-i-n-] inter-

vention could rescue him from his _____ [d-e-s-p-r-t-]

plight.

■ The famished wolves were _____ [d-e-s-p-r-t-]

desperate
dangerous
disastrous

and _____ [d-a-n-g-r-s-], and an encounter with

them could prove _____ [d-s-a-s-t-r-s].

■ *"...here's a marvelous* _____ [c-o-n-v-e-n-t]
place for our rehearsal"

convenient

(A Midsummer-Night's Dream, III, i, 2)

DIRECTIONS: Continue as before. Study the spelling carefully. Write each
word three times.

21. eccentric _____ _____ _____

22. eligible _____ _____ _____

23. excellent _____ _____ _____

24. exhausted _____ _____ _____

25. extraordinary _____ _____ _____

26. extremely _____ _____ _____

27. familiar _____ _____ _____

28. feminine _____ _____ _____

29. feasible _____ _____ _____

30. genuine _____ _____ _____

Review words 21-30. Then take the quiz.

QUIZ

**COVER
THIS STRIP**

FILL THE BLANKS

feminine
eccentric

■ Cousin Claribel has _____ [f-e-m-n-n-] charm,

but wearing curlers to the opera house struck me as a bit

_____ [e-e-n-t-r-c-].

page 167

- We think your _____ [e-x-t-r-d-n-y] plan to

reach India by sailing west is _____ [-x-t-m-1-y]

   extraordinary
   extremely
   feasible

ingenious, Mr. Columbus, but the experiment hardly seems

_____ [f-e-s-b-1-].

- It was without _____ [g-e-n-i-n-] pleasure

that Mr. Snavely recognized several _____ [f-m-1-r]

   genuine
   familiar
   feminine

faces as he was buying the _____ [f-e-m-n-n-]

lingerie.

- Although a bit _____ [e-e-n-t-r-c-], "Skate-

board" Snopes is an _____ [e-1-g-b-1-] bachelor

   eccentric
   eligible
   excellent

of _____ [-x-1-n-t] character.

- To become _____ [e-1-g-b-1-] for football,

Hank _____ [-x-a-s-t-d] every means at his

   eligible
   exhausted

disposal, except study.

- Welding didn't seem to be a _____ [f-e-m-n-n-]

occupation, but Lockheed found that hiring female welders

   feminine
   extremely
   feasible

was _____ [-x-t-m-1y] _____ [f-e-s-b-1-].

- "This gives me more _____ [g-e-n-i-n-] pain

than it does you," said Father, and he gave me an

   genuine
   extraordinary
   exhausted

_____ [e-x-t-r-d-n-y] clobbering until he was

_____ [-x-a-s-t-d].

- "Your credentials are _____ [-x-1-n-t]," said

the warden, "and you should be _____ [e-1-g-b-1-]

   excellent
   eligible

for parole in seventeen years."

- An _____ [e-e-n-t-r-c-] fellow named Orville

Wright made the _____ [e-x-t-r-d-n-y] claim that

   eccentric
   extraordinary
   feasible

heavier than air flight was _____ [f-e-s-b-1-].

exhausted
familiar
extremely

- The _____ [-x-a-s-t-d] swimmer reached the

    _____ [f-m-l-r] beach. Because the water was

    _____ [-x-t-m-l-y] cold, he had decided not to

drown himself.

excellent
genuine

- "A most _____ [-x-l-n-t] fellow! It was a

    _____ [g-e-n-i-n-] pleasure to have him to dinner,"

said the cannibal.

excellent

-   "O, it is _____ [-x-l-n-t]
  To have a giant's strength; but it is tyrannous
  To use it like a giant."
         (Measure for Measure, II, ii, 107)

20

ASTR: STAR

31. **asterisk** (as′tər isk) *n.* a starlike sign (*) used to indicate footnotes, omissions, etc.

    The author used *asterisks* in place of profanity.
    An *asterisk* directed my eye to an explanatory footnote.

    <u>starry asterisk</u> _____ _____
    (copy twice)

32. **asteroid** (as′tər oid′) *n.* a very small planet; a planetoid

    Thousands of *asteroids* revolve around the sun.
    An *asteroid* measures one to 480 miles in diameter.

    <u>tiny asteroids</u> _____ _____

33. **astrology** (ə strol′ə jē) *n.* a study that claims to interpret the influence of stars and planets on human affairs

    Your birthday, according to *astrology*, influences your personality.
    Astrology is not considered a true science.

    <u>medieval astrology</u> _____ _____

34. **astronaut** (as′trə nôt′) *n.* a person trained to travel in outer space;
a cosmonaut

> American *astronauts* landed on the moon.
> Within the speeding rocket, the *astronaut* is weightless.

skilled astronauts _____ _____

35. **astronomy** (ə stron′ə mē) *n.* the science that deals with stars,
planets, and other heavenly bodies

> Galileo's telescope was a boon to *astronomy*.
> *Astronomy* made it possible to predict eclipses.

science of astronomy _____ _____

Review words 31-35. Then go on.

QUIZ

DIRECTIONS: Fill the blanks with words we studied that are derived from the
Greek root ASTR (star). Be sure you spell the words correctly.

COVER
THIS STRIP

	■ Scholarly articles such as your term paper usually use a footnote number now instead of an _____ [a-s-s-k].
asterisk	
	■ The signs of the zodiac are basic in a study of
astrology	_____ [a-s-1-g-].
	■ The professor of _____ [a-s-n-m-] said that the
astronomy astronaut asteroid	_____ [a-s-n-t-] was headed toward a tiny planet known as an _____ [a-s-o-d].
	■ According to _____ [a-s-1-g-], every planet and _____ [a-s-o-d] affects your personality and
astrology asteroid	fate depending on whether you were born March 3 or July 29.
	■ An article in an _____ [a-s-n-m-] journal deals with the _____ [a-s-o-d]; and here and there
astronomy asteroid asterisk	an old-fashioned _____ [a-s-s-k] directs your eye to a scholarly footnote.

page 171

astronaut
asterisk

■ The rocket carrying the _____ [a-s-n-t-] was

now a speck in the sky, no bigger than an _____

[a-s-s-k].

■ To paraphrase the words of one _____ [a-s-n-t-]:

"Surely _____ [a-s-n-m-] is a marvelous science,

astronaut
astronomy
astrology

whereas _____ [a-s-l-g-] is a steaming pile of

manure."

■ *"O, learn'd indeed were that astronomer*
That knew the stars as I his characters"
(Cymbeline, III, ii, 27)

Non-test examples

OTHER DERIVATIVES OF ASTR (STAR):

astral (as′trəl) *adj.* pertaining to or like the stars; starry [*an astral body such as Saturn*]

astrocompass (as′trə kum′pəs) *n.* a device which sights upon a heavenly body to help direct the flight of aircraft

astrodome (as′trō dōm′) *n.* a transparent dome on top of an aircraft for observation of heavenly bodies

astrodynamics (as′trō dī nam′iks) *n.* the study of motion and gravitation of objects in space

astrogate (as′trə gāt′) *v.* to navigate in outer space [*Computers enabled us to astrogate toward the distant planet.*]

astrograph (as′trə graf′) *n.* a navigational device for charting the shifting positions of planets and stars

astrolabe (as′trə lāb′) *n.* an ancient astronomical instrument used for measuring the altitude of the sun and stars

The root ASTR (star) is used to form other compound words, particularly in science. Examples:

aster	astrogeology	astronomical
astrionics	astromancy	astrophotography
astrobiology	astrometry	astrophysics
astrobotany	astronavigation	disaster

36. **autobiography** (ô′tə bī og′rə fē) *n.* the story of a person's life written by that same person

> James Thurber wrote a hilarious *autobiography*.
> Charles Dickens' novels contain *autobiographical* elements.

candid autobiography _____ _____
    (copy twice)

37. **autocrat** (ô′tə krat′) *n.* a ruler with absolute power over others; a dictator; a domineering person

> Nobody argues with our boss. He's an *autocrat*.
> We want democracy, not *autocratic* government.

ruthless autocrat _____ _____

38. **autograph** (ôt′ə graf′) *n.* a person's signature; a thing written in one's own hand *v.* to write one's name on or in something

> We asked for the actor's *autograph*.
> Fernando *autographed* this baseball.

rare autograph _____ _____

39. **autohypnosis** (ôt′ō hip nōs′is) *n.* self-induced hypnosis

> Bad habits are sometimes cured by *autohypnosis*.
> Techniques of *autohypnosis* are not hard to master.

cured by autohypnosis _____ _____

40. **automation** (ôt′ə mā′shən) *n.* a system of production in which all processes are performed by self-operating machinery

> Bottles are capped by *automation*.
> *Automation* has taken jobs from some people.

efficient automation _____ _____

41. **autopsy** (ô top′sē) *n.* [lit., a seeing for oneself, from *auto* (self) and *opsis* (a seeing)] inspection and dissection of a corpse, usually to discover the cause of death; a post-mortem; detailed analysis of a book, play, or event

> If foul play is suspected, an *autopsy* must be performed.
> An *autopsy* disclosed that a bullet had hit Smithers' navel.

thorough autopsy _____ _____

Review words 36-41. Then go on.

QUIZ

DIRECTIONS: Fill the blanks with words we studied that are derived from the Greek root AUTO (self). Be sure you spell the words correctly.

COVER
THIS STRIP

autopsy	■ The coroner performed many an _____ [a-t-p-y], but never found a broken heart.
autobiography autohypnosis	■ The captain's _____ [a-t-b-g-y] told how he had used _____ [a-h-p-n-o-s] to stop swearing.
automation autograph	■ Nick admired the engineer who introduced _____ [a-m-a-t-n] at the bean factory, so he got his _____ [a-g-r-a-p-].
autopsy	■ After the play folded, a panel of critics conducted an _____ [a-t-p-y] to find out what killed it.
autocrat automation	■ Henry Ford, the _____ [a-t-c-r-t] of the automobile industry, would have loved the cool efficiency of modern _____ [a-m-a-t-n].
autohypnosis autobiography	■ The ex-president had to use _____ [a-h-p-n-o-s] to get in the mood to write his _____ [a-t-b-g-y].
autohypnosis autograph	■ Bill bought a book on _____ [a-h-p-n-o-s] which was guaranteed to improve his memory, and he even got the author to _____ [a-g-r-a-p-] it, but now he can't remember where he put the book.
autocrat autograph autobiography	■ I asked the _____ [a-t-c-r-t] who ruled that little nation to _____ [a-g-r-a-p-] my copy of his fast-selling _____ [a-t-b-g-y].
automation	■ The system of _____ [a-m-a-t-n] broke down at the sauerkraut cannery.

■ An _____ [a-t-p-y] on the corpse of the hated

_____ [a-t-c-r-t] revealed that he had eaten a

poisoned mackerel.

autopsy
autocrat

Non-test examples

OTHER DERIVATIVES OF AUTO (SELF):

autobahn (ô'tə bän') *n.* in Germany, a superhighway

autocatharsis (ô'tō kə thär'sis) *n.* purging oneself of psychiatric
problems by writing about one's experience and impressions

autoerotism (ô'tō er'ə tiz əm) *n.* satisfying of sexual emotion by oneself

autogenesis (ôt'ō jen'i sis) *n.* spontaneous generation; born of itself

autogiro (ôt'ə jī'rō) *n.* an aircraft similar to a helicopter

autoharp (ôt'ō härp') *n.* a zither that plays its own chord accompaniment
through a system of dampers

autoignition (ô'tō ig nish'ən) *n.* the spontaneous self-ignition of fuel
in an internal-combustion engine as a result of heat of compression, etc.

automat (ô'tə mat') *n.* a restaurant in which food is obtained
automatically from small, coin-operated compartments

automaton (ô tom'ə ton') *n.* a self-moving machine; an apparatus that
operates automatically in response to programed instructions; a person who
acts in a monotonous, mechanical way, without active thought

autonomy (ô ton'ə mē) *n.* self-government; independence; freedom [*a
revolt to win autonomy*]

autoplasty (ô'tə plas'tē) *n.* the surgical repair of defects by grafting
tissue from another part of the patient's body

The root AUTO (self) is used to form many other compound words. Examples:

autoanalysis	autohybridization	automobile
autobus	autoinduction	automotive
autocombustion	autoinfection	autoradiograph
autoconduction	autoinoculation	autosepticemia
autocracy	autointoxication	autostability
autodiagnosis	autokinetic	autosuggestion
autodiffusion	autoluminescence	autotoxemia

42. **antibiotic** (an'tī bī ot'ik) *n.* a chemical substance which destroys bacteria, used in treatment of infections

> My doctor prescribed *antibiotics*.
> The *antibiotic* known as penicillin was found in moldy bread.

antibiotic drugs _____ _____
   (copy twice)

43. **biography** (bī og'rə fē) *n.* a written account of another person's life

> Boswell wrote a classic *biography* of Samuel Johnson.
> *Who's Who* provides concise *biographical* data.

biography of Lincoln _____ _____

44. **biology** (bī ol'ə jē) *n.* the scientific study of plants and animals; the science of living matter in all its phases

> *Biology* students have cut up fifty million frogs.
> Maria specialized in marine *biology*.

biology laboratory _____ _____

45. **biopsy** (bī op'sē) *n.* the diagnostic examination of bits of living tissue taken from a patient's body

> The surgeon conducted a *biopsy*.
> The *biopsy* showed that the lump was benign.

a favorable biopsy _____ _____

Review words 42-45. Then go on.

QUIZ

DIRECTIONS: Fill the blanks with words we studied that are derived from the Greek root BIO (life). Be sure you spell the words correctly.

COVER
THIS STRIP
_____

biopsy	■ A malignancy can be detected by a _____ [b-p-s-].
	■ As a student of _____ [b-l-g-y], Lydia was
biology biography	inspired by a _____ [b-g-r-y] of Charles Darwin.

biology antibiotic	■ The _____ [b-l-g-y] professor warns that venereal diseases are now resistant to _____ [a-b-i-c] drugs.
biography	■ Become famous, and your dressmaker will write a _____ [b-g-r-y] exposing your sins.
biology	■ Botany and zoology are branches of _____ [b-l-g-y].
biopsy	■ It's better to have a _____ [b-p-s-] today than an autopsy tomorrow.
antibiotic	■ Tetracycline is an _____ [a-b-i-c] which can interact dangerously with other drugs.
biography	■ The gangster was so tough that we had to print his _____ [b-g-r-y] on sandpaper.
biopsy antibiotic	■ After doing a _____ [b-p-s-] on Jasper's infected lung, the doctor prescribed an _____ [a-b-i-c].

OTHER DERIVATIVES OF BIO (LIFE): *Non-test examples*

biodegradable (bī ō də grā′də bəl) *adj.* able to be decomposed by bacterial action [*Use biodegradable detergents.*]

bioecology (bī′ō e kol′ə jē) *n.* the science that deals with the interrelations between living things and their environment

biogenesis (bī′ō jen′ə sis) *n.* the doctrine that living organisms are generated only by other similar living organisms

biometry (bī om′ə trē) *n.* the calculating of the probable length of human life

bionics (bī on′iks) *n.* the study of human and animal behavior which may aid in applications to the design of computers and other electronic devices

biorhythm (bī′ō rith′əm) *n.* the various cycles whereby one's physical, emotional, and intellectual energy levels are presumed to rise and fall

biosphere (bī′ə sfēr′) *n.* the zone of the earth and its atmosphere that can sustain life

biosynthesis (bī′ō sin′thə sis) *n.* the formation of chemical compounds by living organisms

biotherapy (bī'ō ther'ə pē) *n.* the treatment of disease by substances such as penicillin that are derived from living organisms

symbiosis (sim'bī ō'sis) *n.* the living together of two different organisms, to the advantage of both

The root BIO (life) is used to form many other scientific terms. Examples:

bioastronautics	bioelectric	bioplasm
biocatalyst	bioflavenoid	biopsychic
biocentric	biogeography	biosatellite
biochemist	bioluminescence	bioscope
biocide	biomagnetism	biosocial
bioclimatology	biomedicine	biotechnology
biodynamics	biophysics	biotin

CHRON: TIME

46. **anachronism** (ə nak'rə niz'əm) *n.* the representing of something as existing at the wrong time in history; a person or thing appearing after its own time

> Showing George Washington in a helicopter is an *anachronism.*
> Farmer Fingle's horse and buggy are an *anachronism* in city traffic.

Avoid anachronisms. _____   _____
   (copy twice)

47. **chronic** (kron'ik) *adj.* lasting a long time; constant; having long had a disease

> If you have *chronic* headaches, find the cause.
> It's hard to love a *chronic* grouch.

chronic ills _____   _____

48. **chronicle** (kron'i kəl) *n.* a story; a historical record of events in order of time *v.* to relate the history of

> Rolvaag *chronicled* the hardships of the pioneer.
> For a *chronicle* of the French Revolution, read Thomas Carlyle.

ancient chronicle _____   _____

49. chronological (kron′ə loj′i kəl) *adj*. arranged in time order

> Leah named the presidents in *chronological* order.
> American history is usually studied *chronologically*.

chronological order _____ _____

50. synchronize (sin′krə nīz′) *v*. to cause to happen at the same time; regulate so as to agree in rate and phase

> The plotters *synchronized* their watches.
> The film editor must *synchronize* sound and action.

synchronize action _____ _____

Review words 46–50. Then go on.

QUIZ

DIRECTIONS: Fill the blanks with words we studied that are derived from the Greek root CHRON (time). Be sure you spell the words correctly.

COVER
THIS STRIP

chronicle chronic	■ Mark Twain wrote a _____ [c-r-n-c-l-] of the Mississippi, starring Huck Finn and that _____ [c-r-n-c-] prankster, Tom Sawyer.
anachronism	■ Abe Lincoln signing the Emancipation with a ballpoint pen? What a droll _____ [a-n-c-s-m]!
chronic chronological	■ The hillbilly, a _____ [c-r-n-c] alcoholic, was unable to name his eleven children in _____ [c-l-g-l] order.
chronicle synchronize anachronism	■ We enjoyed the _____ [c-r-n-c-l-] of Puritan days, especially the farcical scene where the Mathers all _____ [s-n-c-n-z-] their digital watches. An amusing _____ [a-n-c-s-m]!
chronicle chronological	■ The Bible student can _____ [c-r-n-c-l-] events of the Old Testament in _____ [c-l-g-l] order.

anachronism	■ Our inky old mimeograph machine is an _____ [a-n-c-s-m] among the desk-top duplicators.
synchronize chronic	■ The ballet dancers can _____ [s-n-c-n-z-] their movements perfectly, except for the clown with the _____ [c-r-n-c-] backache.
chronological synchronize	■ Although he can name the world chess champions in _____ [c-r-n-c-l-] order, Figley can't _____ [s-n-c-n-z-] his own pawns and bishops.
chronicle	■ *"For 'tis a* _____ [*c-r-n-c-l-*] *of day by day"* *(The Tempest, V, i, 163)*

Non-test examples

OTHER DERIVATIVES OF CHRON (TIME):

chronograph (kron′ə graf′) *n.* a timepiece that records graphically--possibly by means of a stylus and a revolving drum--the moment and duration of an event; a stopwatch

chronology (krə nol′ə jē) *n.* a listing of events in the order of their occurrence

chronometry (krə nom′ə trē) *n.* the science of measuring time accurately

chronoscope (kron′ə skōp′) *n.* an instrument for precise measurement of extremely small intervals of time, as in determining the speed of projectiles

---

Review words 1-50, spelling and vocabulary. Then take the Chapters 19-20 Self-Test.

CHAPTERS 19-20: SELF-TEST

DIRECTIONS: Write the words in full. Complete this entire test before you check and grade your answers.

_____ 1. Every bird thinks its own voice is [d-v-i-n-].
_____ 2. The bear [c-r-t-n-l-y] enjoyed Mom's jelly.
_____ 3. "You have [-x-t-r-d-n-r-y] eyes," he whispered.
_____ 4. My alarm clock is [a-c-u-r-t-] once in a while.
_____ 5. Driving across your tulips was [a-k-w-r-d] of me.
_____ 6. The mosquitoes are [-x-t-r-m-l-y] affectionate.
_____ 7. A frilly dress is more [f-e-m-n-n-] than overalls.
_____ 8. A whale watchers' club isn't [f-e-s-b-l-] in Iowa.
_____ 9. The tramp was so [d-s-p-r-t-] that he asked for work.
_____ 10. My [e-c-n-t-r-c] neighbor sleeps in a tree house.

_____ 11. The world belongs to a student who is [a-m-b-i-u-s].
_____ 12. The strikers thought a salary raise was [d-e-s-r-b-1-].
_____ 13. A fly has [a-c-d-n-t-1-y] drowned in my soup.
_____ 14. Our water supply was [e-h-a-s-t-d], and so was I.
_____ 15. Hiram's head is [a-b-s-1-t-y] perfect for a rock garden.
_____ 16. Nobody is [c-o-n-s-u-s] of his own odor.
_____ 17. The jeweler advertised "[g-e-n-i-n] simulated pearls."
_____ 18. Backing off the cliff was [d-s-a-s-t-r-s-].
_____ 19. Bullfighting is a [d-a-n-g-r-s-] pastime.
_____ 20. Our weather is [c-h-a-g-b-1-], from bad to worse.
_____ 21. He's an [e-1-g-b-1-] bachelor...for welfare money.
_____ 22. I forgot the Turk's name, but his fez is [f-m-i-1-r].
_____ 23. Who built these very old, these [a-n-i-n-t] pyramids?
_____ 24. The cannibals ate a [d-e-1-i-u-s] missionary.
_____ 25. The operation was a [c-m-p-1-e-t-] success, but Joe died.
_____ 26. The moon is [a-p-r-n-t-1-y] not made of green cheese.
_____ 27. Three helpings of turkey seemed [a-d-q-a-t-].
_____ 28. The shark had an [e-x-e-1-n-t] set of teeth.
_____ 29. A rich father-in-law can be quite [c-o-n-v-i-n-t].
_____ 30. Improve your writing and you'll have a [b-r-i-1-n-t] career.

Write correctly the words we studied that are derived from the Greek roots
ASTR, AUTO, BIO, and CHRON.

_____ 31. Streptomycin is a powerful [a-t-i-b-t-c-].
_____ 32. Most scientists regard [a-s-1-g-y] as a hoax.
_____ 33. Casanova describes his love life in his [a-t-b-g-r-y].
_____ 34. A footnote used to be indicated by an [a-s-t-r-s-].
_____ 35. Cancer can be detected by means of a [b-o-p-y].
_____ 36. Some football coaches are [c-r-n-c] complainers.
_____ 37. The marching band should [s-n-c-r-n-z-] their movements.
_____ 38. The coroner's [a-t-p-s-] uncovered foul play.
_____ 39. Poets are always glad to [a-t-g-r-h-] a book.
_____ 40. The TV set in that nativity play is an [a-n-c-r-n-s-m].

Write the letter that indicates the best definition.

( ) 41. asteroid   a. science of living things
( ) 42. astronaut   b. science of heavenly bodies
( ) 43. astronomy   c. a historical record; story
( ) 44. autocrat   d. a space traveler
( ) 45. autohypnosis   e. a written life story
( ) 46. automation   f. in order of time
( ) 47. biography   g. a state of self-suggestion
( ) 48. biology   h. a ruler; an arrogant person
( ) 49. chronicle   i. a tiny planet
( ) 50. chronological   j. self-operating machinery

ANSWER KEY: 1. divine; 2. certainly; 3. extraordinary; 4. accurate;
5. awkward; 6. extremely; 7. feminine; 8. feasible; 9. desperate; 10. eccentric;
11. ambitious; 12. desirable; 13. accidentally; 14. exhausted; 15. absolutely;
16. conscious; 17. genuine; 18. disastrous; 19. dangerous; 20. changeable;
21. eligible; 22. familiar; 23. ancient; 24. delicious; 25. complete;
26. apparently; 27. adequate; 28. excellent; 29. convenient; 30. brilliant;
31. antibiotic; 32. astrology; 33. autobiography; 34. asterisk; 35. biopsy;
36. chronic; 37. synchronize; 38. autopsy; 39. autograph; 40. anachronism;
41. i; 42. d; 43. b; 44. h; 45. g; 46. j; 47. e; 48. a; 49. c; 50. f

DESCRIPTIVE WORDS: "IGNORANT" TO "WICKED"

21

DIRECTIONS: Study the spelling of each word carefully, giving special attention to the trouble spots (underlined letters). Then write each word neatly three times.

1. ignorant _____ _____ _____

2. imaginary _____ _____ _____

3. immediately _____ _____ _____

4. incidentally _____ _____ _____

5. incredible _____ _____ _____

6. independent _____ _____ _____

7. infinite _____ _____ _____

8. innocent _____ _____ _____

9. lovely _____ _____ _____

10. mischievous _____ _____ _____

Review words 1-10 until you are sure you can spell them. Then go on and take the quiz.

COVER
THIS STRIP   FILL THE BLANKS

lovely
innocent
incredible

infinite
imaginary

independent
mischievous

incidentally
ignorant

lovely
incredible
immediately

incidentally
infinite
innocent

ignorant
imaginary

incredible
lovely
immediately

independent
mischievous

■ Ben's blind date proved to be a _____ [l-v-l-y-]
freshman coed with an _____ [i-n-c-n-t-] smile.
"What _____ [i-n-c-r-d-b-l-] luck!" muttered Ben.

■ Gaze at the _____ [i-n-f-n-t-] stars, and your
earthly troubles will seem _____ [i-m-g-n-r-y-].

■ Thomas Paine, who urged the colonies to fight to be
_____ [i-n-d-p-n-d-t-], was regarded by England as
a _____ [m-s-c-h-v-s-] radical.

■ No one, _____ [i-n-c-d-n-t-y], is as
_____ [i-g-n-r-n-t-] as the fellow who thinks he
knows it all.

■ We bought a _____ [l-v-l-y-] cottage with an
_____ [i-n-c-r-d-b-l-] view, and _____
[i-m-e-d-t-l-y-] began to worry about the mortgage.

■ The ocean, _____ [i-n-c-d-n-t-y], is not
_____ [i-n-f-n-t-] in size, and we would be
_____ [i-n-c-n-t-] indeed to conclude that it cannot be contaminated.

■ An _____ [i-g-n-r-n-t-] person is often haunted
by fears, most of them _____ [i-m-g-n-r-y].

■ "It's _____ [i-n-c-r-d-b-l-] how _____
[l-v-l-y-] you are," he murmured, and he _____
[i-m-e-d-t-l-y-] sank his teeth into the roast turkey.

■ A tornado has an _____ [i-n-d-p-n-d-t-] mind
and it can be quite _____ [m-s-c-h-v-s-].

incidentally
imaginary

■ On the voyage, _____ [i-n-c-d-n-t-y], I learned

that the equator is an _____ [i-m-g-n-r-y] line.

■ The baby sitter _____ [i-m-e-d-t-l-y] realized

immediately
independent
mischievous

that Junior had an _____ [i-n-d-p-n-d-t] and

_____ [m-s-c-h-v-s] spirit, and she hated him.

■ Our greatest scientists are like _____

[i-g-n-r-n-t] and _____ [i-n-c-n-t] children

ignorant
innocent
infinite

sticking their toes into the _____ [i-n-f-n-t-]

ocean of the unknown.

■ *"Age cannot wither her, nor custom stale*

infinite

Her _____ *[i-n-f-n-t-] variety"*
(Antony and Cleopatra, II, ii, 241)

DIRECTIONS: Continue as before. Study the spelling carefully. Write each word three times.

11. mod<u>e</u>rn _____ _____ _____

12. m<u>y</u>sterious _____ _____ _____

13. notic<u>ea</u>ble _____ _____ _____

14. occa<u>si</u>onally _____ _____ _____

15. opt<u>i</u>mistic _____ _____ _____

16. para<u>ll</u>el _____ _____ _____

17. p<u>a</u>rticul<u>a</u>r _____ _____ _____

18. phy<u>s</u>ical _____ _____ _____

19. r<u>i</u>diculous _____ _____ _____

20. sincer<u>e</u>ly _____ _____ _____

Review words 11-20. Then take the quiz.

QUIZ

COVER THIS STRIP	FILL THE BLANKS
parallel ridiculous	■ "Any _____ [p-a-r-1-e-1-] between man and the ape is _____ [r-d-i-c-1-u-s-]," said the ape.
sincerely noticeable	■ I _____ [s-n-c-r-1-y-] hoped that the rip in my pants was not _____ [n-o-t-c-b-1-].
sincerely optimistic	■ Until he sat down, the condemned man was _____ [s-n-c-r-1-y-] _____ [o-p-t-m-s-t-c-] that he would be pardoned.
parallel physical occasionally noticeable	■ If two people lead _____ [p-a-r-1-e-1-] lives, a _____ [p-h-s-c-1-] resemblance may _____ [o-c-a-s-n-1-y-] become _____ [n-o-t-c-b-1-].
sincerely optimistic modern	■ "I am _____ [s-n-c-r-1-y-] very _____ [o-p-t-m-s-t-c] about _____ [m-d-r-n-] science," whispered the radiation victim.
particular ridiculous	■ The rich child who is very picky and _____ [p-r-t-i-c-1-r] about his food will seem _____ [r-d-i-c-1-u-s] to a hungry brother.
modern mysterious occasionally	■ Many _____ [m-o-d-r-n] novels deal with _____ [m-s-t-e-r-u-s] crime, yet such stories _____ [o-c-a-s-n-1-y-] have startling originality.
particular parallel ridiculous	■ I remember in _____ [p-r-t-i-c-1-r] that Charlie Chaplin's feet weren't _____ [p-a-r-1-e-1-]. but that they stuck out at a _____ [r-d-i-c-1-u-s] angle.

modern
mysterious
physical
noticeable

- The _____ [m-o-d-r-n-] maiden in her bikini is

not as _____ [m-s-t-e-r-u-s-] as her grandmother

was, but her _____ [p-h-s-c-1-] features are more

_____ [n-o-t-c-b-1-].

occasionally
optimistic

- We _____ [o-c-a-s-n-1-y-] see acts of altruism

that make us _____ [o-p-t-m-s-t-c-] about the

human race.

- "Do you remember any _____ [p-h-s-c-1-]

features of the _____ [m-s-t-e-r-u-s-] robber?"--

physical
mysterious
particular

"Yes, sir, I remember, in _____ [p-r-t-i-c-1-r-],

his fat finger on the trigger."

-                 *"New customs,*
Though they be never so _____ [r-d-i-c-l-u-s],
Nay, let 'em be unmanly, yet are follow'd."
              (Henry VIII, I, iii, 3)

ridiculous

DIRECTIONS: Continue as before. Study the spelling carefully. Write each word three times.

21. stric**t**ly   _____   _____   _____

22. su**bt**le   _____   _____   _____

23. su**cc**essfu**l**   _____   _____   _____

24. sup**reme**   _____   _____   _____

25. terr**i**ble   _____   _____   _____

26. undoubte**d**ly   _____   _____   _____

27. valu**a**ble   _____   _____   _____

28. vis**i**ble   _____   _____   _____

29. w**ei**rd   _____   _____   _____

30. wi**c**ked   _____   _____   _____

Review words 21-30. Then take the quiz.

QUIZ

COVER
THIS STRIP   FILL THE BLANKS

supreme
terrible

- The soldiers made the _____ [s-u-p-r-m-]

sacrifice; they ate the mess sergeant's _____

[t-e-r-b-l-] fish stew.

wicked
subtle

- The rich are as _____ [w-i-k-d-] as the poor,

but their sins are more _____ [s-u-t-l-].

undoubtedly
weird
visible

- Ichabod Crane was _____ [u-n-d-o-u-t-l-y-] as

_____ [w-e-r-d-] as any scarecrow _____

[v-s-b-l-] in the cornfields.

successful
valuable
strictly

- A businessman said that to be _____

[s-u-c-s-f-l-] you should sell a _____ [v-a-l-b-l-]

product, yes, and _____ [s-t-r-c-l-y] for cash.

wicked
subtle
terrible

- The serpent in the Garden was both _____

[w-i-k-d-] and _____ [s-u-t-l-], and Eve gave in

to the _____ [t-r-b-l-] temptation.

valuable
visible
undoubtedly

- A diamond is less _____ [v-a-l-b-l-] if flaws

are _____ [v-i-s-b-l-], and the same is

_____ [u-n-d-o-u-t-l-y-] true of a student essay.

weird
visible
valuable
wicked

- Radium, a _____ [w-e-r-d-] substance, is

_____ [v-s-b-l-] in darkness. It can be

_____ [v-a-l-b-l-] in cancer treatment, but it can

also have rather _____ [w-i-k-d-] side effects.

strictly
supreme
successful

- These eggs are _____ [s-t-r-c-l-y] fresh, the

_____ [s-u-p-r-m-] contribution of our highly

_____ [s-u-c-s-f-l-] chickens.

undoubtedly
subtle
successful
terrible

■ Some cartoonists _____ [u-n-d-o-u-t-l-y] are

too _____ [s-u-t-l-] to be _____

[s-u-c-s-f-l], a _____ [t-r-b-l-] mistake.

■ My roommate tasted the _____ [w-e-r-d-]

seedcake I had baked and, in a moment of _____

weird
supreme
strictly

[s-u-p-r-m-] honesty, said that it was "_____

[s-t-r-c-l-y] for the birds."

■ "...these _____ [w-e-r-d-] *sisters saluted
me, and referred me to the coming on of time, with 'Hail,
king, that shalt be!'"*

weird

(Macbeth, I, v, 8)

22

DĒC: TEN

31. **decade** (dek'ād) *n.* a period of ten years

     A **week** away from you is like a *decade*.
     It was the *decade* of Babe Ruth, Jack Dempsey, and Calvin Coolidge.

     jazz decade _____ _____
     (copy twice)

32. **decagon** (dek'ə gon') *n.* a plane figure with ten angles and ten sides

     The park was a grassy *decagon*.
     The baker cut out some *decagonal* cookies.

     shapely decagon _____ _____

33. **decathlon** (di kath'lon) *n.* an athletic contest consisting of ten track and field events

     The *decathlon* includes the pole vault, shot put, and dashes.
     Bruce Jenner won the Olympic *decathlon*.

     decathlon winner _____ _____

34. **decimal** (des'ə məl) *adj.* based on the number ten   *n.* a fraction such as 17.395 based on the number ten.

> The computer calculated interest to three *decimals*.
> The *decimal* fraction *.7* equals seven tenths.

decimal system   _____   _____

35. **decimate** (des'ə māt') *v.* to kill a great number of; originally, to pick by lot and kill every tenth man of

> The Great Plague *decimated* London in 1665.
> Lumber companies will *decimate* our huge redwoods.

to decimate cities   _____   _____

Review words 31-35. Then go on.

QUIZ

DIRECTIONS: Fill the blanks with words we studied that are derived from the Greek root DEC (ten). Be sure you spell the words correctly.

COVER
THIS STRIP
_____

decathlon	■ It takes a truly great all-around athlete to star in the _____ [d-c-t-l-n-].
decimate	■ Greedy fishermen continue to _____ [d-c-m-] the whales.
decagon	■ If the Pentagon is only half as efficient as it should be, maybe we should build a _____ [d-c-g-n-].
decagon decimal	■ In mathematics class we had to figure the area of a _____ [d-c-g-n-] to two _____ [d-c-m-l-] places.
decade decimate	■ We graciously brought our civilization to the South Sea islands, and within a _____ [d-c-d-] our diseases had begun to _____ [d-c-m-t-] the natives.

decimal decade decathlon	■ Because man has ten fingers, he devised the _____ [d-c-m-l-] system and began to think of ten years as a _____ [d-c-d-] and of a ten-event athletic contest as a _____ [d-c-t-l-n-].
decagon decimate	■ In World War III some generals huddled somewhere in a pentagon or a _____ [d-c-g-n-] may unleash the radioactive bombs that will _____ [d-c-m-t-] the world.
decade decathlon decimal	■ After practicing the ten events for an entire _____ [d-c-d-], Joe Shlupp competed in the _____ [d-c-t-l-n-] and was a mere _____ [d-c-m-l-] point short of winning thirteenth place.

Non-test examples

OTHER DERIVATIVES OF DEC (TEN):

decagram (dek'ə gram') *n.* ten grams

decahedron (dek'ə hē'drən) *n.* a solid figure that has ten plane surfaces

decaliter (dek'ə lēt'ər) *n.* ten liters

Decalogue (dek'ə lôg') *n.* the Ten Commandments

Decameron (di kam'ər ən) *n.* a collection of tales (1353) by Boccaccio, presumably told by ten travelers during a ten-day period

decameter (dek'ə mē'tər) *n.* ten meters

decapod (dek'ə pod) *n.* a ten-legged crustacean such as a lobster, crab, or crayfish

decasyllable (dek'ə sil'ə bəl) *n.* a ten-syllable line of poetry

December (di sem'bər) *n.* the twelfth month of the year; originally the tenth month of the ancient Roman year

decemvir (di sem'vər) *n.* a member of a ten-man ruling council

decennial (di sen'ē əl) *adj.* occurring every ten years *n.* a tenth anniversary

decibel (des'ə bel') *n.* a unit expressing the intensity of a sound wave

decigram (des'ə gram') *n.* one-tenth gram

deciliter (des'ə lē'tər) *n.* one-tenth liter

decillion (di sil'yən) *n.* a number written in the United States as 1 followed by thirty-three zeros.

decimeter (des'ə mē'tər) *n.* one-tenth meter

DERM: SKIN

36. **dermatitis** (dur'mə tīt'is) *n.* inflammation of the skin

> The poison oak caused our *dermatitis*.
> *Dermatitis* made him scratch like a chicken.

severe dermatitis _____ _____
 (copy twice)

37. **dermatologist** (dur'mə tol'ə jist) *n.* a specialist in skin and its diseases

> Dr. Skinner, as you might guess, was a *dermatologist*.
> The *dermatologist* cured the baby's skin rash.

skilled dermatologist _____ _____

38. **epidermis** (ep'ə dur'mis) *n.* the outermost layer of skin, covering the true skin

> Sunburn causes the *epidermis* to peel.
> The scratch barely tore the *epidermis*.

flaky epidermis _____ _____

39. **hypodermic** (hī'pə dur'mik) *adj.* injected under the skin *n.* an injection under the skin

> The diabetic patient was given a *hypodermic*.
> A *hypodermic* injection preceded surgery.

hypodermic needle _____ _____

40. **pachyderm** (păk'ə dûrm') *n.* a large thick-skinned animal such as the elephant, hippopotamus, or rhinoceros

On the *pachyderm's* head sat the trainer.
Mervin cleaned up behind the *pachyderms*.

a huge pachyderm _____ _____

Review words 36-40. Then go on.

QUIZ

DIRECTIONS: Fill the blanks with words we studied that are derived from the Greek root DERM (skin). Be sure you spell the words correctly.

COVER
THIS STRIP

pachyderm	■ Knute knew that this was a traveling elephant because the _____ [p-a-d-m-] was carrying a trunk.
epidermis dermatitis	■ Dave applied a dab of butter to his facial _____ [e-p-d-s-] and cured his _____ [d-m-t-s-].
hypodermic dermatitis	■ Mary didn't think that getting a _____ [h-p-d-c-] to treat her _____ [d-m-t-s-] was such a sharp idea.
dermatologist hypodermic pachyderm	■ The _____ [d-m-t-g-t-] bent three needles trying to give a _____ [h-y-d-c-] to a _____ [p-a-d-m-].
hypodermic epidermis	■ A _____ [h-p-d-c-] needle has to go in way past the _____ [e-p-d-s-], and that hurts.
dermatologist epidermis dermatitis	■ The _____ [d-m-t-g-t-] took one look at the _____ [e-p-d-s-] of my finger and said, "A nice case of _____ [d-m-t-s-]. Thirty dollars please."

■ An elephant doesn't mind being insulted by a

dermatologist
pachyderm

_____ [d-m-t-g-t-] because a _____

[p-a-d-m-] is not thin-skinned.

Non-test examples

OTHER DERIVATIVES OF DERM (SKIN):

derma (dur'mə) *n.* beef casing that is stuffed and roasted; kishka

dermatoid (dur'mə toid') *adj.* resembling skin

dermatophyte (dər mat'ə fīt') *n.* a parasitic plant on the skin, such as the fungus that causes ringworm

dermatoplasty (dər mat'ə plas'tē) *n.* skin grafting

dermatosis (dər'mə tō'sis) *n.* any skin disorder

endoderm (en'də durm') *n.* the inner cells of the embryo from which various inner linings are formed

---

DYN: POWER

41. dynamic (dī nam'ik) *adj.* energetic; forceful; relating to energy

> La Guardia had a *dynamic* personality.
> We must find *dynamic* fuels other than oil.

a dynamic woman
(copy twice)

_____ _____

42. dynamite (di'nə mīt') *n.* a powerful explosive *v.* to blow up with dynamite

> Miners blasted the rocks with *dynamite*.
> A soldier is sent to *dynamite* the bridge.

sticks of dynamite

_____ _____

43. dynamo (dī'nə mō') *n.* an electric generator; an energetic, forceful person

> The electric plant installed a huge *dynamo*.
> Al Lamson was a *dynamo* at left guard.

a human dynamo

_____ _____

44. dynasty (dī'nə stē) *n.* a series of rulers who are of the same family; the period of reign of a certain family

He was founder of the illustrious Ming *dynasty*.
A Ford *dynasty* developed in Detroit.

<u>a banking dynasty</u> _____ _____

Review words 41-44. Then go on.

QUIZ

DIRECTIONS: Fill the blanks with words we studied that are derived from the Greek root DYN (power). Be sure you spell the words correctly.

COVER
THIS STRIP

dynamo	■ The generator in an automobile was once referred to as a _____ [d-n-o-].
dynasty	■ A nation headed by presidents, instead of emperors, is not likely to produce a ruling _____ [d-n-y-].
dynamic dynamite	■ In 1866 a _____ [d-n-m-c-] Swede named Alfred Nobel invented _____ [d-n-m-t-].
dynamo dynasty	■ Joseph Kennedy, a _____ [d-n-m-o-] of industry, headed a _____ [d-n-y-] of statesmen.
dynamite dynamo dynamic	■ A gang of extortionists tried to plant some _____ [d-n-m-t-] under the huge _____ [d-n-o-], but their plot was foiled by a _____ [d-n-m-c-] detective named Ginsburg.
dynasty dynamic dynamite	■ The American stage has had its _____ [d-n-y] of Barrymores, a _____ [d-n-m-c-] family of actors who were _____ [d-n-m-t-] at the box office.

OTHER DERIVATIVES OF DYN (POWER):

dynameter (dī nam'ə tər) *n.* a device for finding the magnifying power of a telescope

dynamics (dī nam'iks) *n.* the branch of mechanics dealing with the effects of forces on the motion of bodies

dynamism (dī'nə miz'əm) *n.* the theory that energy rather than mass is the basic principle of nature

dynamoelectric (di'nə mō i lek'trik) *adj.* having to do with changing electrical energy into mechanical energy, or vice versa

dynamometer (di'nə mom'ə tər) *n.* a device that measures mechanical power

dyne (dīn) *n.* a standard unit of force

dynode (dī'nōd) *n.* an electrode in an electron tube that increases the power of incoming signals

electrodynamics (i lek'trō dī nam'iks) *n.* the branch of physics that deals with the relationship of electric currents and magnetic forces

hydrodynamics (hī'drō dī nam'iks) *n.* the branch of physics that deals with the motions and forces of liquids

superheterodyne (sōō'pər het'ər ə dīn') *adj.* involving a type of radio reception which amplifies the power of carrier waves by special circuits

thermodynamics (thur'mō dī nam'iks) *n.* the branch of physics that deals with the transformation of heat into mechanical energy and vice versa

---

GRAM, GRAPH: WRITE

45. calligraphy (kə lig'rə fē) *n.* beautiful handwriting; the art of fancy penmanship

> The art department offers a course in *calligraphy*.
> The doctor's *calligraphy* looked like pigeon tracks.

<u>neat calligraphy</u> _____ _____
(copy twice)

46. **epigram** (ep′ə gram′) *n.* a short, witty, quotable statement, often
with a surprise twist

> Her essay was colorful and *epigrammatic*.
> Oscar Wilde's *epigrams* were on every lip.

witty epigram _____   _____

47. **graffiti** (grə fē′tē) *n.* crude drawings or scribblings on public walls

> The gangs marked their boundaries with *graffiti*.
> Hideous *graffiti* marred the walls and fences.

weird graffiti _____   _____

48. **grammar** (gram′ər) *n.* a body of rules for writing and speaking a given
language

> The lower grades are known as *grammar* school.
> Latin *grammar* includes a dative case and an ablative case.

grammar rules _____   _____

49. **graphic** (graf′ik) *adj.* vivid; realistic; giving a clear picture;
written or drawn

> Linda gave a *graphic* description of the accident.
> The sailor's language was unnecessarily *graphic*.

graphic arts _____   _____

50. **seismograph** (sīz′mə graf′) *n.* an instrument that records the
intensity of earthquakes

> The *seismograph* registered a major shock.
> The *seismographer* located the epicenter of the quake.

seismograph record _____   _____

Review words 45-50. Then go on.

QUIZ

DIRECTIONS: Fill the blanks with words we studied that are derived from the Greek root GRAM-GRAPH (write). Be sure you spell the words correctly.

COVER
THIS STRIP

seismograph	■ The inventor of the _____ [s-i-s-m-g-] got a big bang out of it.
graphic graffiti	■ In _____ [g-r-c-] language the butcher swore that he'd carve up the next kid who painted _____ [g-f-t-] on the walls of his shop.
epigram calligraphy	■ Alonzo threw an original _____ [e-p-g-] into his composition now and then, so the teacher happily forgave his miserable _____ [c-1-g-y].
grammar graphic epigram	■ A textbook of _____ [g-r-m-r-] would be more exciting if it included a few _____ [g-p-c-] illustrations and an occasional _____ [e-p-g-].
seismograph graphic	■ The Caltech _____ [s-i-s-m-g-] had made a _____ [g-p-c-] record of the huge earthquake.
graffiti grammar calligraphy	■ The lavatory walls were besmirched with obscene _____ [g-f-t-] scrawled in bad _____ [g-r-m-r-] and wretched _____ [c-1-g-y].
calligraphy epigram grammar	■ In impressive _____ [c-1-g-y] the author wrote a brief _____ [e-p-g-] on the flyleaf of my _____ [g-r-m-r-] book.
graffiti seismograph	■ Some of the _____ [g-f-t-] on the subway walls were so earthshaking that one expected them to register on a _____ [s-i-s-m-g-].

OTHER DERIVATIVES OF GRAM-GRAPH (WRITE):

cryptogram (krip'tə gram') *n.* a message written in code or cipher

diagram (dī'ə gram') *n.* a sketch, graph, or geometrical figure that explains or illustrates an idea

geography (jē og'rə fē) *n.* the science that deals with the earth--its physical features, climate, crops, people, etc; the surface features of a region [*the geography of Alaska*]; a book dealing with these things

graph (graf) *n.* a diagram which presents the relationship of variable quantities by means of bars, curves, etc. [*a cost-of-living graph*]

graphite (graf'īt) *n.* a soft black form of carbon used in lead pencils, lubricants, etc.

graphology (gra fol'ə jē) *n.* the study of handwriting, especially as a reflection of the writer's character

holograph (hol'ə graf') *adj.* handwritten entirely by its author [*a holograph will*] *n.* a document so written

lithograph (lith'ə graf') *n.* a print made by a process involving a flat stone or metal plate, on which a design has been made with a greasy material

mimeograph (mim'ē ə graf') *n.* a machine that prints copies by means of a stencil fastened to a drum containing ink

phonograph (fō'nə graf') *n.* an instrument that reproduces sound recorded on a flat disc or a cylinder

photograph (fō'tə graf') *n.* a picture taken with a camera *v.* to take a picture of [*to photograph the bride*]

ungrammatical (un'grə mat'i kəl) *adj.* breaking the rules of grammar [*ungrammatical sentences*]

telegraph (tel'ə graf') *n.* a system for transmitting coded impulses by wire or radio *v.* to send a message by such means

typography (tī pog'rə fē) *n.* the art of printing with type; the style and appearance of printed matter [*clean typography*]

Review words 1-50, spelling and vocabulary. Then take the Chapters 21-22 Self-Test.

DIRECTIONS: Write the words in full. Complete this entire test before you check and grade your answers.

_____ 1. Your most [v-a-l-b-l-] asset is your education.
_____ 2. On smogless days the mountains are [v-s-b-l-].
_____ 3. If you are happy, you are [s-u-c-s-f-l-].
_____ 4. A baby has [i-n-f-n-t-e-] beauty to its mother.
_____ 5. Some people are [w-i-k-d-] and some are like you.
_____ 6. Railroad tracks should be exactly [p-r-l-e-l-].
_____ 7. Lucy has a [l-v-l-y-] face and a heart to match.
_____ 8. From the chemistry lab came a [m-s-t-e-r-u-s-] odor.
_____ 9. Children should not be told about [t-e-r-b-l-] dragons.
_____ 10. By December 26, Santa is a [p-h-s-c-l-] wreck.
_____ 11. My black eye may be [n-o-t-c-b-l-].
_____ 12. Much illness is [i-m-a-g-n-r-y-].
_____ 13. All religions are [r-d-c-u-l-s-] except our own.
_____ 14. When you're sixteen, your parents seem very [i-g-n-r-n-t-].
_____ 15. Bring the butterfly net [i-m-e-d-t-l-y-] for Benny.
_____ 16. Don't become a victim of [m-o-d-r-n-] comforts.
_____ 17. His last words were "I am [i-n-o-c-n-t-]!"
_____ 18. To run a four-minute mile seemed [i-n-c-r-d-b-l-].
_____ 19. The neighbor's dog [s-i-n-c-r-l-y-] loves our garbage.
_____ 20. Dickens was the [s-u-p-r-m-] novelist of his era.
_____ 21. Our ship captain was [o-c-a-s-n-l-y-] sober.
_____ 22. Many women prefer to be [i-n-d-p-d-n-t-].
_____ 23. Fleagle is as [s-u-t-l-] as a foghorn.
_____ 24. Ben Franklin, [i-n-c-d-n-t-l-y-], invented a stove.
_____ 25. The salami was [s-t-r-c-l-y-] kosher.
_____ 26. It costs nothing to be [o-p-t-m-s-t-c-].
_____ 27. A child that isn't [m-i-s-c-h-v-s-] is probably sick.
_____ 28. Eat at Sloppy Sam's, if you aren't [p-r-t-c-l-r-].
_____ 29. The Martians found [w-e-r-d-] two-legged beasts on earth.
_____ 30. Mother is [u-n-d-o-u-t-l-y-] your best friend.

Write correctly the words we studied that are derived from the Greek roots DEC, DERM, DYN, and GRAM—GRAPH:

_____ 31. The coal miner set off a charge of [d-n-m-t-].
_____ 32. Our library uses the Dewey [d-e-m-l-] system.
_____ 33. Teddy Roosevelt was an extremely [d-n-m-c-] president.
_____ 34. The tiger was tranquilized by a [h-p-d-r-c-] injection.
_____ 35. The flapper age began during the [d-c-d-] of the 1920s.
_____ 36. I had a big zoo job. I washed the [p-a-c-d-m-].
_____ 37. We noticed some nasty phrases among the [g-r-a-f-i-].
_____ 38. This insecticide will [d-c-m-t-] the roaches.
_____ 39. Hemingway wrote punchy, [g-r-c-] prose.
_____ 40. A writer must master the rules of [g-r-m-r-].

Write the letter that indicates the best definition.

( ) 41. calligraphy   a. an earthquake recorder
( ) 42. decagon   b. a skin specialist
( ) 43. decathlon   c. an era of family rule
( ) 44. dermatitis   d. fancy handwriting
( ) 45. dermatologist   e. the top layer of skin
( ) 46. dynamo   f. a clever, quotable statement
( ) 47. dynasty   g. a ten-sided figure
( ) 48. epidermis   h. inflammation of the skin
( ) 49. epigram   i. an electric generator
( ) 50. seismograph   j. a ten-event contest

ANSWER KEY

Check your test answers by the following key. Deduct 2% per error from 100%.

1. valuable	11. noticeable	21. occasionally	31. dynamite	41. d
2. visible	12. imaginary	22. independent	32. decimal	42. g
3. successful	13. ridiculous	23. subtle	33. dynamic	43. j
4. infinite	14. ignorant	24. incidentally	34. hypodermic	44. h
5. wicked	15. immediately	25. strictly	35. decade	45. b
6. parallel	16. modern	26. optimistic	36. pachyderm	46. i
7. lovely	17. innocent	27. mischievous	37. graffiti	47. c
8. mysterious	18. incredible	28. particular	38. decimate	48. e
9. terrible	19. sincerely	29. weird	39. graphic	49. f
10. physical	20. supreme	30. undoubtedly	40. grammar	50. a

Score: _____ %

Review carefully any words which you have missed in the foregoing Self-Test.

Your instructor will give you a final test on words 1-50 in Chapters 17 and 18.

23

DIRECTIONS: Study the spelling of each word carefully, giving special attention to the trouble spots (underlined letters). Then write each word neatly three times.

1. absen_c_e _____ _____ _____

2. admi_ss_ion _____ _____ _____

3. al_co_hol _____ _____ _____

4. app_e_tite _____ _____ _____

5. arriv_a_l _____ _____ _____

6. a_u_tomobile _____ _____ _____

7. bic_y_cle _____ _____ _____

8. Brit_ai_n _____ _____ _____

9. bur_gl_ar _____ _____ _____

10. calend_a_r _____ _____ _____

Review words 1-10 until you are sure you can spell them. Then go on and take the quiz.

COVER THIS STRIP	FILL THE BLANKS

automobile	■ Repairing _____ [a-t-m-b-l-] mufflers is exhausting work.
alcohol	■ Boozers always find _____ [a-l-c-h-l]; they have a "fifth" sense.
absence	■ If _____ [a-b-s-n-] makes the heart grow fonder, teacher must love Johnny.
calendar	■ Take this _____ [c-a-l-n-d-r]. Its days are numbered.
burglar bicycle automobile	■ The _____ [b-r-g-l-r] said he stole the _____ [b-i-c-l-] and the _____ [a-t-m-b-l-] because money alone doesn't bring happiness.
arrival Britain automobile	■ Upon his _____ [a-r-i-v-l] in Great _____ [B-r-t-n], the amateur tennis star was given an expensive _____ [a-t-m-b-l-] for his very own.
calendar burglar alcohol bicycle	■ Next on the court _____ [c-a-l-n-d-r] was an old _____ [b-r-g-l-r] who had snatched a pint of _____ [a-l-c-h-l] and wobbled off on his _____ [b-i-c-l-].
admission appetite	■ The old boarding house charged thirty cents _____ [a-d-m-i-s-n], and one ate until one's _____ [a-p-t-i-t] said, "I surrender, dear."
automobile burglar bicycle	■ Somebody took Clem's _____ [a-t-m-b-l-], the one with the _____ [b-r-g-l-r] alarm, and Clem had to ride home on a _____ [b-i-c-l-].
absence	■ "I'd visit you, dear," wrote Joe, "but my _____ [a-b-s-n-] from this jail might cause comment."

admission
arrival

■ The lunatic was granted _____ [a-d-m-i-s-n]

to Happy Meadows on _____ [a-r-i-v-l].

■ Laborers in Great _____ [B-r-i-t-n] have a

Britain
appetite

splendid _____ [a-p-t-i-t-] for beef.

■ The early movies cost five cents _____

admission

[a-d-m-i-s-n], and they were worth it, too.

■ A guzzler in Great _____ [B-r-i-t-n] was

indulging his _____ [a-p-t-i-t-] for cheap

Britain
appetite
alcohol

_____ [a-l-c-h-l], then fell off a building

and hasn't had a drop since.

■ According to my _____ [c-a-l-n-d-r], our baby's

calendar
arrival

_____[a-r-i-v-l] will be on Groundhog Day.

absence

■ Your _____ [a-b-s-n-] won't improve your grades.

■ *"...but doth not the _____ [a-p-t-i-t-]*
alter? a man loves the meat in his youth that he cannot
endure in his age."

appetite

(Much Ado About Nothing, II, viii, 247)

DIRECTIONS: Continue as before. Study the spelling carefully. Write each
word three times.

11. can_di_date _____ _____ _____

12. car_ee_r _____ _____ _____

13. cat_e_gory _____ _____ _____

14. cem_e_tery _____ _____ _____

15. _c_er_ea_l _____ _____ _____

16. chara_c_ter _____ _____ _____

17. chauv_i_nism _____ _____ _____

18. con_sci_ence _____ _____ _____

19. counsel_o_r _____ _____ _____

20. c_ou_rage _____ _____ _____

Review words 11-20. Then take the quiz.

COVER THIS STRIP	FILL THE BLANKS
character	■ I bought venetian blinds from a shady _____ [c-a-r-a-t-r].
courage category	■ Some folks are timid; some have _____ [c-u-r-g-e]. In which _____ [c-a-t-g-r-y] do you belong?
career cemetery	■ Gray's "Elegy" says that every _____ [c-r-e-r-], great or lowly, ends in the _____ [c-m-t-r-y].
cereal chauvinism	■ The housewife cooks the breakfast _____ [-e-r-el], and the man eats it; and that, too, is male _____ [c-a-v-n-s-m].
category conscience counselor	■ A certain _____ [c-a-t-g-r-y] of people can let their _____ [c-o-n-s-n-c-] be their guide; but I need a more reliable _____ [c-o-n-s-l-r].
candidate conscience	■ When a political _____ [c-a-n-d-a-t-] wrestles with his _____ [c-o-n-s-n-c-], it's a lightweight match.
courage cereal cemetery	■ Someone with _____ [c-u-r-g-e] should point out on TV that sugary _____ [-e-r-e-1] and salty snacks can nudge us toward the _____ [c-m-t-r-y].
chauvinism cemetery	■ Male _____ [c-a-v-n-s-m] began with Adam, and it should be buried in the _____ [c-m-t-r-y] of the dead past.
character candidate category	■ Abe Lincoln had lofty _____ [c-a-r-a-t-r] and therefore, as a _____ [c-a-n-d-a-t-] for office, did not fall into any common _____ [c-a-t-g-r-y].
cemetery	■ In my new job I have a thousand people under me. I cut grass at the _____ [c-m-t-r-y].

■ A folksy _____ [c-a-r-a-t-r] in the TV

commercial confided that he was a success in his

character
career
cereal

_____ [c-r-e-r-] because he ate a packaged

_____ [-e-r-e-1] with a nutty flavor.

■ As for the _____ [c-a-r-a-t-r] of a good

character
counselor
courage
conscience

student _____ [c-o-n-s-1-r], she should have

_____ [c-u-r-g-e], yes, and a _____

[c-o-n-s-n-c-], too.

■ Betty was a _____ [c-a-n-d-a-t-] for the

candidate
counselor
chauvinism
career

position of _____ [c-o-n-s-1-r], but the male

[c-a-v-n-s-m] of the school board forestalled that possible

_____ [c-r-e-r-].

■   "The play's the thing
          Wherein I'll catch the _____ [c-o-n-s-n-c-]

conscience

             of the king."   (Hamlet, II, ii, 641)

DIRECTIONS: Continue as before. Study the spelling carefully. Write each word three times.

21. criticism _____ _____ _____

22. curiosity _____ _____ _____

23. decision _____ _____ _____

24. democracy _____ _____ _____

25. description _____ _____ _____

26. discipline _____ _____ _____

27. electricity _____ _____ _____

28. entrance _____ _____ _____

29. environment _____ _____ _____

30. excitement _____ _____ _____

Review words 21-30. Then take the quiz.

COVER
THIS STRIP   FILL THE BLANKS
_____

curiosity
electricity

■ Although _____ [c-u-r-s-t-y] killed the cat,

it also led men to harness _____ [e-l-c-t-r-t-y].

description
environment

■ Fanny the Firefly wrote a glowing _____

[d-s-c-p-t-n] of her new _____ [e-n-v-r-m-n-t].

democracy
criticism

■ A genuine _____ [d-e-m-c-r-y] welcomes

_____ [c-r-i-t-s-m].

entrance
discipline

■ Don't seek _____ [e-n-t-r-n-c-] to West Point

unless you enjoy strict _____ [d-i-c-p-l-n-].

description
excitement

■ The _____ [d-s-c-p-t-n] of California's

gold nuggets aroused intense _____

[e-x-i-t-m-n-t] in the East.

■ Horses should have a stable _____

environment

[e-n-v-r-m-n-t].

■ Ben Franklin wrote a graphic _____ [d-s-c-p-t-n]

description
curiosity
electricity

of his _____ [c-u-r-s-t-y] about lightning and

_____ [e-l-c-t-r-t-y].

■ At the _____ [e-n-t-r-n-c-] to Muir Woods,

Paula posted a sharp _____ [c-r-i-t-s-m] of

entrance
criticism
environment

factories that would pollute and destroy our lovely

natural _____ [e-n-v-r-m-n-t].

■ The fight fans roared in _____ [e-x-i-t-m-n-t]

as the referee awarded the _____ [d-e-s-i-o-n]

excitement
decision

to Moosejaw Mulligan.

democracy
environment
decision
discipline

■ American _____ [d-e-m-c-r-y] provides an

ideal _____ [e-n-v-r-m-n-t] for people of

_____ [d-e-s-i-o-n] and self-_____

[d-i-c-p-l-n-], as well as for bums.

■ As election day nears, you feel an _____

[e-x-i-t-m-n-t] because our great _____

excitement
democracy
decision

[d-e-m-c-r-y] is about to make an historic

_____ [d-e-s-i-o-n].

■ The landlord turned off my _____

[e-l-c-t-r-t-y], just because I gave him some honest

electricity
criticism

_____ [c-r-i-t-s-m].

■ "Mr. Edison, I have traits of _____ [c-u-r-s-t-y]

and _____ [d-i-c-p-l-n-]," I said, "and I

crave _____ [e-n-t-r-n-c-] to the field of

science." But Edison, being deaf, did not hear me; so he

curiosity
discipline
entrance
electricity

went right on inventing something—I think it was

_____ [e-l-c-t-r-t-y]—without me.

■   "...we do admire
          This virtue and this moral _____ [d-i-c-p-l-n-]"
discipline   *(Taming of the Shrew, I, i, 30)*

GREEK ROOTS: "LOG" TO "PAN"

24

LOG: WORD; STUDY

31. **dialogue** (dī'ə log) *n.* a talking together of two or more persons; conversation between characters of a story or play; an exchange of ideas for the purpose of settling an issue

> Abbott and Costello's *dialogue* began, "Who's on first?"
> The statesmen began a *dialogue* at the summit meeting.

witty dialogue _____ _____
(copy twice)

32. **eulogy** (yōō'lə jē) *n.* high praise of a person or event; a speech praising someone who has died

> The oil man began a warm *eulogy* of Texas.
> The munitions maker *eulogized* the dead soldiers.

lofty eulogy _____ _____

33. **geology** (jē ol'ə jē) *n.* the science that deals with the physical structure of the earth, including rock formations and their origins; the physical features of a given region

> Ms. Perkins discussed the *geology* of Peru.
> The *geologist* found oil-bearing shale.

geology major _____ _____

34. prologue (prō'lŏg) *n.* an introduction to a play or poem; a preface; a preamble

        The curtain rose, and an actor read the *prologue*.
        The wedding-day quarrel was *prologue* to a stormy marriage.

<u>brief prologue</u>   _____   _____

35. theology (thē ŏl'ə jē) *n.* the study of God and of religious truths; the beliefs of a particular religion

        The seminary was open to students of *theology*.
        The *theologian* discussed the gospels.

<u>Christian theology</u>   _____   _____

Review words 31–35. Then go on.

QUIZ

DIRECTIONS: Fill the blanks with words we studied that are derived from the Greek root LOG (word; study). Be sure you spell the words correctly.

COVER
THIS STRIP

prologue dialogue	■ The drama opened with a _____ [p-r-l-g-], after which came a comic _____ [d-i-l-o-g-].
eulogy geology	■ Our loose-jawed guide delivered a sugary _____ [-u-l-g-y] of the Alpine _____ [g-o-l-g-y].
prologue theology	■ Emily read the Bible as a _____ [p-r-l-g-] to her study of _____ [t-h-e-l-g-].
dialogue eulogy	■ Sandra ended her _____ [d-i-l-o-g-] with the chef with a _____ [-u-l-g-y] of the apple strudel.
prologue	■ The earthquake was merely _____ [p-r-l-g-] to greater disasters.
dialogue theology geology	■ We listened to an angry _____ [d-i-l-o-g-] between the professors of _____ [t-h-e-l-g-] and of _____ [g-o-l-g-y].

theology eulogy geology	■ The minister, well versed in _____ [t-h-e-l-g-], delivered a _____ [-u-l-g-y] over the battered body of the _____ [g-o-l-g-y] student.

Non-test examples

OTHER DERIVATIVES OF LOG (WORD; STUDY):

apology (ə pol'ə jē) *n.* an expression of regret for having wronged another

anthology (an thol'ə jē) *n.* a collection of selected stories, poems, or excerpts

anthropology (an'thrə pol'ə jē) *n.* the study of man, his origins, physical characteristics, culture, and customs

cardiology (kär'dē ol'ə jē) *n.* the study of the heart

cetology (si tol'ə jē) *n.* the study of whales

conchology (kong kol'ə jē) *n.* the study of shells and mollusks

craniology (krā nē ol'ə jē) *n.* the study of human skulls

doxology (dok sol'ə jē) *n.* a hymn or verse of praise to God

embryology (em'brē ol'ə jē) *n.* the study of embryos

eschatology (es'kə tol'ə jē) *n.* the branch of theology that deals with death, judgment, future state of the soul, etc.

ethnology (eth nol'ə jē) *n.* the study of racial and ethnic groups

genealogy (jē'nē ol'ə jē) *n.* the study of family ancestries

graphology (gra fol'ə jē) *n.* the study of handwriting, especially as a clue to the writer's character

gynecology (gī'nə kol'ə jē) *n.* the study of the functions and diseases peculiar to women

hippology (hi pol'ə jē) *n.* the study of horses

histology (hi stol'ə jē) *n.* the study of organic tissues

hydrology (hi drol'ə jē) *n.* the study of the waters of the earth

logic (loj'ik) *n.* the study of correct reasoning; valid induction and deduction

logorrhea (log'ə rē'ə) *n.* excessive talkativeness

martyrology (mär'tə rol'ə jē) *n.* the study of the lives of religious martyrs mineralogy (min'ə ral'ə jē) *n.* the study of minerals

mythology (mi thol'ə jē) *n.* the study of myths

necrology (ne krol'ə jē) *n.* a list of those who have died

oology (ō ol'ə jē) *n.* the study of birds' eggs

paleontology (pā'lē on tol'ə jē) *n.* the study of ancient forms of life

pathology (pə thol'ə jē) *n.* the study of diseases

petrology (pə trol'ə jē) *n.* the study of rocks

pharmacology (fär'mə kol'ə jē) *n.* the study of drugs

philology (fi lol'ə jē) *n.* the study of written records to determine authenticity and meaning

phrenology (fri nol'ə jē) *n.* the study of the skull's shape as a clue to character

sexology (seks ol'ə jē) *n.* the study of human sexual behavior

sociology (sō'sē ol'ə jē) *n.* the study of human society

symbology (sim bol'ə jē) *n.* the study of symbols; symbolism

tautology (tô tol'ə jē) *n.* unnecessary repetition of an idea in different words, as in "small little midget" and "some reading books"

technology (tek nol'ə jē) *n.* the ways by which material things are produced in industry, manufacturing, commerce, and the arts

terminology (tûr'mə nol'ə jē) *n.* the system of terms used in a science, art, or specialized subject

tetralogy (te tral'ə jē) *n.* a series of four related literary works

trilogy (tril'ə jē) *n.* a series of three related literary works

volcanology (vol'kən ol'ə jē) *n.* the study of volcanoes

zoology (zō ol'ə jē) *n.* the study of animals

METR, METER: MEASURE

36. barometer (bə rom'ə tər) *n.* an instrument that measures atmospheric pressure; anything that indicates change

> A falling *barometer* suggests rain.
> *Barometric* pressure can indicate elevation.

mercury barometer _____ _____
(copy twice)

37. chronometer (krə nom'ə tər) *n.* a timepiece such as a very accurate clock or watch, possibly used for scientific purposes

> The navigator consulted the *chonometer*.
> The Swiss have excelled in *chronometry*.

precise chronometer _____ _____

38. metric (met'rik) *adj.* using the meter and gram as units of measurement

> Scientists use the *metric* system.
> A thousand kilograms equal a *metric* ton.

metric units _____ _____

39. micrometer (mi krom'ə tər) *n.* an instrument for measuring tiny angles, distances, etc., as in connection with a microscope or telescope

> I adjusted the *micrometer* of my telescope.
> Measure the thickness of the wire with a *micrometer*.

micrometer reading _____ _____

40. pentameter (pen tam'ə tər) *adj.* consisting of five metrical feet; *n.* a line of verse containing five metrical feet or measures

> Bryant's "Thanatopsis" uses the classic *pentameter* verse.
> The *pentameter* line has more dignity than the shorter tetrameter.

iambic pentameter _____ _____

Review words 36-40. Then go on.

QUIZ

DIRECTIONS: Fill the blanks with words we studied that are derived from the Greek root METR, METER (measure). Be sure you spell the words correctly.

COVER
THIS STRIP

metric	■ The meter is the basic unit of the _____ [m-t-c] system.
barometer chronometer	■ Captain Crock checked the falling _____ [b-r-m-r] and then his _____ [c-r-n-m-r], and muttered: "We're in for a bit of a blow!"

pentameter	■ Shakespeare's blank verse is in iambic _____ [p-n-t-m-r].
metric micrometer	■ The optometrist measured the thickness of my broken lens in _____ [m-t-c] units with a _____ [m-i-c-m-r].
chronometer pentameter	■ The poet took five hours by the village _____ [c-r-n-m-r] to complete the poem in iambic _____ [p-n-t-m-r].
metric	■ What will we call footnotes when we adopt the _____ [m-t-c] system?
chronometer micrometer	■ For exact time, use a _____ [c-r-n-m-r]; for exact measurement, use a _____ [m-i-c-m-r].
pentameter	■ Add one measure to a tetrameter (four metrical feet), and your line of poetry becomes a _____ [p-n-t-m-r].
barometer metric	■ A mercury _____ [b-r-m-r] will give readings in inches if it is not on the _____ [m-t-c] system.
micrometer	■ Looey the lab technician carefully adjusted the _____ [m-i-c-m-r] of his Swiss microscope.

OTHER DERIVATIVES OF METR, METER (MEASURE):   *Non-test examples*

ammeter (am'mē tər) *n.* an instrument for measuring amperes of electrical current

geometry (jē om'ə trē) *n.* the branch of mathematics that deals with space and its relations

hydrometer (hī drom'ə tər) *n.* an instrument for measuring the specific gravity of a liquid

metrology (mə trol'ə jē) *n.* the science of weights and measures

metronome (me'trə nōm') *n.* an instrument for marking musical rhythm

seismometer (sīz mom'ə tər) *n.* an instrument for recording and measuring earthquakes; a seismograph

spectrometer (spek trom'ə tər) *n.* an instrument for measuring the wave length of a ray of light

speedometer (spi dom'ə tər) *n.* an instrument for measuring the speed of a vehicle

telemeter (tə lem'ə tər) *n.* an instrument for measuring distance to a remote object

thermometer (thər mom'ə tər) *n.* an instrument for measuring temperature

trigonometry (trig'ə nom'ə trē) *n.* the branch of mathematics that deals with the relations of the angles and sides of triangles

The root METER is used in measures of length:

meter (mē'tər) *n.* a unit of length equal to 39.37 inches.

decameter (dek'ə mē'tər) *n.* ten meters

hectometer (hek'tə mē'tər) *n.* one hundred meters

kilometer (ki lom'ə tər) *n.* one thousand meters

decimeter (des'ə mē'tər) *n.* one tenth of a meter

centimeter (sen'tə mē'tər) *n.* one hundredth of a meter

millimeter (mil'ə mē'tər) *n.* one thousandth of a meter

The root METER is used in terms that identify types of poetic verse:

dimeter (dim'ə tər) *n.* a line of verse consisting of two metrical feet

trimeter (trim'ə tər) *n.* a verse consisting of three metrical feet

tetrameter (te tram'ə tər) *n.* a verse consisting of four metrical feet

pentameter (pen tam'ə tər) *n.* a verse consisting of five metrical feet

hexameter (hek sam'ə tər) *n.* a verse consisting of six metrical feet

heptameter (hep tam'ə tər) *n.* a verse consisting of seven metrical feet

octameter (ok tam'ə tər) *n.* a verse consisting of eight metrical feet

41. **neuralgia** (nyoo ral′jē ə) *n.* sharp pain along the course of a nerve

> The old man was tortured by *neuralgia*.
> *Neuralgic* pains sent her to the aspirin bottle.

chronic neuralgia　　——————————————　　——————————————
　(copy twice)

42. **neurologist** (nyoo rol′ə jist) *n.* a doctor who deals with disorders of the nervous system

> The *neurologist* discovered a pinched nerve.
> The pitcher's elbow was checked by a *neurologist*.

skillful neurologist　　——————————————　　——————————————

43. **neurosis** (nyoo rō′sis) *n.* an emotional disorder less serious than a psychosis but marked by feelings of anxiety, depression, compulsions, obsessions, or phobias; psychoneurosis

> Nancy's *neurosis* involved a morbid fear of germs.
> Mama's worry about her unmarried daughter became a *neurosis*.

minor neurosis　　——————————————　　——————————————

44. **neurotic** (nyoo rot′ik) *adj.* suffering from an emotional disorder or neurosis *n.* a person with a neurosis

> Everybody is, to some extent, *neurotic*.
> My *neurotic* uncle has four bolts on each door.

neurotic traits　　——————————————　　——————————————

Review words 41-44. Then go on.

QUIZ

DIRECTIONS: Fill the blanks with words we studied that are derived from the Greek root NEUR (nerve). Be sure you spell the words correctly.

COVER
THIS STRIP

———

	■ Although he's extremely afraid of cats, my ————————
neurotic	[n-r-t-c] friend has made no attempt to rid himself of that
neurosis	———————————— [n-r-o-s-].

	■ The noted _____ [n-r-l-g-t] was himself quite
neurologist neurotic	_____ [n-r-t-c]; he was in constant fear of being sued.
	■ My stuttering is an embarrassing _____
neurosis neuralgia	[n-r-o-s-], but it's preferable to the agony of _____ [n-r-a-1-g-].
	■ Let's name ten _____ [n-r-t-c] people to a
neurotic	best-stressed list.
	■ If you have _____ [n-r-a-1-g-], go to a
neuralgia neurologist neurosis	_____ [n-r-l-g-t]; if you have an annoying _____ [n-r-o-s-], go to a psychiatrist; if you have money, kiss it goodby.
	■ "Aha, inflamed nerves," said the _____
neurologist neuralgia	[n-r-l-g-t]. "A lovely case of _____ [n-r-a-1-g-]."

OTHER DERIVATIVES OF NEUR (NERVE):   *Non-test examples*

neural (nyoor'əl) *adj*. pertaining to the nerves

neurasthenia (nyoor'əs thē'nē ə) *n*. nervous exhaustion and physical distress, possibly due to emotional conflicts

neuritis (nyoo rī'tis) *n*. inflammation of a nerve

neuron (nyoor'on) *n*. the basic unit of the nervous system, consisting of a nerve cell body and its processes

neurosurgery (nyoor'ō sûr'jə rē) *n*. surgery of nerve tissue

The root NEUR (nerve) occurs in many other combinations. Examples:

neurectomy	neurolysis	neuropsychiatry
neuroanatomy	neuromuscular	neuropsychosis
neurocirculatory	neuropath	neurotoxic
neurogenic	neurophysiology	neurovascular

45. **panacea** (pan'ə sē'ə) *n.* a supposed remedy for all diseases or troubles; a cure-all

     The medicine man sold me a *panacea* for baldness and cancer.
     Every politician has his *panacea* for our national problems.

     <u>simple panacea</u> _____ _____
     (copy twice)

46. **pandemic** (pan dem'ik) *adj.* epidemic everywhere; universal
     a worldwide disease

     Europeans died like flies. It was the *pandemic* Black Plague.
     The rock-and-roll craze was *pandemic*.

     <u>pandemic disease</u> _____ _____

47. **pandemonium** (pan'də mō'nē əm) *n.* wild disorder and uproar; a scene of chaos; hell

     The World Series victory ended in *pandemonium*.
     Pandemonium broke loose.

     <u>scene of pandemonium</u> _____ _____

48. **panegyric** (pan'ə jir'ik) *n.* elaborate, flowing praise; a formal eulogy, spoken or written

     Chaplin's comic role has been the subject of *panegyrics*.
     The minister's *panegyric* would have pleased the dead man.

     <u>endless panegyric</u> _____ _____

49. **panorama** (pan'ə ram'ə) *n.* a complete view in all directions; a continuously passing scene or unfolding of events

     H.G. Wells presents a *panorama* of world history.
     From the helicopter we saw a *panorama* of disaster.

     <u>huge panorama</u> _____ _____

50. **pantheism** (pan'thē iz'əm) *n.* the belief that the whole world is God and that God is present in all aspects of nature

     A *pantheist* sees God in trees, lakes, and flowers.
     William Wordsworth wrote *pantheistic* poetry.

     <u>pure pantheism</u> _____ _____

Review words 45-50. Then go on.

QUIZ

DIRECTIONS: Fill the blanks with words we studied that are derived from the Greek root PAN (all). Be sure you spell the words correctly.

COVER
THIS STRIP

pandemonium

> ■ The baseball just cleared the fence, and then--
>
> _____ [p-n-d-n-m]!

panegyric
panorama

> ■ Sir Hilary went into a _____ [p-n-g-r-c]
>
> about the _____ [p-n-r-m-a] visible from the peak.

> ■ Unemployment during the '30s was _____

pandemic
panacea

> [p-n-d-m-c-], and President Roosevelt had to find a
>
> _____ [p-n-e-a].

pantheism

> ■ Tony gave up on the philosophy of _____
>
> [p-n-t-h-m] because he hated the dirty forest.

> ■ After his encore, "Lungs" Lipton threw kisses to the

panorama
pandemonium

> _____ [p-n-r-m-a] of rock fans and caused sheer
>
> _____ [p-n-d-n-m].

panegyric
pantheism

> ■ The nature poet wrote a _____ [p-n-g-r-c] to
>
> the glories of _____ [p-n-t-h-m], then got hay fever.

pandemic
panacea

> ■ In 1918 influenza was _____ [p-n-d-m-c-], and
>
> physicians had no _____ [p-n-e-a].

> ■ Herr Goebbels delivered a _____ [p-n-g-r-c]

panegyric
pandemic

> to the glories of war, ignoring the miseries that were
>
> already _____ [p-n-d-m-c-].

panorama
panacea

> ■ Gazing at the _____[p-n-r-m-a] of ocean can
>
> serve as a _____ [p-n-e-a] for our petty troubles.

pantheism
pandemonium

> ■ The grizzly attacked the disciples of _____
>
> [p-n-t-h-m], causing instant _____ [p-n-d-n-m].

page 219

OTHER DERIVATIVES OF PAN (ALL):

Pan-American (pan'ə mer'ə kən) *adj*. of North, Central, and South America [*a Pan-American alliance*]

panchromatic (pan'krō mat'ik) *adj*. sensitive to all colors [*panchromatic film*]

pancreas (pan'krē əs) *n*. a large gland situated near the stomach which secretes insulin and digestive juice

Pandora's box (pan dôr'əz) a source of all troubles when opened [*The new casino was a Pandora's box of crimes.*]

Panhellenic (pan'hə len'ik) *adj*. of all Greeks; of all Greek-letter fraternities and sororities

panic (pan'ik) *n*. a sudden, hysterical fear that often spreads quickly *v*. to become frantic with fear [*The crowd panicked.*]

panoply (pan'ə plē) *n*. the complete, magnificent covering, such as a warrior's equipment

panoptic (pan op'tik) *adj*. permitting an all-inclusive view [*panoptic photography*]

pantheon (pan'thē on') *n*. a temple dedicated to all the gods or honoring the nation's dead heroes

The root PAN (all) is used quite freely to form new terms, especially those suggesting the union of all branches of a group. Examples:

Pan-African	Pan-Christian	Pan-Slavism
Pan-Arabian	Pan-Germanic	pansophy
Pan-Asian	Pan-Islamic	pantonality
panatrophy	panpsychism	pantoscope
pancarditis	Pan-Russian	pantropical

Review words 1-50, spelling and vocabulary. Then take the Chapters 23-24 Self-Test.

CHAPTERS 23-24: SELF-TEST

DIRECTIONS: Write the words in full. Complete this entire test before you check and grade your answers.

_____ 1. The midget bought a child's [a-d-m-s-n] ticket.
_____ 2. A soft tomato hit one of the [a-m-t-u-r] singers.
_____ 3. We need a [c-a-l-n-d-r] with longer weekends.
_____ 4. What is a watt of [e-l-e-c-t-y]?
_____ 5. Sweeter than wine is a person's good [c-r-c-t-r].
_____ 6. Her final [d-e-s-i-o-n] was to keep the baby.
_____ 7. We like [c-r-i-t-s-m], if it's favorable.
_____ 8. That fellow in the gutter drank too much [a-l-h-o-l].
_____ 9. We are shaped by our [e-n-v-i-r-m-n-t].
_____ 10. The little voice that says "Be good" is your [c-o-n-s-n-c-].
_____ 11. My new [b-r-g-l-r] alarm rings when I take a shower.
_____ 12. Joggers compete in their age [c-a-t-g-r-y].
_____ 13. A child needs [d-i-c-p-l-i n-] as well as food.
_____ 14. Beggars greeted the tourists promptly on [a-r-i-v-l-].
_____ 15. Americans prefer [d-e-m-o-c-y].
_____ 16. Old Lem's teeth looked like a run-down [c-e-m-t-r-y].
_____ 17. The bandaged bride went to a marriage [c-o-n-s-l-r].
_____ 18. The fly in the soup did not improve my [a-p-t-i-t-].
_____ 19. Every girl dreams of a [c-r-e-r-] in the movies.
_____ 20. Great novels came from Great [B-r-i-t-n].
_____ 21. Villagers who craved [e-x-i-t-m-n-t] watched haircuts.
_____ 22. Daniel Defoe wrote a graphic [d-s-c-r-t-n] of the plague.
_____ 23. One [c-a-n-d-a-t-] for Congress plays the banjo.
_____ 24. My black eye aroused Mother's [c-u-r-s-t-y].
_____ 25. We bought a rattling good [a-t-m-b-l-].
_____ 26. To wipe out male [c-a-v-n-i-s-m], wipe out males.
_____ 27. Our big watchdog has the [c-u-r-g-e] of a rabbit.
_____ 28. We pedaled along on our [b-c-c-l-e] built for three.
_____ 29. Two lions and a chimp guarded the [e-n-t-r-n-e] and exit.
_____ 30. Oatmeal is a wholesome breakfast [-e-r-e-l].

Write correctly the words we studied that are derived from the Greek roots
LOG, METR-METER, NEUR, and PAN.

_____ 31. Don't break your [c-r-n-m-t-r]. It's a waste of time.
_____ 32. She swore that a fur coat would be a [p-a-n-e-a] for her woes.
_____ 33. Always worrying? He must be [n-u-r-t-c].
_____ 34. Ernest Hemingway wrote believable [d-i-l-o-g-].
_____ 35. Painful nerves! It's my [n-u-r-a-l-g-].
_____ 36. The honey-sweet [-u-l-g-y] made the corpse turn over.
_____ 37. Some nature lovers believe in [p-n-t-h-m].
_____ 38. Milton's _Paradise Lost_ was written in iambic [p-t-m-t-r].
_____ 39. "Blaster" Briggs had studied [t-h-l-g-y] before turning to sin.
_____ 40. The soccer game ended in riot and [p-n-d-m-n-].

Write the letter that indicates the best definition.

( ) 41. barometer
( ) 42. geology
( ) 43. metric
( ) 44. micrometer
( ) 45. neurologist
( ) 46. neurosis
( ) 47. pandemic
( ) 48. panegyric
( ) 49. panorama
( ) 50. prologue

a. a sweeping, all-around view
b. a measurer of tiny distances
c. spreading everywhere, as a disease
d. the science of rocks and earth surfaces
e. flowery praise
f. a measurer of air pressure
g. an emotional disorder
h. dealing with scientific measurements
i. the preface to a play or poem
j. a specialist in nerve disorders

ANSWER KEY

Check your test answers by the following key. Deduct 2% per error from 100%.

1. admission	11. burglar	21. excitement	31. chronometer	41. f
2. amateur	12. category	22. description	32. panacea	42. d
3. calendar	13. discipline	23. candidate	33. neurotic	43. h
4. electricity	14. arrival	24. curiosity	34. dialogue	44. b
5. character	15. democracy	25. automobile	35. neuralgia	45. j
6. decision	16. cemetery	26. chauvinism	36. eulogy	46. g
7. criticism	17. counselor	27. courage	37. pantheism	47. c
8. alcohol	18. appetite	28. bicycle	38. pentameter	48. e
9. environment	19. career	29. entrance	39. theology	49. a
10. conscience	20. Britain	30. cereal	40. pandemonium	50. i

Score: _____ %

Review carefully any words which you have missed in the foregoing Self-Test.

Your instructor will give you a final test on words 1-50 in Chapters 23 and 24.

25

DIRECTIONS: Study the spelling of each word carefully, giving special attention to the trouble spots (underlined letters). Then write each word neatly three times.

1. expe<u>ns</u>e   _____ _____ _____

2. exp<u>er</u>ience _____ _____ _____

3. expl<u>ana</u>tion _____ _____ _____

4. Feb<u>ru</u>ary _____ _____ _____

5. fu<u>tu</u>re   _____ _____ _____

6. garb<u>ag</u>e   _____ _____ _____

7. gasol<u>in</u>e _____ _____ _____

8. gove<u>rn</u>or _____ _____ _____

9. g<u>u</u>ardian _____ _____ _____

10. hypocri<u>sy</u> _____ _____ _____

Review words 1-10 until you are sure you can spell them. Then go on and take the quiz.

COVER
THIS STRIP   FILL THE BLANKS
_____

governor   ■ Our bald _____ [g-v-e-n-r] had a hair-raising
experience
                    _____ [e-x-p-e-r-n-c-].

                    ■ "Spare no _____ [e-x-p-e-n-]," said my

                    tight-fisted _____ [g-a-r-d-n]. "It's
expense
guardian   _____ [-e-b-u-a-r-y]; give the canary another
February
                    seed."

                    ■ In the _____ [f-u-t-r-] we may be making

future   _____ [g-a-s-l-n] out of _____
gasoline
garbage   [g-a-r-b-g-].

                    ■ A master of _____ [h-p-o-c-r-y] always seems

                    to have a convincing _____ [e-x-p-l-n-t-n] for
hypocrisy
explanation   his questionable actions.

                    ■ "Am I late for the _____ [g-a-r-b-g-] pickup?"--

garbage   "No, jump in."

                    ■ Grandpa's _____ [e-x-p-e-n-] account shows

expense   that he used two gallons of _____ [g-a-s-l-n]
gasoline
February   in _____ [-e-b-u-a-r-y].

                    ■ Mike's _____ [e-x-p-l-n-t-n] about the
explanation
hypocrisy   lipstick on his collar was sheer _____ [h-p-o-c-r-y].

                    ■ My _____ [g-a-r-d-n] predicted that I'd be the
guardian
future   _____ [f-u-t-r-] _____ [g-v-e-n-r],
governor
garbage   but that was a lot of _____ [g-a-r-b-g-].

                    ■ Bill rode a bike to avoid the _____ [e-x-p-e-n-]
expense
gasoline   of _____ [g-a-s-l-n-], but now he ate more.

experience
guardian

■ Our _____ [e-x-p-e-r-n-c-] tells us not to

appoint a wolf to be _____ [g-a-r-d-n-] of

the chicken coop.

■ In spite of the painter's _____ [e-x-p-1-n-t-n]

that he had years of _____ [e-x-p-e-r-n-c-],

explanation
experience
February

it took him all of _____ [-e-b-u-a-r-y] to paint

the kitchen.

■ The Indians were to learn at a _____ [f-u-t-r-]

future
governor
hypocrisy

date that the promises of the colonial _____

[g-v-e-n-r] were sheer _____ [h-p-o-c-r-y].

■   *"Why what's the matter,
    That you have such a _____ [-e-b-u-a-r-y] face,
    So full of frost, of storm, and cloudiness?*
February
                (Much Ado About Nothing, V, iv, 41)

DIRECTIONS: Continue as before. Study the spelling carefully. Write each
word three times.

11. insurance _____ _____ _____

12. jealousy _____ _____ _____

13. knowledge _____ _____ _____

14. language _____ _____ _____

15. leisure _____ _____ _____

16. library _____ _____ _____

17. lightning _____ _____ _____

18. literature _____ _____ _____

19. luxury _____ _____ _____

20. magazine _____ _____ _____

Review words 11-20. Then take the quiz.

COVER THIS STRIP	FILL THE BLANKS
magazine literature language	■ Melvin subscribed to a _____ [m-a-g-z-n-] that printed the finest German _____ [l-i-t-u-r-], but found he couldn't read the _____ [l-a-n-g-g-].
leisure library knowledge	■ If you spend your _____ [l-e-s-r-] hours in the _____ [l-i-b-r-y], you'll pick up a mass of _____ [-n-o-l-e-g-].
lightning library magazine	■ A bolt of _____ [l-i-t-n-i-g] hit the _____ [l-i-b-r-y], but nothing burned except a fire prevention _____ [m-a-g-z-n-].
luxury jealousy	■ One teacher drove up in a _____ [l-x-r-y] limousine; and the college president, in his battered VW, felt a pang of _____ [j-e-l-s-y].
lightning insurance luxury	■ After Fritz was struck by _____ [l-i-t-n-i-g], his widow was able to collect life (but not fire) _____ [i-n-s-r-n-] on him; and so, for once, he provided her with a bit of _____ [l-x-r-y].
knowledge insurance	■ Acquire mastery or _____ [-n-o-l-e-g-] of a special craft, and you have _____ [i-n-s-r-n-] against poverty.
leisure luxury	■ Those who dream of _____ [l-e-s-r-] and _____ [l-x-r-y) should dream less and work more.
knowledge lightning jealousy language	■ When Gary received _____ [-n-o-l-e-g-] that Mary was unfaithful, bolts of _____ [l-i-t-n-i-g] shot from his eyes and, in a fit of _____ [j-e-l-s-y], he used _____ [l-a-n-g-g-] that melted the wax in Mary's ears.

magazine
jealousy
literature

■ The love story _____ [m-a-g-z-n-] described

the secret _____ [j-e-l-s-y] of Siamese twins

who were both in love with their _____ [l-i-t-u-r-]

teacher.

■ "Watch your _____ [l-a-n-g-g-]!" snapped

language

the counselor, and I answered, "English."

■ The _____ [i-n-s-r-n-] salesman was wearing a

_____ [l-e-s-r-] suit when his body was found in

insurance
leisure
library
literature

the city _____ [l-i-b-r-y] under a pile of romantic

_____ [l-i-t-u-r-].

■ *"O, beware, my lord, of* _____ [*j-e-l-s-y*];
It is the green-eyed monster"

jealousy

(Othello, III, iii, 165)

DIRECTIONS: Continue as before. Study the spelling carefully. Write each
word three times.

21. math**e**matics _____ _____ _____

22. med**i**cine _____ _____ _____

23. mosqu**i**to _____ _____ _____

24. mus**c**le _____ _____ _____

25. n**ei**ghb**o**r _____ _____ _____

26. ni**c**ke**l** _____ _____ _____

27. nu**i**sance _____ _____ _____

28. o**c**ean _____ _____ _____

29. pas**s**ion _____ _____ _____

30. philos**op**hy _____ _____ _____

Review words 21-30. Then take the quiz.

COVER THIS STRIP	FILL THE BLANKS
	■ "Do I have problems!" exclaimed the _____
mathematics	[m-a-t-h-m-t-s] teacher.
	■ Werther's hopeless _____ [p-a-s-n] for Lotte
passion ocean medicine	gave him an illness that an _____ [o-c-a-n] of _____ [m-e-d-i-n-] could not cure.
	■ People once rode the el (elevated train) for a
nickel	_____ [n-i-k-l-].
	■ One rich invalid has a walk-in _____
medicine	[m-e-d-i-n-] chest.
	■ Our professor of _____ [p-h-i-l-s-y] went
philosophy ocean mosquito	fishing in the _____ [o-c-a-n], but the only bites he got were _____ [m-s-q-i-t-o-] bites.
	■ I swallowed a _____ [n-i-k-l-], and the
nickel	doctor made me cough up twenty dollars.
	■ Edgar Allan Poe describes how Ligeia's deathless
passion	_____ [p-a-s-n] brings her back from the grave.
	■ Since it's a _____ [n-u-s-n-c-e] to take
nuisance medicine philosophy	_____ [m-e-d-i-n-], my _____ [p-h-i-l-s-y] is "Stay healthy!"
	■ Capone swore at a _____ [m-s-q-i-t-o-] that was
mosquito nuisance muscle	a _____ [n-u-s-n-c-e], so it bit him on the leg _____ [m-u-s-l-].
	■ My _____ [n-e-b-r], who believes in a
neighbor philosophy nickel	_____ [p-h-i-l-s-y] of pleasure, is now down to his last _____ [n-i-k-l-].

passion
mathematics
nuisance

■ Some students have a _____ [p-a-s-n] for

_____ [m-a-t-h-m-t-s]; others consider it a

_____ [n-u-s-n-c-e].

neighbor
ocean

■ My conceited _____ [n-e-b-r] nearly drowned

in the _____ [o-c-a-n], trying to walk on water.

■ "Don't _____ [m-u-s-1-] into my territory,"

growled Scarface, "or your life ain't worth a

muscle
nickel

_____ [n-i-k-1-]."

■ The _____ [m-a-t-h-m-t-s] tutor told my

_____ [n-e-b-r]: "You might be a man of

mathematics
neighbor
muscle
mosquito

_____ [m-u-s-1-], but you don't have the brains

of a _____ [m-s-q-i-t-o-]."

■ *"The miserable have no other _____ [m-e-d-i-n-]*
But only hope"

medicine
                                    (Measure for Measure, III, i, 2)

26

PATH: DISEASE; FEELING

31. **antipathy** (an tip'ə thē) *n.* a strong dislike; an aversion; a feeling of hostility

    The hobo had an *antipathy* toward profitable labor.
    Flo and Joe displayed an *antipathy* **for ea**ch other.

    natural antipathy _____ _____
        (copy twice)

32. **apathy** (ap'ə thē) *n.* a lack of feeling or emotion; indifference; unconcern

    The class president criticized student *apathy*.
    Apathetic clerks don't make many sales.

    chronic apathy _____ _____

33. **empathy** (em'pə thē) *n.* ability to share somebody else's feelings

    We winced or cheered in *empathy* for our cowboy hero.
    The women wept in *empathy* for the grieving widow.

    genuine empathy _____ _____

34. **pathologist** (pə thol'ə jist) *n.* a specialist in the nature of diseases; one who is skilled in diagnosis of disease

> The *pathologist* detected cancer cells.
> A coroner must be a skilled *pathologist*.

expert pathologist _____ _____

35. **telepathy** (tə lep'ə thē) *n.* transference of thought through space without use of normal sensory channels

> *Telepathy* is a form of ESP (extrasensory perception).
> Is *telepathic* communication possible?

Was it telepathy? _____ _____

Review words 31-35. Then go on.

QUIZ

DIRECTIONS: Fill the blanks with words we studied that are derived from the Greek root PATH (disease; feeling). Be sure you spell the words correctly.

COVER
THIS STRIP
_____

pathologist empathy antipathy	■ The _____ [p-t-g-s-t] felt an _____ [e-m-p-y] for the dying miners and an _____ [a-t-p-y] for the coal dust that poisoned their lungs.
telepathy apathy antipathy	■ Many scientists doubt the existence of _____ [t-l-p-y] and regard the concept with _____[a-p-t-y] if not with utter _____ [a-t-p-y].
pathologist apathy antipathy empathy	■ Some of the drug victims looked at the _____ [p-t-g-s-t] with vacant eyes and _____ [a-p-t-y], others with sullenness and _____ [a-t-p-y]; but he was compassionate and felt _____ [e-m-p-y] for them in their plight.
telepathy empathy	■ If _____ [t-l-p-y] really exists, surely those mental signals would be between lovers or others who feel strong _____ [e-m-p-y] for one another.

- Suddenly he felt that Sally needed help. Could this be

  _____ [t-l-p-y]? At once the listlessness and

telepathy
apathy
pathologist

  _____ [a-p-t-y] left him, and the young

  _____ [p-t-g-s-t] ran toward the river.

- *"No contraries hold more* _____ [a-t-p-y]
  Than I and such a knave"

antipathy

  (King Lear, II, ii, 93)

Non-test examples

OTHER DERIVATIVES OF PATH (DISEASE; FEELING):

allopathy (ə lop'ə thē) *n.* treatment of disease by remedies that tend to produce symptoms opposite to those of the disease

homeopathy (hō'mē op'ə thē) *n.* treatment of disease by remedies that tend to produce symptoms similar to those of the disease

osteopathy (os'tē op'ə thē) *n.* a system of healing that stresses manipulation of the musculo-skeletal system

pathetic (pə thet'ik) *adj.* tending to arouse compassion; pitiful

pathetic fallacy the literary device of ascribing human feeling to things of nature, as in "sullen clouds" and "the smiling sun"

pathological (path'ə loj'i kəl) *adj.* involving disease; compulsive [*a pathological trait*]

pathos (pā'thos) *n.* a quality that arouses pity

PHIL: LOVING

36. **Anglophile** (ang'glə fīl') *n.* a person who admires England, its people, customs, etc.

    Most *Anglophiles* are fond of the tidy English gardens.
    Read Shakespeare and you become an *Anglophile*.

    <u>loyal Anglophile</u>   _____   _____
    (copy twice)

37. **bibliophile** (bib'lē ə fīl') *n.* one who loves or collects books

    The rich leather bindings delighted the *bibliophile*.
    Some *bibliophiles* collect a specialty such as old Bibles.

    <u>wealthy bibliophile</u>   _____   _____

38. **philander** (fĭ lăn'dər) *v.* to make love insincerely: said of a man

> The maiden was betrayed by a *philandering* salesman.
> Did Prince Hamlet love Ophelia or was he a *philanderer*?

Don't philander. _____ _____

39. **philanthropy** (fĭ lăn'thrə pē) *n.* an affection for mankind, especially as shown by donations for socially useful purposes

> Carnegie and Strauss were *philanthropic* citizens.
> One *philanthropist* founded a mission for drug addicts.

public philanthropy _____ _____

40. **philatelist** (fĭ lăt'ə list) *n.* a stamp collector; a hobbyist who collects postage stamps, postmarks, stamped envelopes, etc.

> Franklin D. Roosevelt was an avid *philatelist*.
> As a *philatelist* you soak up facts of world history.

amateur philatelist _____ _____

Review words 36-40. Then go on.

QUIZ

DIRECTIONS: Fill the blanks with words we studied that are derived from the Greek root PHIL (loving). Be sure you spell the words correctly.

COVER
THIS STRIP

bibliophile philander	■ The _____ [b-i-b-p-l-] purchased a first edition of the memoirs of Casanova, the handsome bounder whose hobby was to _____ [p-l-d-r] shamelessly among the Italian women.
philatelist	■ The _____ [p-l-t-s-t] invested in triangular stamps because he thought he saw an angle.
philanthropy philatelist bibliophile	■ When not engaged in _____ [p-l-t-p-y], the wealthy woman was an active _____ [p-l-t-s-t] and _____ [b-i-b-p-l-].

bibliophile
Anglophile
philanthropy

- I concluded that the _____ [b-i-b-p-l-] was

also an _____ [A-n-g-p-l-], since most of her

books dealt with the _____ [p-l-t-p-y] of Queen

Victoria and Florence Nightingale.

philatelist
Anglophile
philanthropy

- The dying _____ [p-l-t-s-t], being an

_____ [A-n-g-p-l-], left his rare stamps to

the British Museum, an admirable act of _____

[p-l-t-p-y].

Anglophile
philander

- Perceiving that the _____ [A-n-g-p-l-] was

trifling with Agatha's affections, I warned him not to

_____ [p-l-d-r].

"Did you come to buy stamps," she asked, "or to

philander
philatelist

_____ [p-l-d-r]?"--"You mean," replied the

_____ [p-l-t-s-t], "that I've got a choice?"

Non-test examples

OTHER DERIVATIVES OF PHIL (LOVING):

Francophile (fran'ke fīl') *n.* a person who admires France, its people, customs, etc.

hemophilia (hē'mə fil'ē ə) *n.* a hereditary disorder in males, characterized by prolonged bleeding from minor cuts

philharmonic (fil'har mon'ik) *adj.* devoted to music; loving music [*the philharmonic society*] *n.* symphony orchestra

philhellene (fil hel'ēn) *n.* a person who admires the Greeks

philodendron (fil'ə den'drən) *n.* a tropical climbing plant with thick evergreen vine leaves (lit., fond of trees)

philogynist (fi loj'ə nist) *n.* one who is extremely fond of women

philoprogenitive (fil'ə prō jen'ə tiv) *adj.* loving children, especially one's own; prolific [*a philoprogenitive tribe*]

philosophy (fi los'ə fē) *n.* love of wisdom; the inquiry into the principles of reality; practical wisdom [*a philosophy of government*]

philter (fil'tər) *n.* a magic potion thought to arouse sexual love; a love potion

PHOB: FEAR; HATRED

41. **acrophobia** (ak'rə fō'bē ə) *n.* an abnormal fear of heights

> The *acrophobe* refused to work on the twentieth floor.
> For you I'd climb the highest mountain--except for my *acrophobia*.

acute acrophobia   _____   _____
    (copy twice)

42. **claustrophobia** (klos'trə fō'bē ə) *n.* an abnormal fear of being in a
a closed or confined space

> The *claustrophobe* said that a small room feels like a coffin.
> Clifford wants outdoor work; he has *claustrophobia*.

claustrophobia agony   _____   _____

43. **pyrophobia** (pī'rə fō'bē ə) *n.* an abnormal fear of fire

> Don't become a fireman if you have *pyrophobia*.
> The *pyrophobe* slept with a fire extinguisher under his pillow.

extreme pyrophobia   _____   _____

44. **Russophobia** (rus'ə fō'bē ə) *n.* strong fear or hatred of Russia

> Joe McCarthy, a *Russophobe*, saw two communists in every garage.
> Russian arms buildup has fanned our *Russophobia*.

pervasive Russophobia   _____   _____

45. **xenophobia** (zen'ə fō'bē ə) *n.* strong fear or hatred of foreigners
and strangers

> Luke's hostility to newcomers amounted to *xenophobia*.
> I tried to befriend the *xenophobic* hermit.

small-town xenophobia   _____   _____

Review words 41-45. Then go on.

DIRECTIONS: Fill the blanks with words we studied that are derived from the Greek root PHOB (fear; hatred). Be sure you spell the words correctly.

COVER
THIS STRIP

claustrophobia

- Lock little Buster into a closet to punish him, and he may develop _____ [c-l-s-p-b-a].
- My cousin Clarence is afflicted with both _____

acrophobia
pyrophobia

[a-c-r-p-b-a] and _____ [p-r-p-b-a], and he has nightmares about falling in a burning plane.

- Jim's hatred of Moscow, or _____ [R-s-o-p-b-a],

Russophobia
xenophobia

is part of his general distrust of all foreigners, or _____ [-e-n-p-b-a].

- Your little darling may fall off a ladder and develop _____ [a-c-r-p-b-a], burn his pinky and

acrophobia
pyrophobia
xenophobia

develop _____ [p-r-p-b-a], or get clobbered by a strange boy and develop _____ [-e-n-p-b-a].

- Truly unhappy is the mountain climber with _____ [a-c-r-p-b-a], also the elevator

acrophobia
claustrophobia
Russophobia

operator with _____ [c-l-s-p-b-a]; nor do I envy the prisoner in Siberia with _____ [R-s-o-p-b-a].

- Agonies and tensions are felt by those who have a fear of small rooms, or _____ [c-l-s-p-b-a]; a fear

claustrophobia
pyrophobia
xenophobia

of flames, or _____ [p-r-p-b-a]; a fear of strangers, or _____ [-e-n-p-b-a].

- Our nation has wavered between periods of cool friendship with Russia and periods of _____

Russophobia

[R-s-o-p-b-a].

Fear or hatred of--

agoraphobia	open spaces	hydrophobia	water (rabies)
ailurophobia	cats	hypnophobia	sleep
androphobia	men	musophobia	mice
astrophobia	stars	necrophobia	dead bodies
autophobia	being alone	neophobia	new things
ballistophobia	missiles	nyctophobia	darkness
bathophobia	depths	ophidiophobia	snakes
ceraunophobia	thunder	phonophobia	noise
cynophobia	dogs	psychrophobia	cold
demophobia	crowds	taphephobia	being buried alive
gamophobia	marriage	thanatophobia	death
gynophobia	women	toxicophobia	poison
haptephobia	being touched	triskaidekaphobia	number 13
hemophobia	blood	zoophobia	animals

PSYCH: MIND; SPIRIT

46. **psychiatrist** (sī kī'ə trist) *n.* a doctor of medicine who specializes in the treatment of mental disorders

> The *psychiatrist* testified at the sanity hearing.
> The disturbed youth needs *psychiatric* help.

Freudian psychiatrist _____ _____
    (copy twice)

47. **psychology** (sī kol'ə jē) *n.* the science of the mind, including mental and emotional processes; human behavior

> Every parent should understand child *psychology*.
> Job applicants take *psychological* tests.

sales psychology _____ _____

48. **psychopath** (sī'kō path) *n.* a person who is mentally unstable and possibly has criminal tendencies

> Police hunted for a *psychopathic* killer.
> A *psychopath* is not an ideal roommate.

weird psychopath _____ _____

49. **psychosomatic** (sī'kō sō mat'ik) *adj.* referring to a physical disorder caused by the emotions

> Ulcers are a common *psychosomatic* ailment.
> Worries can cause *psychosomatic* illness.

psychosomatic aches _____ _____

50. **psychotherapy** (sī'kō ther'ə pē) *n.* the treatment of mental disorder by psychological methods such as psychoanalysis, hypnosis, suggestion, and counseling

> Sigmund Freud founded a school of *psychotherapy*.
> *Psychotherapeutic* methods differ widely.

psychotherapy session _____ _____

Review words 46-50. Then go on.

QUIZ

DIRECTIONS: Fill the blanks with words we studied that are derived from the Greek root PSYCH (mind; spirit). Be sure you spell the words correctly.

COVER
THIS STRIP

	■ My study of _____ [-s-c-o-1-g-y] taught me that it's unwise to argue with a _____ [-s-c-o-p-t-h] in a dark alley.
psychology psychopath	■ Convinced that her migraine headaches were _____ [-s-c-o-s-m-t-c], Kathy decided to undergo _____ [-s-c-o-t-r-p-y].
psychosomatic psychotherapy	■ Mervin was given _____ [-s-c-o-t-r-p-y] by a skilled _____ [-s-c-i-t-r-i-t], and his _____ [-s-c-o-s-m-t-c] stammer disappeared.
psychotherapy psychiatrist psychosomatic	

psychiatrist psychology	▪ Desiring to become a _____ [-s-c-i-t-r-i-t], Karen majored in _____ [-s-c-o-l-g-y].
psychotherapy psychopath	▪ After extended _____ [-s-c-o-t-r-p-y], the _____ [-s-c-o-p-t-h] was released. A week later he strangled three boys and a cat.
psychiatrist	▪ Please serve no liquor to that _____ [-s-c-i-t-r-i-t]. He's too Jung.
psychosomatic	▪ Soldiers are sometimes literally paralyzed by fear, a _____ [-s-c-o-s-m-t-c] reaction.
psychology psychopath	▪ A course in abnormal _____ [-s-c-o-l-g-y] deals with eccentric people such as the _____ [-s-c-o-p-t-h].

Non-test examples

OTHER DERIVATIVES OF PSYCH (MIND; SPIRIT):

metempsychosis (met'əm sī kō'sis) *n.* the passage of the soul at death into another body

parapsychology (par'ə sī kol'ə jē) *n.* the branch of psychology that deals with telepathy, ESP, and other psychic phenomena

psyche (sī'kē) *n.* the human soul; the mind

psychedelic (sī'kə del'ik) *adj.* causing extreme mental changes, such as hallucinations and enhanced sensory awareness

psychic (sī'kik) *adj.* having to do with the mind; apparently sensitive to extrasensory phenomena [*psychic predictions*] *n.* one who is apparently sensitive to extrasensory phenomena

psychoanalysis (sī'kō ə nal'ə sis) *n.* a method of treating mental disorders, developed by Sigmund Freud and others, through the use of such techniques as free association and dream analysis

psychobiography (sī'kō bī og'rə fe) *n.* a biography that deals largely with the psychological aspects and development of the central character

psychochemical (sī'kō kem'i kəl) *adj.* pertaining to a drug such as LSD that affects mental activity *n.* a drug that affects the mind

psychodrama (sī'kō dräm'ə) *n.* a method of group therapy in which a patient acts out a situation related to his problem

psychograph (sī'kō graf') *n*. a chart which graphically outlines the relative strength of one's personality traits; a biographical sketch which stresses personality tests

psychokinesis (sī'kō ki nē'sis) *n*. the alleged ability to control physical objects or events by mental power

psychometry (sī kom'ə trē) *n*. mental testing

psychosis (sī kō'sis) *n*. a major mental disorder with or without organic disease such as brain damage; insanity

More examples of PSYCH (mind; spirit) derivatives:

psychasthenia	psychogenic	psychosexual
psychoacoustics	psychoneurosis	psychosurgery
psychobiology	psychopathology	psychotic
psychodynamics	pyschopharmacology	psychotoxic

Review words 1-50, spelling and vocabulary. Then take the Chapters 25-26 Self-Test.

CHAPTERS 25-26: SELF-TEST

DIRECTIONS: Write the words in full. Complete this entire test before you check and grade your answers.

_____ 1. One [m-s-q-t-o-] took more blood than the Red Cross.
_____ 2. Every hero was once a family [n-u-s-n-c-].
_____ 3. The shortest month is [-e-b-u-r-y].
_____ 4. Robert Frost and his [n-e-b-r] mended a wall.
_____ 5. The dog learned a foreign [l-a-n-g-e]: "Meow."
_____ 6. We bought a [n-i-k-l-] candy bar--for fifty cents.
_____ 7. The bolt of [l-i-t-n-i-g] melted his fillings.
_____ 8. Sally, take your [m-e-d-c-n-e] like a lady.
_____ 9. "Three a.m.," said Dad. "I demand an [e-x-p-l-n-t-n]."
_____ 10. England had a working class and a [l-e-s-r-] class.
_____ 11. Lefty had a bad [e-x-p-r-n-c-e] with a crocodile.
_____ 12. In the waiting room I read an aged [m-a-g-z-n-].
_____ 13. Albert Einstein had a genius for [m-a-t-h-m-t-s].
_____ 14. I'd visit Europe, except for the [e-x-p-e-n-].
_____ 15. A man with a past hasn't much of a [f-u-t-r-].
_____ 16. Russians regard an automobile as a [l-x-r-y].
_____ 17. Every [g-v-r-n-r] dreams of becoming president.
_____ 18. Rich? Even their [g-a-r-b-g-] is gift wrapped.
_____ 19. Yasha has a deep [p-a-s-n] for Mozart's music.
_____ 20. Develop creativity as well as [-n-o-l-e-g-].
_____ 21. The Russian promises were sheer [h-p-o-c-r-i-y].
_____ 22. I sent her "an [o-c-e-n-] of love" on a wet postcard.
_____ 23. This moped goes ten miles on a drop of [g-a-s-l-n-].

_____ 24. The beating heart of a college is the [l-i-b-r-y].
_____ 25. Sick people can't buy health [i-n-s-r-n-c-].
_____ 26. Depend on yourself, not on a [g-a-r-d-n] angel.
_____ 27. Socrates shared his [p-h-l-s-p-y] with Athenian youths.
_____ 28. Emily Dickinson added to our poetic [l-i-t-r-t-r-].
_____ 29. To fling the discus, you must develop [m-u-s-1-].
_____ 30. Six of the Sultan's seven wives felt [j-e-l-o-s-y].

Write correctly the words we studied that are derived from the Greek roots
PATH, PHIL, PHOB, and PSYCH:

_____ 31. Teacher reads my mind. It must be [t-e-l-p-t-y].
_____ 32. An old one-cent stamp cost the [p-l-t-l-s-t] a pretty penny.
_____ 33. The lad was listless, the picture of [a-p-t-y].
_____ 34. This ancient book will gladden a [b-i-b-p-l-].
_____ 35. Avoid parachute jumping if you have [a-c-p-b-a].
_____ 36. Your fear of marriage may require [-s-c-o-t-r-p-y].
_____ 37. Junior has an [a-t-i-p-t-y] for wholesome foods.
_____ 38. Slasher Sam, a dangerous [p-c-o-p-t-h-], has escaped.
_____ 39. Headaches caused by tension are [p-c-o-s-m-c].
_____ 40. The tiny jail cell is agony for somebody with [c-l-p-b-a].

Write the letter that indicates the best definition.

( ) 41. Anglophile   a. extreme fear of fire
( ) 42. empathy   b. to flirt and seduce
( ) 43. pathologist   c. benevolence; charity to society
( ) 44. philander   d. hatred of Russia
( ) 45. philanthropy   e. the study of the mind and human behavior
( ) 46. psychiatrist   f. one who loves England
( ) 47. psychology   g. abnormal fear of strangers
( ) 48. pyrophobia   h. sharing the feelings of another
( ) 49. Russophobia   i. a doctor who treats mental disorders
( ) 50. xenophobia   j. a specialist in bodily diseases

ANSWER KEY

Check your test answers by the following key. Deduct 2% per error from 100%.

1. mosquito	11. experience	21. hypocrisy	31. telepathy	41. f
2. nuisance	12. magazine	22. ocean	32. philatelist	42. h
3. February	13. mathematics	23. gasoline	33. apathy	43. j
4. neighbor	14. expense	24. library	34. bibliophile	44. b
5. language	15. future	25. insurance	35. acrophobia	45. c
6. nickel	16. luxury	26. guardian	36. psychotherapy	46. i
7. lightning	17. governor	27. philosophy	37. antipathy	47. e
8. medicine	18. garbage	28. literature	38. psychopath	48. a
9. explanation	19. passion	29. muscle	39. psychosomatic	49. d
10. leisure	20. knowledge	30. jealousy	40. claustrophobia	50. g

Score: _____ %

Review carefully any words which you have missed in the foregoing Self-Test.

Your instructor will give you a final test on words 1-50 in Chapters 25 and 26.

27

DIRECTIONS: Study the spelling of each word carefully, giving special attention to the trouble spots (underlined letters). Then write each word neatly three times.

1. physician   _____ _____ _____

2. poison   _____ _____ _____

3. possession   _____ _____ _____

4. prejudice   _____ _____ _____

5. procedure   _____ _____ _____

6. professor   _____ _____ _____

7. quantity   _____ _____ _____

8. reference   _____ _____ _____

9. repetition   _____ _____ _____

10. restaurant   _____ _____ _____

Review words 1-10 until you are sure you can spell them. Then go on and take the quiz.

COVER THIS STRIP	FILL THE BLANKS

COVER THIS STRIP

professor
restaurant

prejudice
quantity
possession

physician
reference
repetition

procedure
restaurant
prejudice

professor
poison
possession

repetition

restaurant

procedure
repetition

physician

professor
reference
procedure

FILL THE BLANKS

- I talked to my _____ [p-r-o-f-s-r] at the _____ [r-e-s-t-r-n-t] over a hot cup of Sanka.

- Grazing the trees, I felt some _____ [p-r-j-d-i-c-] toward our pilot when I saw a _____ [q-a-n-t-y] of liquor in his _____ [p-o-s-e-s-n].

- The _____ [p-h-s-i-a-n] made constant _____ [r-e-f-r-n-c-] to dieting, and the _____ [r-e-p-t-i-t-n] worried Big Ben.

- The hiring _____ [p-r-c-d-u-r-] at the new _____ [r-e-s-t-r-n-t] gives off a smell of _____ [p-r-j-d-i-c-].

- "Rats!" said the chemistry _____ [p-r-o-f-s-r] when asked what he was going to kill with the _____ [p-o-i-s-n] in his _____ [p-o-s-e-s-n].

- We'll get a _____ [r-e-p-t-i-t-n] of the earthquake soon, and you can shake on that.

- A penny _____ [r-e-s-t-r-n-t] would make lots of cents.

- Any _____ [p-r-c-d-u-r-] such as spelling can be mastered by constant _____ [r-e-p-t-i-t-n].

- A _____ [p-h-s-i-a-n] should never lose his patients.

- The physics _____ [p-r-o-f-s-r] made a _____ [r-e-f-r-n-c-] to the _____ [p-r-c-d-u-r-] for making telescopes.

restaurant
poison
quantity

■ "This _____ [r-e-s-t-r-n-t] food is absolute

_____ [p-o-i-s-n]," complained Joe, "and such a

small _____ [q-a-n-t-y] of it, too!"

■ When David gets a low grade, he always makes a

_____ [r-e-f-r-n-c] to _____

reference
prejudice

[p-r-j-d-i-c].

■ One _____ [p-h-s-i-a-n] claims that an excess

physician
quantity
poison

_____ [q-a-n-t-y] of salt in our food is sheer

_____ [p-o-i-s-n].

■ *"I loved Ophelia: forty thousand brothers*

quantity

Could not, with all their _____ [q-a-n-t-y] *of love,*
Make up my sum."   (Hamlet, V, i, 293)

DIRECTIONS: Continue as before. Study the spelling carefully. Write each word three times.

11. rhythm   _____ _____ _____

12. roommate   _____ _____ _____

13. scene   _____ _____ _____

14. schedule   _____ _____ _____

15. scissors   _____ _____ _____

16. secretary   _____ _____ _____

17. sergeant   _____ _____ _____

18. sheriff   _____ _____ _____

19. society   _____ _____ _____

20. stomach   _____ _____ _____

Review words 11-20. Then take the quiz.

COVER
THIS STRIP   FILL THE BLANKS

roommate
rhythm
scissors

■ My _____ [r-o-m-a-t-e] said that my poem had

poor _____ [r-t-h-m], so I destroyed it with a

pair of _____ [s-i-s-r-s].

scene
rhythm

■ George Gershwin came on the _____ [s-e-n-e]

claiming he had "plenty of _____ [r-t-h-m]."

sergeant
society
stomach

■ The army _____ [s-r-g-e-n-t] went to the

nutrition _____ [s-o-c-t-y] dinner and got a

_____ [s-t-m-c-]-ache.

secretary
schedule
scissors

■ Our _____ [s-e-c-t-r-y] snipped out the dull

TV _____ [s-c-e-d-u-1-] with a pair of dull

_____ [s-i-s-r-s].

scene
roommate
sheriff
stomach

■ In the third _____ [s-e-n-e], my _____

[r-o-m-a-t-e] plays the role of a _____ [s-h-e-r-f]

with a big heart and a _____ [s-t-m-c-] to

match.

secretary
schedule
society

■ By mistake our _____ [s-e-c-t-r-y] sent the

_____ [s-c-e-d-u-1-] of bullfights to a

be-kind-to-animals _____ [s-o-c-t-y].

sheriff
schedule
scissors

■ At high noon the _____ [s-h-e-r-f] faced the

desperado right on _____ [s-c-e-d-u-1-], but the

lawman had forgotten his gun so he fought with a pair of

_____ [s-i-s-r-s].

roommate
stomach

■ The final exam in Personal Health 1A gave my _____

[r-o-m-a-t-e] a nervous _____ [s-t-m-c-].

sergeant

■ The army _____ [s-r-g-e-n-t] tried to

drown his sorrows but found they could swim.

rhythm
scene
sheriff

■ The _____ [r-t-h-m] band whipped up a wild

_____ [s-e-n-e]--until the _____

[s-h-e-r-f] arrived.

sergeant
secretary
society

■ Our army _____ [s-r-g-e-n-t] married, then

soon divorced, the _____ [s-e-c-t-r-y] of

the temperance _____ [s-o-c-t-y].

scene

■   *"Last _____ [s-e-n-e] of all,*
   That ends this strange eventful history,
   Is second childishness"
                        (As You Like It, II, vii, 163)

DIRECTIONS: Continue as before. Study the spelling carefully. Write each word three times.

21. surgeon   _____ _____ _____

22. sympathy   _____ _____ _____

23. system   _____ _____ _____

24. telephone   _____ _____ _____

25. tobacco   _____ _____ _____

26. tragedy   _____ _____ _____

27. vacuum   _____ _____ _____

28. victim   _____ _____ _____

29. violence   _____ _____ _____

30. welfare   _____ _____ _____

Review words 21-30. Then take the quiz.

QUIZ

COVER
THIS STRIP   FILL THE BLANKS
_____

telephone
system

■ Alexander Graham Bell gave us the _____

[t-e-l-p-h-n-] _____ [s-s-t-m], thus

making Friday night dates possible.

surgeon

- The tree _____ [s-r-g-e-n] had a

branch office.

victim
violence
welfare

- The _____ [v-i-c-t-m] of the gang

_____ [v-i-l-n-c-] was carried into the

_____ [w-e-l-f-r-] office.

vacuum
sympathy

- Outer space is a lonely _____ [v-a-c-u-m-],

and anybody out there has my _____ [s-m-p-t-h-y].

tragedy
surgeon
telephone

- After the car _____ [t-r-a-g-y] I tried to

call a hospital _____ [s-r-g-e-n] on the public

_____ [t-e-l-p-h-n-], but I didn't have a dime.

welfare
tobacco

- By taking some food stamps from _____

[w-e-l-f-r-] citizens, we were able to give firmer support

to _____ [t-o-b-a-c-o-] growers.

vacuum
violence

- Luke returned the _____ [v-a-c-u-m-] tubes to

the old TV set, to avoid family _____ [v-i-l-n-c-].

telephone

- In Hongkong I tried to use the _____

[t-e-l-p-h-n-], but I kept getting a Wong number.

surgeon
victim
tobacco
system

- An eminent lung _____ [s-r-g-e-n] says he

often operates on a _____ [v-i-c-t-m] of

_____ [t-o-b-a-c-o-]. "It's a lousy

_____ [s-s-t-m]," he admits, "but smokers are

my best customers."

violence
tragedy
sympathy

- Gang _____ [v-i-l-n-c-] results in bloody

_____ [t-r-a-g-y], after which we wring our

hands and express our _____ [s-m-p-t-h-y].

surgeon
victim
tragedy

- The hospital _____ [s-r-g-e-n] began to

repair a _____ [v-i-c-t-m] of the racing car

_____ [t-r-a-g-y].

welfare
sympathy

- The _____ [w-e-l-f-r-] office gave the mother

of ten much _____ [s-m-p-t-h-y] but little aid.

- In the ads all _____ [t-o-b-a-c-o-] smokers

are handsome and virile. What a clever advertising

tobacco
system

_____ [s-s-t-m]!

- "Look, teacher, a perfect _____ [v-a-c-u-m-]!"--

vacuum

"That's nothing."

- *"They will by* _____ *[v-i-l-n-c-] tear him from*
  your palace,
  And torture him with grievous lingering death."
  (2 King Henry VI, III, ii, 246)

violence

28

ANTI: AGAINST; OPPOSITE

31. antagonize (an tag'ə nīz') *v.* to make unfriendly; make an enemy of

> His midnight parties *antagonized* the neighbors.
> England's tax on tea met with *antagonism* in Boston.

Why antagonize?   _____   _____
  (Copy twice)

32. antihero (an'tī hēr'ō) *n.* a main character in fiction who is lacking in noble spirit or heroic qualities

> The *antihero* of *Catch-22* shuns all military dangers.
> Benchley depicts himself as a blundering, *antiheroic* simpleton.

shabby antihero   _____   _____

33. antiseptic (an ti sep'tik) *adj.* working against infection; clean
n. something that fights germs

> The hospital halls smelled of *antiseptic*.
> Lover Boy gargled the *antiseptic* mouthwash.

antiseptic drugs   _____   _____

34. **antisocial** (an′ti sō′shəl) *adj.* unfriendly toward others; harmful to society

> The drifters often engaged in *antisocial* activities.
> Rodney bites his playmates. He's *antisocial*.

<u>antisocial behavior</u>   _____   _____

35. **antonym** (an′tə nim) *n.* a word that is opposite in meaning to another word

> "Beautiful" is an *antonym* of "ugly."
> "Brave" and "cowardly" are *antonyms*.

<u>pair of antonyms</u>   _____   _____

Review words 31–35. Then go on.

QUIZ

DIRECTIONS: Fill the blanks with words we studied that are derived from the Greek root ANTI (against; opposite). Be sure you spell the words correctly.

COVER
THIS STRIP

	■ The TV commercial urges us to gargle with Perfumo
antiseptic antisocial	_____ [a-t-s-p-c], because bad breath is _____ [a-t-s-o-1].
	■ In fiction, what main character saves the drowning girl?
	Why, the hero. Who pushed her into the river? Why, the
antihero	_____ [a-t-h-o].
antonym antagonize	■ "Befriend" is an _____ [a-t-n-m] for the word "_____ [a-t-g-n-z-]."
	■ A sad movie! Deprived of his whiskey, the wretched
antihero antiseptic	alcoholic _____ [a-t-h-o] gulps the bottle of _____ [a-t-s-p-c].
antonym	■ "Smart" is an _____ [a-t-n-m] for "stupid."
	■ My dog "Biting Bowser" is a great watchdog, but he's
antisocial	rather _____ [a-t-s-o-1].

page 250

antihero antagonize antisocial	■ The novel's rowdy _____ [a-t-h-o] begins to _____ [a-t-g-n-z-] the neighborhood by his _____ [a-t-s-o-1] behavior.
antonym	■ A word with the same meaning is a synonym; a word with the opposite meaning is an _____ [a-t-n-m].
antagonize antiseptic	■ Nancy, I don't want to _____ [a-t-g-n-z-] your cook, but did she pour _____ [a-t-s-p-c] into this coffee?

Non-test examples

OTHER DERIVATIVES OF ANTI (AGAINST; OPPOSITE):

antibiotic (an'ti bī ot'ik) *n.* a chemical such as penicillin which tends to destroy bacteria

anticlimax (an'ti kli'maks) *n.* an event or statement that is much less powerful or striking than expected; a weak, disappointing conclusion

antifebrile (an'tē fē'brəl) *adj.* effective against a fever

antinovel (an'tē nov'əl) *n.* a literary work which rejects traditional structure of the novel with regard to plot, form, etc.

antipodes (an tip'ə dēz') *n.* places that are located on opposite sides of the globe from one another

antithesis (an tith'i sis) *n.* the direct opposite; a contrast in two phrases, as in "The rich get richer; the poor get children."

antivivisection (an'ti viv i sek'shən) *n.* opposition to the practice of subjecting living animals to cutting operations for scientific purposes

The prefix ANTI (against; opposite) is extremely common. Examples:

anti-aircraft	anticoagulant	antievolutionist
anti-American	anticommunist	anti-Fascism
antibacterial	anticorrosive	antifederalist
antiballistic	anticyclone	antifeminism
anti-British	anti-Darwinian	antifeudal
anti-Catholic	antidemocratic	antifreeze
Antichrist	antidepressant	anti-French
anticlerical	antidraft	anti-Freudian

antifriction	antimagnetic	antipolitical
antigambling	antimalarial	antipollution
anti-German	antimatter	antipope
antigovernment	anti-Mexican	antiproton
antihistamine	antimilitarist	antireform
antihumanist	antimissile	antireligious
antihypnotic	antimodern	anti-Russian
anti-idealistic	antimonarchist	antirust
anti-intellectual	antimoral	anti-Semitic
anti-Irish	anti-Negro	antiskid
antiknock	antineutron	antislavery
antilabor	antinicotine	antistatic
antiliberal	antinoise	antitank
antiliquor	antioxidant	antitobacco
antilottery	antipersonnel	antitoxin
antilogarithm	antiperspirant	antitrust
antimachine	anti-Platonic	antiwar

EU: GOOD; WELL

36. **eugenics** (yoo jen'iks) *n.* the science of improving mental and physical qualities of the human race by controlled selection of parents; the movement to improve the human species through control of hereditary factors

> Sir Francis Galton was an early advocate of *eugenics*.
> Can *eugenics* improve the human race?

eugenics society   _____   _____
    (copy twice)

37. **euphemism** (yoo'fə miz əm) *n.* a mild word or phrase that is substituted for another that seems blunt or offensive

> "Powder room" is a *euphemism* for "toilet."
> Advertisements for deodorants are usually *euphemistic*.

dainty euphemism　　　　_____　_____
　　　(copy twice)

38.　euphony　(yo͞o′fə ne)

　　　　　Poe's verses have remarkable *euphony*.
　　　　　From the pipe organ came *euphonious* chords.

　　　verbal euphony　　　　_____　_____

39.　euphoria　(yo͞o fôr′ē ə)　*n.* an exaggerated feeling of well-being and
　　　happiness

　　　　　A hot bath after the marathon was pure *euphoria*.
　　　　　Our winning coach was *euphoric*, on cloud nine.

　　　sheer euphoria　　　　_____　_____

40.　euthanasia　(yo͞o thə nā′zhə)　*n.* the act of causing an easy, painless
　　　death, so as to end suffering; mercy killing

　　　　　Euthanasia ended the cancer patient's agony.
　　　　　Should our state legalize *euthanasia*?

　　　euthanasia debate　　　　_____　_____

Review words 36-40.　Then go on.

QUIZ

DIRECTIONS: Fill the blanks with words we studied that are derived from the
Greek prefix EU (good; well).　Be sure you spell the words correctly.

COVER
THIS STRIP

	■ Some people feel that "mercy killing," also known as
	_____ [-u-t-h-n-s-a], is merely a
euthanasia euphemism	_____ [-u-p-h-s-m] for "murder."
	■ Some people claim that superior beings could be produced
eugenics	if we applied the principles of _____ [-u-g-n-c-].
	■ Lulled by the majestic _____ [-u-p-h-n-y]
	of Beethoven's Fifth, Oswald sank into _____
euphony euphoria	[-u-p-h-r-a].

eugenics euthanasia	■ An authoritarian government would probably abuse the principles of _____ [-u-g-n-c-] and _____ [-u-t-h-n-s-a].
euphoria euphony	■ While in a condition of _____ [-u-p-h-r-a], Samuel Coleridge composed "Kubla Khan," a poem of remarkable _____ [-u-p-h-n-y].
eugenics euphemism	■ People are not cattle, and they won't submit to _____ [-u-g-n-c-], which term is a _____ [-u-p-h-s-m] for planned breeding.
euphemism	■ In 1900 a woman might be "in a delicate condition," a _____ [-u-p-h-s-m] for "pregnant."
euphony	■ The old-time orator was often more interested in _____ [-u-p-h-n-y] than content.
euphoria euthanasia	■ An overdose of morphine given to the suffering patient produced _____ [-u-p-h-r-a], but the result was _____ [-u-t-h-n-s-a].

Non-test examples

OTHER DERIVATIVES OF EU (GOOD; WELL):

Eucharist (yōō′kə rist) *n.* the consecrated bread and wine used in Holy Communion; Holy Communion

eupepsia (yōō pep′sē ə) *n.* good digestion (antonym: *dyspepsia*)

euphonium (yōō fō′nē əm) *n.* a brass musical instrument with a mellow tone

euphuism (yōō′fyōō iz′əm) *n.* an artificial, flowery literary style in imitation of John Lyly's "Euphues"

eupnea (yōōp nē′ə) *n.* normal, easy breathing (antonym: *dispnea*)

eurhythmics (yoo rith′miks) *n.* the art of bodily movement in interpretation of musical rhythms

eutheniks (yōō then′iks) *n.* the science of improving the mental and physical qualities of the human race by control of environmental factors

KILO: THOUSAND

41. **kilocycle** (kǐl'ə sī kəl) *n.* a unit of one thousand cycles per second, equal to a unit of electromagnetic wave frequency; a kilohertz

    Radio frequencies are measured in *kilocycles*.
    Tune to 980 *kilocycles* for KFWB newscasts.

    kilocycle frequency   _____ _____
         (copy twice)

42. **kilogram** (kǐl'ə gram) *n.* one thousand grams, a unit of weight

    A *kilogram* is equal to 2.2046 pounds.
    We bought a *kilogram* of overripe tomatoes.

    kilogram of bread   _____ _____

43. **kilometer** (kǐ lom'ə tər) *n.* one thousand meters, a unit of distance

    A *kilometer* is equal to 3280.8 feet, or about five-eighths of a mile.
    Walk a *kilometer* in an Indian's moccasins.

    ten-kilometer run   _____ _____

44. **kilowatt** (kǐl'ə wot) *n.* one thousand watts, a unit of electrical power

    A hundred-watt bulb uses one-tenth of a *kilowatt*.
    We were charged six cents per *kilowatt*-hour.

    kilowatt-hour   _____ _____

Review words 41-44. Then go on.

QUIZ

DIRECTIONS: Fill the blanks with words we studied that are derived from the Greek prefix KILO (thousand). Be sure you spell the words correctly.

COVER
THIS STRIP

	■ Bruno walked a _____ [k-l-m-t-r] to the
	butcher shop and bought a _____ [k-l-g-m] of
kilometer kilogram	boloney.

kilocycle kilowatt	■ The unit of radio wave frequency is the _____ [k-1-c-1-], and the unit of electrical power is the _____ [k-1-w-t].
kilogram kilometer	■ A pound is smaller than a _____ [k-1-g-m], but a mile is bigger than a _____ [k-1-m-t-r].
kilocycle kilowatt	■ The tuner indicated the _____ [k-1-c-1-] frequency; meanwhile the radio set was using one-tenth of a _____ [k-1-w-t] of power.
kilometer kilogram	■ After I ran a quick _____ [k-1-m-t-r], each shoe began to weigh a _____ [k-1-g-m].
kilowatt	■ Will the new refrigerator blow out a fuse? Better check its _____ [k-1-w-t] rating.
kilocycle	■ Can you count to a thousand in one second? If not, don't expect to count the radio impulses in a _____ [k-1-c-1-].

OTHER DERIVATIVES OF KILO (THOUSAND):   *Non-test examples*

A unit of--

kiloampere	electrical current	kiloliter	capacity
kilobar	pressure	kilolumen	luminous flux
kilocalorie	heat	kilomegacycle	frequency
kilocurie	radioactivity	kilomole	molecular weights
kilodyne	force	kilo-oersted	magnetic intensity
kilogauss	magnetic induction	kiloparsec	distance
kilograin	weight	kilopoise	viscosity
kilohm	resistance	kilopound	weight
kilojoule	work	kiloton	explosive force
kiloline	magnetic flux	kilovolt	electromotive force

45. **monocle** (mon'ə kəl) *n.* an eyeglass for one eye

   The *monocle* has lost its former popularity.
   His eyebrows shot up, and the *monocle* fell.

   shiny monocle   _____   _____
   (copy twice)

46. **monogamy** (mə nog'ə mē) *n.* the practice of having only one husband or wife at a time

   Monogamy is common to most civilized nations.
   The sultan, with five wives, scoffed at *monogamy*.

   custom of monogamy   _____   _____

47. **monograph** (mon'ə graf') *n.* a highly detailed treatise written on a limited area of a subject; a scholarly study on a particular topic

   One *monograph* deals with the life cycle of the Japanese beetle.
   Mr. Hinkle wrote a *monograph* on sausage additives.

   scholarly monograph   _____   _____

48. **monopolize** (mə nop'ə līz') *v.* to get control of; to have exclusive possession of

   The United States *monopolized* the Olympic medals.
   Marcus *monopolized* the conversation.

   monopolize water   _____   _____

49. **monotone** (mon'ə tōn') *n.* the uttering of words or sounds in a single tone; a tiresome sound without harmony or change of pitch

   The secretary read the minutes in a rapid *monotone*.
   The prayers were chanted in *monotone*.

   a dull monotone   _____   _____

50. **monotonous** (mə not'ə nəs) *adj.* having a tiresome lack of variety; boring in its uniformity

   Prisoners follow a *monotonous* routine.
   TV commercials are repeated with *monotonous* regularity.

   monotonous labor   _____   _____

Review words 45-50. Then go on.

QUIZ

DIRECTIONS: Fill the blanks with words we studied that are derived from the Greek prefix MONO (one). Be sure you spell the words correctly.

COVER
THIS STRIP

---

monocle

■ A single handcuff is a manacle; a single eyeglass is a

_____ [m-n-c-l-].

monotone
monotonous

■ A variation of musical tones can be fascinating, but a

_____ [m-n-t-o-n-] is _____ [m-n-t-n-s].

■ The professor published a _____ [m-n-g-p-h]

on the railroad barons who managed to _____

monograph
monopolize

[m-n-p-l-z-] the western rail industry.

■ My chess-playing machine is very smart, but it talks in

monotone

a flat _____ [m-n-t-o-n-].

■ The gist of Mona's _____ [m-n-g-p-h] on

monograph
monogamy
monotonous

causes of divorce was that _____ [m-n-g-m-y]

can become _____ [m-n-t-n-s].

■ "I'll stick to _____ [m-n-g-m-y]," said the

Romeo with the _____ [m-n-c-l-], "but my heart

monogamy
monocle

is a polygamist."

■ At the boarding house table Jumbo Jim would

monopolize
monotonous

_____ [m-n-p-l-z-] the chicken legs with

_____ [m-n-t-n-s] regularity.

■ The scientist adjusted his _____ [m-n-c-l-]

monocle
monotone
monograph

and, in a low _____ [m-n-t-n-], he read his

_____ [m-n-g-p-h] on oak tree fungus.

■ No believers in _____ [m-n-g-m-y], the rich

monogamy
monopolize

sheiks _____ [m-n-p-l-z-] the marriageable girls.

page 258

OTHER DERIVATIVES OF MONO (ONE):

    monarch (mon'ərk) *n.* the single ruler of a government

    monatomic (mon'ə tom'ik) *adj.* having only one atom in the molecule

    monism (mō'niz əm) *n.* the doctrine that reality consists of only one basic substance or principle

    monochrome (mon'ə krōm') *n.* a drawing in shades of a single color

    monodrama (mon'ə drä'mə) *n.* a drama to be acted by a single performer

    monody (mon'ə dē) *n.* a song or poem of lament in which a single voice predominates

    monogram (mon'ə gram') *n.* a single design consisting usually of interlaced initials and used on stationery, clothing, etc.

    monogyny (mə noj'ə nē) *n.* the practice of having one wife at a time

    monokini (mon'ə kē'nē) *n.* a woman's topless bathing suit

    monolingual (mon'ə ling'gwəl) *adj.* speaking only one language [*a monolingual nation*]

    monolith (mon'ə lith) *n.* a single large block of stone, as used in an obelisk, column, or statue

    monologue (mon'ə log') *n.* a long talk by one speaker; a recitation by one actor

    monomial (mō nō'mē əl) *n.* an algebraic expression consisting of only one term, such as 7xy.

    mononucleosis (mon'ə nōō'klē ō'sis) *n.* a disease in which the blood has an excessive number of single-nucleus cells

    monoplane (mon'ə plān) *n.* a airplane with only one supporting surface

    monopode (mon'ə pōd') *n.* a creature with only one foot

    monosodium (mon'ə sō'dē əm) *adj.* containing a single atom of sodium

    monosyllable (mon'ə sil'ə bəl) *n.* a one-syllable word such as *run* or *am*

    monotheism (mon'ə thē'iz əm) *n.* the belief that there is only one God

The prefix MONO (one) occurs in scores of technical terms.

Review words 1-50, spelling and vocabulary. Then take the Chapters 27-28 Self-Test.

DIRECTIONS: Write the words in full. Complete this entire test before you check and grade your answers.

_____ 1. The astronomy [p-r-o-f-s-r] bumped his head and saw stars.
_____ 2. Wendy walked five miles to a [t-e-l-p-n-].
_____ 3. The football star demanded an easy [s-c-e-d-u-l-].
_____ 4. The poor need jobs, not just [s-m-p-t-h-y]
_____ 5. *Othello* is a Shakespearean [t-r-a-g-y].
_____ 6. Huck Finn caught a [q-a-n-t-y] of catfish.
_____ 7. The hospital [s-r-g-n] made a cutting remark.
_____ 8. A good [s-e-c-t-y] has to be a good speller.
_____ 9. Norton trimmed his toenails with [s-i-s-r-s].
_____ 10. In *Moby Dick*, Ishmael has a cannibal for a [r-o-m-a-t-e].
_____ 11. "Name your [p-o-s-n]," said the bartender.
_____ 12. Velma's diamond ring is in the [v-a-c-u-m-] cleaner.
_____ 13. He's a [p-h-s-c-n] and familiar with many tongues.
_____ 14. The [r-e-s-t-r-n-t] food was all cold, except the ice water.
_____ 15. No Dodge City [s-h-r-i-f-] had to provide for his old age.
_____ 16. The band was arrested for [p-o-s-e-s-n] of banned things.
_____ 17. The library [r-e-f-r-n-c-] room is not a social center.
_____ 18. Habits become automatic through [r-e-p-t-t-n].
_____ 19. For some reason my [s-t-m-c-] couldn't handle nine hot dogs.
_____ 20. Everybody has some [p-r-e-j-d-c-] except you and me.
_____ 21. Rescuers gathered the bomb [v-i-t-m] into a basket.
_____ 22. I like the [s-e-n-e-] where Hamlet meets the ghost.
_____ 23. Picking a jury is a glacier-slow [p-r-o-c-d-r-].
_____ 24. One doesn't belch in high [s-o-c-t-y].
_____ 25. Industrial leaders must consider the public [w-e-l-f-r-].
_____ 26. Asylum inmates loved the [r-t-h-m-] band.
_____ 27. This mess was cooked by the mess [s-r-g-n-t].
_____ 28. Teacher used the honor [s-s-t-m], and everybody got a hundred.
_____ 29. The dear departed had smoked [t-b-a-c-o-] near a gas tank.
_____ 30. The French Revolution was blotched by mob [v-i-l-n-c-e].

Write correctly the words we studied that are derived from the Greek prefixes ANTI, EU, KILO, and MONO:

_____ 31. It is unwise to [a-n-t-g-n-z-] a hungry tiger.
_____ 32. One wife to one husband is known as [m-o-n-g-y].
_____ 33. "Rich" is an [a-n-t-n-m] for "poor."
_____ 34. A large bread might weigh one [k-l-g-m-].
_____ 35. A shabby-spirited main character is an [a-t-i-h-o-].
_____ 36. Pumping gas for thirty years becomes [m-n-o-t-n-s-].
_____ 37. "Passed away" is a [-u-p-h-s-m] for "died."
_____ 38. Five-eighths of a mile equals one [k-l-m-t-r-].
_____ 39. Speeches delivered in a [m-o-n-t-o-n-] are boring.
_____ 40. Terminal suffering might be shortened by [-u-t-h-n-s-a].

Write the letter that indicates the best definition.

( ) 41. antiseptic   a. a smooth, pleasant sound
( ) 42. antisocial   b. to have exclusive control of
( ) 43. eugenics   c. unfriendly to other people
( ) 44. euphony   d. a very pleasant feeling
( ) 45. euphoria   e. working against germs
( ) 46. kilocycle   f. a treatise on a limited topic
( ) 47. kilowatt   g. improvement of human species
( ) 48. monocle   h. a unit of radio wave frequency
( ) 49. monograph   i. a single eyeglass
( ) 50. monopolize   j. a unit of electrical power

ANSWER KEY

Check your test answers by the following key. Deduct 2% per error from 100%.

1. professor	11. poison	21. victim	31. antagonize	41. e
2. telephone	12. vacuum	22. scene	32. monogamy	42. c
3. schedule	13. physician	23. procedure	33. antonym	43. g
4. sympathy	14. restaurant	24. society	34. kilogram	44. a
5. tragedy	15. sheriff	25. welfare	35. antihero	45. d
6. quantity	16. possession	26. rhythm	36. monotonous	46. h
7. surgeon	17. reference	27. sergeant	37. euphemism	47. j
8. secretary	18. repetition	28. system	38. kilometer	48. i
9. scissors	19. stomach	29. tobacco	39. monotone	49. f
10. roommate	20. prejudice	30. violence	40. euthanasia	50. b

Score: _____ %

Review carefully any words which you have missed in the foregoing Self-Test.

Your instructor will give you a final test on words 1-50 in Chapters 27 and 28.

SUPPLEMENTARY SPELLING LISTS (AVERAGE AND ADVANCED)

These five hundred words are a supplement to the programed spelling in this textbook. These words are often misspelled, causing college teachers to wince and moan. The two lists, average and advanced, are presented here as a special challenge to serious students who wish to continue beyond the limits of the programed chapters. As with the basic list (p.92), you will earn extra credit for mastering these words. In addition, you may distinguish yourself in another classroom spelldown.

AVERAGE LIST (1-250)

accent	cavalry	disobey	grateful	offense	rumor
aviator	celery	dissolve	gratitude	opportunity	salad
accident	cellar	divide	groan	opposite	satisfied
accusing	champion	divorce	harmony	ounce	saucer
actually	charity	donkeys	hatred	palace	sausage
adjourn	chemistry	druggist	heartily	particularly	science
advantage	choir	eagle	horizon	patriot	senator
adventure		earnest	horrible	peculiar	sensible
advisable	Christian	echoes	hospital	penalty	serious
affair	claim	economy	hymn	perceive	severe
agency	climate	editor	illustrate	period	shriek
agony	cocoa	efficient	improvement	permanent	solemn
agreeable	column	eighth	individual	petition	source
agriculture	commercial	elephant	intimate	pigeon	sparrow
alien	compare	elevator	inventor	pioneer	spectacular
ancestor	comrade		jewelry	position	spirit
antiseptic	condition	emergency	kindergarten	poultry	struggle
arctic	conference	employee	knuckle	practically	studio
assembly	confusion	engineer	label	preach	substitute
attention	conquer	enormous	laundry	preference	sufficient
attractive	consequently	especially	league	previous	surface
authority	considerable	Europe	leather	profession	survivor
autumn	contain	exact	lecture	prominent	sweat
baggage	continuous	exclaim		pronounce	tailor
balance	contrary	exercise	lettuce	proprietor	tenant
ballot	cordial	failure	liar	prosperity	terrible
bankrupt	coward	famine	liquid	purchase	theory
banquet	creature	fatal	liquor	puzzle	threaten
barrel	criminal	faucet	lonesome	radiator	traffic
beverage	crisis	feature	lunatic	raisin	traveler
biscuit	cruel	fertile	machinery	reasonable	trousers
breadth	curve	fierce	manual		typewriter
bruise	cushion	financial	meadow	receipt	urge
budget	decide	fixture	mechanic	recent	useful
bureau	declaration	foreign	memory	recitation	utensil
campaign	decrease	fountain	message	regretted	vision
cannon	delightful	fourteen	narrow	reliable	visitor
capacity	dependable	fried	needle	religious	wrinkle
capable	depth	fuel	neighbor	responsible	worrying
capture	despair	furnace	nephew	revenue	
carriage	diamond	furniture	neutral	review	
cashier	dictionary	grabbed	ninth	riddle	
catalog	dishonest	graduate	official	ruin	

academic	courtesy	indispensable	penicillin	simile
acclaimed	deferred	indivisible	perfectible	snobbish
accommodate	descendant	inevitable	permissible	sophomore
accustomed	diagnosis	inhabitant	persistence	sopranos
acquitted	digestible	innuendo	persuasion	souvenir
allotment	dilapidated	innumerable	phenomenon	sovereign
ambassador	dilemma	inoculate	piazza	specifically
apparatus	dispensary	intelligence	piccolo	sponsor
appearance	dissatisfied	intercede	picnicking	stubborn
architecture	dissimilar	invisible	plausible	subtly
artistically	divisible	iodine	poetically	submitted
ascertain	drunkenness	irrelevant	polygamy	suffrage
attorney	ecstasy	irresistible	potatoes	supervisor
auxiliary	edible	irritable	precede	surroundings
bachelor	ellipsis	isthmus	preparation	susceptible
barbarous	endeavor	judicial	pressure	suspenseful
bestial	equipped	kerosene	primitive	syllable
boundaries	erasure	laboratory	proceed	symbolic
buffaloes	excitable	legislature	proclaim	symmetry
bulletin	exhilarate	leisurely	proficient	tangible
cafeteria	existential	librarian	pronunciation	taxable
cantaloupe	exorbitant	lieutenant	punctuation	technique
ceremony	expatriate	loneliness	quandary	temperament
certificate	exultation	lunar	quarantine	tenement
chauffeur	Fahrenheit	maintenance	quizzes	terror
chocolate	flexible	maneuver	radiance	tolerance
circular	flourish	metaphor	realistically	tomatoes
citizen	forcible	miniature	rebelling	torpedoes
coincidence	forfeit	misshapen	recede	traitor
combustible	frantically	modeled	receivable	transferring
commentator	frivolous	molasses	reconcile	traumatic
commitment	fulfill	monstrous	referred	treasurer
compass	ghetto	municipal	remembrance	typist
compelled	gorgeous	mustache	reminisce	umbrella
competent	government	nuclear	remittance	unnecessary
complexion	grievance	obstacle	renowned	unusual
concede	grievous	occasional	repellent	vaccinate
conceivable	gymnasium	occurrence	repetitive	vandalism
conductor	heretofore	oculist	representative	vengeance
conferred	hindrance	optimism	resistance	vignette
congratulate	hippopotamus	optimistically	responsibility	virgin
contagious	hygiene	orchestra	reversible	voluntary
cooperation	hyperbole	original	rheumatism	voyeur
contemptible	hypothesis	outrageous	rhyme	vulgar
contributor	igloos	parachute	scenario	wherefore
controlling	impromptu	parenthesis	scholar	wield
controversial	inauguration	parliament	seizure	wondrous
convertible	inconvenient	pastime	separation	xylophone
counterfeit	indelible	peaceable	siege	zephyr
courageous	indescribable	peculiar	significance	zodiac

SUPPLEMENTARY GREEK DERIVATIVES

DIRECTIONS: Study the meaning of each Greek prefix and root. One English derivative is given. Fill the blanks at the right with two more derivatives. If in doubt about a word, check its sources in the dictionary.

PREFIX	MEANING	DERIVATIVES		
1. ARCH	chief	*archangel*	_____	_____
2. DIA	through	*diathermy*	_____	_____
3. EPI	upon	*epitaph*	_____	_____
4. HYPER	excessive	*hyperbole*	_____	_____
5. HYPO	under	*hypothesis*	_____	_____
6. META	change; after	*metabolism*	_____	_____
7. NEO	new	*neoclassic*	_____	_____
8. PERI	around	*perimeter*	_____	_____
9. POLY	many	*polygon*	_____	_____
10. SYN, SYM	together	*syndrome*	_____	_____

ROOT	MEANING	DERIVATIVES		
11. ANTHROP	man	*anthropoid*	_____	_____
12. BIBLI	book	*Bible*	_____	_____
13. CHROM	color	*chromatic*	_____	_____
14. COSM	world; order	*cosmic*	_____	_____
15. CRAC, CRAT	power	*plutocrat*	_____	_____
16. CRYPT	secret	*cryptic*	_____	_____
17. CYCL	circle; wheel	*cyclone*	_____	_____
18. DEM	people	*democracy*	_____	_____
19. GAM	marriage	*monogamy*	_____	_____
20. GEN	race; kind	*genetics*	_____	_____
21. GEO	earth	*geometry*	_____	_____
22. GON	corner; angle	*hexagon*	_____	_____

ROOT	MEANING	DERIVATIVES		
23. GYN	woman	*gynecology*	_____	_____
24. HEM	blood	*hemophilia*	_____	_____
25. HETRO	other	*heterodox*	_____	_____
26. HOMO	same	*homosexual*	_____	_____
27. HYDR	water	*hydrant*	_____	_____
28. IATR	heal	*psychiatry*	_____	_____
29. ISO	same	*isobar*	_____	_____
30. LITH	rock	*monolith*	_____	_____
31. MEGA	great	*megaphone*	_____	_____
32. MICRO	small	*microbe*	_____	_____
33. MORPH	form	*amorphous*	_____	_____
34. NECRO	dead	*necrosis*	_____	_____
35. NOM	law; order	*economy*	_____	_____
36. ONYM	name	*antonym*	_____	_____
37. ORTH	right; true	*orthodox*	_____	_____
38. PALEO	ancient	*paleolithic*	_____	_____
39. PHON	sound	*phonetic*	_____	_____
40. PHOS, PHOT	light	*photograph*	_____	_____
41. PHYSI	nature	*physics*	_____	_____
42. POLI	city	*police*	_____	_____
43. PSEUDO	false	*pseudonym*	_____	_____
44. PYR	fire	*pyromaniac*	_____	_____
45. SCOP	see; watch	*periscope*	_____	_____
46. SOPH	wisdom	*sophisticated*	_____	_____
47. TECHN	art; skill	*technique*	_____	_____
48. TELE	far	*telegraph*	_____	_____
49. THE	God	*theocracy*	_____	_____
50. THERM	heat	*thermos*	_____	_____